# The Opera

# The Opera

*Robert Donington*

*King's College*
*University of London*

THE HARBRACE HISTORY OF MUSICAL FORMS

Under the General Editorship of Karl Geiringer

*University of California, Santa Barbara*

**Harcourt Brace College Publishers**

Fort Worth   Philadelphia   San Diego
New York   Orlando   Austin   San Antonio
Toronto   Montreal   London   Sydney   Tokyo

ISBN: 0-15-567536-2

Library of Congress Catalog Card Number: 77-93589

Printed in the United States of America

COVER: *Das Rheingold*. Photo by Tom Lipton / Shostal Associates

PHOTO CREDITS: p. 19, An engraving by A. Carracci based on Buontalenti, 1589; p. 35, photo by Fred Fehl; p. 50, © Beth Bergman; p. 69, Museo Teatrale alla Scala, Milan; pp. 77, 95, 114, © Beth Bergman; p. 130, Archivio dell'Ente Lirico Arena di Verona; p. 159, *Opera News;* p. 173, Louis Melançon Collection; p. 189, photo by Fred Fehl; p. 202, *Opera News;* p. 217, photo by Stuart Robinson

# Table of Contents

# Preface

This book gives an account of opera from its growth out of the ballets and interludes of the sixteenth century down to its varied and often strange developments in the present time. Mere incidental music, however lavishly introduced, does not make a spoken play into an opera. It is the integral combination of words and music, acting and staging, that makes an opera. Thus understood, there has not always been such an art as opera, and we cannot be perfectly sure that there is always going to be. Other varieties of music theater have certainly existed, and others are currently developing. For the purposes of this book, however, the following definition will be proposed: opera is drama unfolding as much in the music as in the words, and as much in the words as in the music.

This book, then, is an introduction to opera that takes into consideration both of its main components: the words that articulate the drama, and the music that expresses it. They are not necessarily of equal value. But the librettos with which Mozart, Verdi, Wagner, and Strauss were so intimately concerned are worth our taking seriously. If we do not pick up enough of the words to keep in touch with what is happening on the stage, we are not getting the whole experience, but only what would come through just as well on the concert platform. It was a poet—Rinuccini—who took the initiative for the earliest opera, and although difficulties have always been encountered in striking a satisfactory balance between words and music, it is this balance that makes the opera.

Important composers will be represented here by a sufficient selection of their operas, taken as samples in depth, to show their places in the long

sweep of operatic history. Other operas, and other less important composers, will be more briefly mentioned. The musical examples, too, are brief and
to the point, since it is expected that they will be supplemented from
available scores and recordings. The historical and artistic ingredients that
went into the development of opera are discussed in Chapter 1. There follow
four parts describing four great periods of opera, each with a short introduction summarizing its main tendencies. In conclusion, the present state and
future prospects of opera are considered.

My warm thanks go to Karl Geiringer, the most constructive of general
editors, to Nina Gunzenhauser and Claire Rubin, who combine just the
right proportions of firm guidance and patient encouragement as editors,
and to my generous colleagues Tom Walker, Paul Griffiths, and Roger
Parker. To have such friends and helpers in writing so inevitably difficult a
book makes all the difference.

Robert Donington

# The Opera

# 1

# The Making of Opera

Opera is drama unfolding as much in the music as in the words. It cannot, therefore, be realistic drama in an outward sense, because in the real world outside conversations are not sung, much less supported by orchestral accompaniment. But this does not necessarily mean that opera is cut off from real life. It may merely mean that opera is concerned with inner realities to which the outer situations and characters are to some extent pointers rather than literal equivalents. That great eighteenth-century rationalist, Dr. Johnson, dismissed the Italian opera of his day as "an exotic and irrational entertainment, which has always been combated and always has prevailed."[1] But this was because he was, by his own admission, quite unmusical. He did not appreciate that music in itself can be intensely dramatic, and that words well set to music can be even more so. The poetry and the music which prevent opera from being outwardly realistic are exactly the qualities which most help it to communicate inwardly real feelings and intuitions. How we feel about things is not something which can be touched or measured or directly observed; but the effect of it on our lives and our actions can be observed in no uncertain manner. It was this which Pascal had in mind when he said that "the heart has its reasons, of which reason knows nothing."[2]

In matters of the heart, music has great powers of persuasion. Even the background music of a film can strongly influence our reactions. In opera, the music is not in the background. It occupies the very forefront of the action. Music seems particularly able to call up associations from our deeper levels, if only because it is so little tied down to literal description, and so close to that ebb and flow of mood which is what it actually feels like to be alive and human. Many of

**1**

our strongest emotions first arose in forgotten situations of childhood, and can be aroused again with mysterious force by any images that touch upon those old experiences, without our necessarily knowing why. There are images, too, that reach us from the childhood of the human race itself. These touch on archetypal themes renewed in every generation. They speak of universal human experiences of birth and death, of love and hate, of hope and fear, which take their individual courses with every one of us. Of such stuff are myths and legends made, and opera has always had an affinity with myth.[3]

Even a straightforward photograph may set up associations. A painting, a sculpture or a poem may deliberately distort the outer facts in order to strengthen our associations with those inner experiences which are also facts; and in opera, what the poetry outlines, the music extends. If we can accept the surface unreality of opera with something of what Coleridge[4] called "that willing suspension of disbelief for the moment, which constitutes poetic faith," then we may find ourselves wide open to those undercurrents of feeling and intuition which may be elusive, but are not unreal.

A drama that is enriched by incidental music, like the typical musical comedy or the so-called *Beggar's Opera*, is not opera. These are spoken plays made more lively—but not more dramatic—by plenty of dancing and lyrics set to popular tunes. In Mozart's *Figaro*, however, we get to know more from the music than from the words about the characters of Figaro and Susanna, young Cherubino, and the erring Count and his forgiving Countess, and about their growth of character as the tangled intrigue unravels. It is because music can show character and the growth of character that drama can unfold as much in the music as in the words. And that is opera.

It is still opera when the more active words are spoken, and only the more reflective words are sung, provided that the drama unfolds as essentially in the music as it does, for example, in Mozart's *Magic Flute*, in Beethoven's *Fidelio*, or in the original and correct version of Bizet's *Carmen*. It is still a sort of light opera when Johann Strauss uses an idiom based on Viennese waltz-music to carry along a sentimental story of slight dramatic interest, as in *Die Fledermaus* ("The Bat"), since what little drama there is does come out directly in the music; the American musical is historically and artistically related to this marginal class of opera, which is known as operetta. On the other hand, it is oratorio rather than opera when costume, scenery, and the full illusion of theatrical staging form no part of the intention. It is ritual when an act of worship is dramatized in music. It is ballet when a drama is mimed wordlessly to music. None of these last add up to opera: they are valuable forms, but different. Classical Greek drama may have been sung throughout in a sort of bardic recitation; but that could not have been music of a kind to carry forward the drama, and this is not opera. The liturgical dramas sung and acted in the Middle Ages, and the mystery plays, miracle plays, and moralities of the Renaissance (seldom sung throughout) are not opera. Not until the threshold of the Modern Age, in late sixteenth-century Italy, just as that paradoxical mixture of culture and violence we call the Renaissance was drawing to its close, did opera emerge.

# Conditions Leading to Opera

One of the conditions most favorable to the emergence of opera was the competitive extravagance that characterized royal courts and other wealthy establishments. Visits and victories, weddings and births, departures and homecomings were celebrated with elaborate pageantry, often amounting to a sort of informal drama. There were showy processions on horse and foot, sometimes including carts to carry emblematic displays, and ending in elaborate receptions; there were banquets and balls, scenes and tableaux, frequently in fancy dress ("disguisings") or with masks ("masquerades") or both. There was also much formal drama, consisting either of tragedies and comedies from the classical Greek and Latin literatures, or of Latin or vernacular imitations or translations; and as if these were not already long enough, there were more or less dramatic interludes before, between, and after the acts. Both in their formal and occasionally even in their informal varieties, these productions made lavish and ingenious use of stage machinery, with ropes and pulleys, handles and windlasses, cams and counterweights, by which gods and goddesses were transported in flight visibly, or in clouds which first hid them and then opened to reveal them. Ships rocked on artificial waves or floated on real water, beset by mechanical sea or river monsters. Other legendary creatures and personages appeared out of hollow mountains or sylvan glades, or rose from subterranean caverns. Hell opened with its flames, or heaven with its celestial bodies. Sieges, conflagrations and all manner of illusions were achieved by this expensive (not to say hazardous) use of stagecraft. The visual display was matched by colorful orchestration and virtuoso singing. The themes were always allegorical, and had frequently some political point to convey. The performers were drawn from the nobility, though with strong professional support. Thus people of high social standing were used to acting out parts which, under the pretense of being mythological, overlapped their actual roles in public affairs. The French kings of the sixteenth and seventeenth centuries, for example, were supposed to be somehow representatives of the sun; and Louis XIV, known as *Le Roi Soleil*, the Sun-King, used as a young man to dance as Apollo, the god of the sun, in court ballets.

A famous instance of this sort of social entertainment—not an opera, but at least indirectly on the way to opera—was the *Ballet Comique de la Royne* ("Dramatic Ballet of the Queen") given in Paris in 1581 under the title of *Circe*.[5] Courtiers in mythological roles flattered the royal family by explaining to them that they now replaced still more beneficently the classical gods and goddesses, among whom the king's sister (in honor of whose marriage the ballet was performed) was specifically identified with Minerva, goddess of wisdom. It seems that Circe, that same infamous seductress and enchantress who was so nearly the ruin of Homer's Odysseus, has recently imprisoned some incautious Frenchmen, one of whom escapes and throws himself upon the king's majesty for assistance as he sits there in the audience. For the moment, Circe has to let her prisoner go; but she soon returns to petrify the entire company with her magic wand. She is rebuffed when Mercury descends in a cloud-machine to restore them all to life and movement; but once more she freezes the scene, and leads Mercury helplessly into her enchanted garden, where she keeps the animals into which she has turned her previous victims. It is all very good ballet and very good theater; but there are undercurrents of meaning to which Circe herself draws our attention. Once upon a time, she tells us, there was a golden age when nature ruled men contentedly by their instincts, like animals without either care or understanding; but when Jupiter presently gave us these human attributes, change and desire came as well, and "I alone," she sings, "am cause of all this change," under the ceaseless revolutions of her father, the Sun. Satyrs and dryads now sing and dance their way to Pan, whom as a power of nature they urge to the rescue; but it takes four not so natural Virtues (familiar companions of the king as they hasten to assure us), together with Minerva and Jupiter, to overcome Circe in a contest fiercely mimed and danced. Thereupon she offers to yield to the king, but to the king alone; and all present are reconciled. A Grand Ballet of forty geometrical figures, allegorically designed, ends the action. There was then general dancing for actors and audience, far into the night.

The political purpose of this lively entertainment, as of some other similar ballets of the time, was to encourage a reconciliation between the factions of the French nobility, who were intermittently but devastatingly involved in civil war. It was really believed that the arts, by the example of their own harmony, might help to restore civil harmony. Thus politics and pageantry overlapped; and such a spectacle made easier the acceptance a few years later of similar scenarios in opera. The artistic purpose of *Circe* went, however, considerably deeper than the political purpose, reflecting as it did the aims of a group of seven poets called the Pleiad (after the seven stars of the constellation Pleiades) and their associates in the first French "Academy of Poetry and Music" (1567-1587). We meet, in the work of this group—with an aim which was typical of the climate of sixteenth-century opinion—the climate in which opera became a possibility. This aim was to restore the classical unity of the arts. The French poetry of the time scans in the normal modern way, by stress: it is the accentuation of the syllables which makes the rhythm. But this could be forced into an arbitrary correspondence with classical poetry, which scanned on quite a different principle, by quantity: it was the duration of the syllables which made the rhythm. The result of this unnatural experiment, which was not maintained strictly for any great while, was called *vers mesuré à l'antique* (verse measured in the antique manner). Then "long" syllables were given long notes, and "short" syllables were given notes of half the length; and the result of that equally unnatural procedure was called *musique mesurée à l'antique*. In *Circe*, written and composed by minor practitioners, the only perceptible effect on the style is a certain stiffness which could not very well have led directly into opera. On the other hand, *Circe* does illustrate a more general theory of the arts, derived ultimately from Plato and still current in Renaissance Neoplatonism, which greatly influenced the origins of opera.

According to this theory, art is a veil which half reveals, in the very act of half concealing, inner meanings such as the art historians have for some time past been able to trace beneath the surface enchantment of Botticelli or Titian or

Michelangelo, without in any way diminishing our immediate appreciation of their sensuous beauty.[6] When Dante,[7] in the late Middle Ages, wrote his vast and allegorical *Divine Comedy*, he wanted us to "consider the teaching which is concealed beneath the strange verses." Boccaccio,[8] in the early Renaissance, gave very lengthy instructions on how to use pagan mythology "to conceal truth in a legendary and fitting covering." Marsilio Ficino,[9] the founder of Renaissance Neoplatonism, taught like Plato that "the inner sense and mind judge all things through certain innate principles," and asked: "how will you ever grasp outer realities if you have lost touch with inner realities?" Ronsard,[10] the greatest poet of the Pleiad, echoed Boccaccio in requiring the artist to "dissemble and conceal fables fitly and disguise well the truth of things with a fabulous cloak," so as to suggest symbolically to ordinary people, "by agreeable and colorful fables, the secrets which they could not understand when the truth is too openly disclosed." Goethe at a later date went even further when he was asked by Eckermann what hidden idea he had tried to symbolize in *Faust,* and replied that he did not know himself, and that "the more impossible for reason to assimilate a work of poetry is, the better."[11] Later still, we shall find Wagner using "mythological symbols" for their "deep and hidden truth," which is felt intuitively rather than rationally; and he also suggested that to reveal too openly that which he himself experienced rather in the manner of a "riddle," would only "get in the way of a genuine understanding."[12]

At the time of *Circe,* Boccaccio's great treatise of mythology was still widely consulted, and there were several more recent and popular compilations from which aspiring artists could draw their pagan allegories. One of these, by Natale Conti,[13] was the acknowledged source of *Circe,* whose printed edition[14] of 1582 includes a summary of Conti's explanation (published in 1567) of "the allegory of Circe." Conti explains Circe as a symbol for that force of life which is always powerful, but for good or for bad according to how we ourselves are taking it. Conti's word for this ambivalent force of life is *libido* (very much as this word was later used by Freud, Jung, and others); and we have here an interesting example of the kind of "truth of things" which Ronsard wanted the artist to suggest. The "fables" which are to suggest the "truth" are those of the pagan gods and goddesses, the heroes and heroines, the nymphs and shepherds, the satyrs and centaurs, the sirens and sea-monsters which crowd round us throughout Renaissance art; but the truth is the truth about ourselves. The shapes that peer out at us through these fantastic personifications are the shapes of our own impulses, projected into mythological images so that we may see there something of our own nature, if not openly, then as through a glass, darkly. That was the Neoplatonic theory of art which passed into the origins of opera, whose first librettists were followers of Ronsard.

## Toward Opera in Florence

It was in Florence that the direct line led on into opera. The courtly masques and interludes there had for a century and more been particularly rich and numerous. None of them became so developed dramatically as *Circe* was in Paris in 1581; but they had even greater advantages in fine poetry, colorful music, and spectacular presentation. In 1565, the interludes for the spoken comedy *La Cofanaria* were dramatically connected episodes from the beautiful fable of Cupid and Psyche, as related by the famous second-century Platonist, Apuleius; early in the next year, the extraordinary pageant on wheels of "the genealogy of the pagan gods" was a visible presentation in costume of Boccaccio's huge Neoplatonic textbook bearing this title, with further complications from Giraldi, Conti, Cartari and that confused but fashionable Egyptologist, Horappolo Niliacus—all Neoplatonists on one level of scholarship or another. In 1586, the climax of the wedding celebrations for Cesare d'Este and Virginia de' Medici was a comedy, *L'Amico Fido* ("The Faithful Friend") and its attendant interludes, contrived by the author of that comedy, Giovanni de' Bardi, whom we shall shortly meet again for his influential contributions in the direction of opera; but he did not make these contributions in connection with the interludes under his care, nor was he responsible for the final transition into opera.

In 1589, Bardi's standing and influence had greatly declined, but he was still remembered for his success in 1586, and he was designated "inventor" of the interludes[15] for Bargagli's comedy *La Pellegrina* at the great dynastic wedding between Ferdinando de' Medici and Christine de Lorraine in 1589. The text of these famous interludes is almost entirely by the young Florentine poet Ottavio Rinuccini (1562-1621), who had already provided some of the poetry in 1586. The music is by composers ranging from the celebrated madrigalist Marenzio to the much more unconventional Caccini and Peri, to whom also we shall be coming back; but very little of the music here points on to the solo melody of opera, since nearly all of it is in dance or madrigal forms—more in chordal part-writing than in close counterpoint, it is true, but nevertheless too polyphonic to unfold an on-going drama in music. The decor and costumes of these interludes of 1589 were derived from one of the many illustrated editions of Cartari's[16] popular Neoplatonic textbook of 1556, as may be seen from surviving prints. The scenarios are all derived directly or indirectly from Plato, but are not otherwise dramatically connected. Since Rinuccini was an ardent admirer of Gabriello Chiabrera (1552-1637), ten years his senior, and since Chiabrera was the most renowned Italian follower of Ronsard, these interludes set a Neoplatonic precedent for opera—of which Rinuccini presently became the first librettist, and Chiabrera the second or perhaps the third. One of the madrigal poems of 1589, and possibly one stage dragon for the much admired conflict of Apollo with the Python, actually turned up again in the earliest opera a few years later. That is how close these brilliant interludes in Florence were to opera. Two further additions were still needed, however, for the final transition into opera. One was a dramatic form suitable for unfolding as much in the music as in the words; the other was a musical texture. The dramatic form was ready at hand, in the shape of pastoral drama; the musical texture was in preparation.

The pastoral drama began as an idyllic poem in vernacular Italian, for acting with incidental music but not for singing in such a way as to be carried forward by its music. In imitation of classical Greek drama (except that Greek poetry did not rhyme), there is regular meter for dialogue and narrative, and a variety of meters and rhyme-schemes for reflective passages and lyrical choruses. This is an arrangement which offers excellent support for a similar variety of musical forms and textures; but it had not as yet occurred to any poet or musician to make a drama in music out of it, if only because there was not as yet any musical form or texture available to carry forward dialogue and narrative with the required dramatic impetus. The thought of a drama all in music and the thought of the forward-moving music to carry it were one and the same thought; and when that thought arrived, opera arrived.

The model for the pastoral drama seems to have been the beautiful little *Orfeo* ("Orpheus") by Angelo Poliziano, produced at Mantua in the latter part of the fifteenth century.[17] Poliziano had been brought as a boy into the household of Lorenzo de' Medici in Florence, where he became Ficino's most brilliant pupil, and actually guided and inspired Botticelli (ten years older than himself) in the proper use of Neoplatonic symbolism.[18] There was a half-playful and half-serious cult of Orpheus at Ficino's villa on the outskirts of Florence, where Plato's Academy, on the outskirts of Athens, was solemnly imitated. In the slightly differing versions of the myth as recounted by Ovid, Virgil, and others, Orpheus the legendary musician (to whom the Neoplatonists also attributed much philosophical and mystic wisdom) descended into the underworld to win by his singing the release of his beloved Euridice, who had died from the bite of a snake. Unable to keep the required condition of not looking round at her during the upward journey, he lost her forever, and was himself (for reasons variously explained by the ancient commentators and their Neoplatonic successors) torn to pieces by the Bacchae, female worshippers of Dionysus, the god of wine and of manic inspiration. Poliziano kept this tragic ending; but after much discussion in the sixteenth century it was generally accepted that such festive occasions should not be marred by anything so sad or ill-omened as a tragic ending. Thus the later pastoral dramas, including the earliest librettos of opera, acquired the remarkable distinction of being tragedies without the tragic ending. They were sometimes called tragi-comedies, which did not imply comic, but happily concluded. They were always supported by much incidental music. A little of the music for Beccari's *Il Sacrificio d'Abramo* ("The Sacrifice of Abraham") survives.[19] The most famous pastoral dramas, and the ones most frequently exploited afterward for opera, were Tasso's[20] *Aminta* and Guarini's[21] *Il Pastor Fido* ("The Faithful Shepherd"). Subsequent imitations of these were on the whole inferior, but numerous.

Meanwhile, the musical texture which, when combined with the pastoral drama, produced opera, was being independently prepared. The chief musical and literary discussion of the sixteenth century, of which we have already seen a rather pedantic sample in the French Pleiad, was on how to recover the intimate classical association of words and music. For to what else could be attributed that power of music, not just over emotion, but over specific emotions such as love or hate or hope or fear, which Plato, Aristotle, and other ancient authorities agreed in ascribing to it? That capacity, by a mere change of prevailing tonality (mode), for making a man first angry, and then calm, or brave and vigorous, or soft and cowardly? Unlike Greek literature, architecture, sculpture, or even painting (in late forms), Greek music has not survived for comparison or inspiration. It was thus natural for the poets to take the lead. Bembo, for instance, the most esteemed successor to the earlier Renaissance genius of Petrarch, drew attention in a fascinating little treatise of 1525 to a basic attribute of language.[22] This is that words in themselves have not only a semantic meaning depending on their usage and grammar, but also a sonorous meaning depending on their actual sound. For example: A word accented three syllables from the end slips off the tongue so easily as to suggest by its mere sound something eager or facile; Bembo called this class of word "slippery," which itself is just such a slippery word. A word accented on the syllable at the end cuts off so abruptly as to suggest something plodding, sluggish, or deliberate; Bembo called it "truncated," as in the word "abate" (or as in the word "truncate" in the English though not in the American pronunciation). And a word accented two syllables from the end comes out so unobtrusively as to suggest something ordinary or intermediate; Bembo called it "level," and this itself is just such a level word.

Poetry has many such resources of sonority. Meters and rhyme-schemes may be simple or complex, regular or irregular. Lines may be of constant length and therefore give an inconspicuous continuity to dialogue or narrative—especially if they are unrhymed, or rhyme only on a concluding couplet. Or lines of mixed length may be used to achieve a more lyrical and sophisticated elegance— especially if grouped into matching stanzas. Syllables may be irregularly added to the meter of the line or subtracted from it. Two syllables, when not separated by a consonant, can be run together (elided) so that they sound almost as one: the more the elisions, the heavier the sonority. The regular pause in the middle of a line (caesura) can be shifted to give an irregular lilt. The natural rise and fall, speed and rhythm of the syllables can be used in a direct and simple way, or manipulated (and even opposed to the prevailing meter) for a more subtle effect. These are all instances of the sonorous meanings of poetry, which on Bembo's principles have to be matched to its semantic meanings.

But music is a language which only has sonorous meanings. In the middle of the sixteenth century, the distinguished composer and theorist Zarlino[23] dis- cussed them very much as Bembo had discussed the sonorous meanings of poetry. For example: Concords fall so smoothly on the ear (this is a physical consequence of the properties of acoustics) that they suggest by their mere sound something restful, or conclusive, or agreeable. Discords fall so harshly on the ear that they suggest something restless, or inconclusive, or disagreeable. Diatonic intervals—those that are native to the prevailing tonality—sound stable or confident. Chromatic intervals—those that are foreign to the prevailing tonality—sound shifting or grievous. Rapid rhythms suggest vigor or agitation; slow rhythms suggest dignity or repose. Repetition may suggest persistence, or (if the repetition is varied) growth. Higher pitches are more acute, and sound more excited; lower pitches are more grave, and sound more relaxed. These are all instances of the sonorous meanings of music, which on Zarlino's principles have to be matched to the sound and sense of the poetry.

For it was commonly agreed that in vocal music, as Plato had insisted, it is for the music to serve the words. But beyond that, a great controversy opened up. On the one hand, Zarlino was followed by the brilliant composers of "modern madrigals"[24] who used mainly a light and relaxed counterpoint, with rising themes for going up to heaven, falling themes for going down to hell, and other almost too literal representations of the words in the music; but they certainly used this counterpoint expressively. On the other hand, there was a small but influential group of mainly amateur musicians and intellectuals who denied that any counterpoint can serve the words or express their meaning. Their patron was that same Florentine nobleman, Giovanni de' Bardi, whom we have already encountered as an organizer of interludes in 1586 and 1589. His group was afterward remembered as Bardi's *Camerata:* a word not found in the contemporary Italian dictionaries,[25] but evidently coined from *camera* (room) as affectionate slang for Bardi's "roomful" or circle of friends. The only trained musicologist among them was Vincenzo Galilei, ironically enough a former pupil of Zarlino. In a brief but brilliantly polemical *Discussion of Ancient and Modern Music*[26] which was published in Florence in 1581, Galilei used an argument provided for him by Girolamo Mei (a distinguished Florentine scholar of the Greek language, then resident in Rome[27]) to the effect that the Greeks had neither counterpoint nor harmony; and that while harmony might be an acceptable modern improvement, counterpoint in vocal music was not. For with counterpoint, it was argued, one part may rise while another falls; one part may move swiftly in short notes while another moves slowly in long notes; one part may be solidly diatonic while another is shiftingly chromatic. These are all sonorous meanings, but not the same sonorous meanings; therefore they cancel one another out; therefore counterpoint cannot serve the words.

As a matter of fact, we do not hear contrapuntal parts as cancelling out or conflicting; we hear them as adding up to that total pattern or *Gestalt* which is itself the counterpoint. Nevertheless, drama is a confrontation of individuals, and opera does need solo melody. Those lightly contrapuntal madrigal comedies of which Orazio Vecchi's *Amfiparnasso*[28] of 1594 is the best known series are amusing little sketches in music, to be sung energetically with mime and gesture; but they are just what Vecchi called them, "a spectacle which one looks at with the mind, where it enters through the ears, and not through the eyes." The historic achievement of Bardi's circle was a style of solo melody for the voice which could lead into opera. It was called at the time the reciting style (*stile recitativo*) or, less often, the representative style (*stile rappresentativo*). Solo singing, of course, was not a novelty. Poems in regular stanzas had long been sung to melodies more or less improvised around traditional formulas. The top or another line of part-songs was also often sung, with instruments supplying more or less the other parts. But the reciting style was composed essentially and exclusively as a solo melody for voice with subordinate accompaniment; and this, though by no means without precedent, had no precedent then known of quite this character.

In the 1570s, Galilei was making early experiments, though none of his in the reciting style survive.[29] He was followed by Giulio Caccini (*c.* 1545-1618), a brilliant young tenor and composer brought from Rome to Florence by Bardi. Caccini's[30] strophic arias are in repeating line-schemes set gracefully to melodies that also repeat, with slight variations, above unobtrusive basses. His solo madrigals are to verses of the poetic form then called madrigal, not repeating but through-composed, except that there may be a couplet treated in the music as a refrain. There are, however, also arias in recitative style, with repeating line-schemes and melodies, but so declamatory that they point toward opera. For the central problem of opera is not in its lyrical passages, to which the normal arts of song apply. The central problem of opera is declamation. The historical solution for this problem was recitative.

## *The Resources of Opera*

The solution brought by *recitative* to the operatic problem of declamation depends upon its capacity for carrying with the utmost continuity and flexibility any swiftness of action, any outpouring of words, any change of mood or clash of temperament which the drama requires, while still keeping music in the picture. The form of recitative is open at the end, so that it can be made as short or as long as the scene requires. The texture is supple, so that it can follow the fluctuations of spoken rhythm, and at least suggest the indefinite outlines of spoken pitch, while still falling recognizably within measure and melody. A rush of notes, one to a syllable, often climaxes on a longer note of higher pitch. Intervals tend to grow wider with excitement, narrower with relaxation. Passing dissonances surge unrestrictedly over a protracted bass note until the next change of harmony is reached. But except in comic scenes (which are often in some local dialect), it is not the speech of the street-corner or even of the drawing-room which is thus stylized in musical equivalents; it is the spoken declamation of the conventional stage, artful in every subtlety of timing and inflection, every sharpening of the consonants and coloring of the vowels, every known trick of the theatrical profession which can be translated into music. The essence of recitative is to be dramatically expressive.

There is an intermediate texture, known as *arioso,* of which the form is also open at the end, but with a more tuneful melody and a more active bass, changing harmony more frequently. The essence of arioso is to hold a balance between dramatic and musical expressiveness.

But *aria* is a form closed at the end by a timely cadence, with a shape of its own which the music itself implies. The words cannot take precedence, as they do in recitative and arioso, but must be somehow accommodated to the music. Passing dissonance is more controlled, and the bass is drawn more into the motion of the melody, with a more regular pulse of harmonic change. The texture is closer, and the rhythm in performance, though not rigid, adheres more nearly to the notated values. Yet there is drama in aria also; for here the music has every opportunity to express the full feeling aroused by the action, and feeling always counts for most in opera. It is the essence of aria to be musically expressive.

The orchestra both supports the singers and spaces out the drama with instrumental passages. Further variety comes from duets and larger ensembles of solo voices, and from choruses—accompanied or unaccompanied, and sometimes danced. Ballets may also be included simply for their entertainment value. But any such marginal features are usually most successful in opera when they are most convincingly incorporated into the dramatic action. With all its varied resourcefulness, opera has always been an art of individuals. Drama is the interplay of individual characters, and character in opera is brought to life by the virtuosity of individual singers.

Now it was the pursuit of individuality, under the stimulus of Greek antiquity rediscovered, that did most to bring Renaissance society away from Medieval Christendom. In music, it was not just the melodic freedom of the reciting style that was relatively novel, but still more so the harmonic freedom which underlay it. The greatest musical innovation of the Renaissance, in practice although not as yet in theory, was modulation—that potentially unrestricted progression through the keys which makes music itself a drama, and which in so doing gave the music of that time an unprecedented capacity for unfolding dramatic character and situation. Individuality in Renaissance society, with modulation and vocal virtuosity in late Renaissance music: these were the underlying reasons why at this period in history, and not before, opera emerged.

## Notes

1. Samuel Johnson, *Lives of the English Poets*, Dublin, 1779-1781, ed. G.B. Hill, Oxford, 1905, p. 160.
2. Blaise Pascal, *Pensées*, publ. only in posthumous collections from 1670.
3. Richard Wagner discussed aspects of this question in *Oper und Drama* ("Opera and Drama"), Leipzig, 1852 (preface dated 1851); *Religion und Kunst* ("Religion and Art"), in *Bayreuther Blätter*, 1880-1881, esp. the first sentence; letter to Liszt (November 25, 1850); letter to Röckel (August 23, 1856). For Engl. translation, see Richard Wagner, *Collected Prose Works*, 8 vols., tr. W.A. Ellis, London, 1892-1899.
4. Samuel Taylor Coleridge, *Biographia Literaria*, London, 1817, Ch. 9.
5. *Circe, ou le Ballet comique de la royne*, ed. Beaujoyeulx, Paris, 1582.
6. See Edgar Wind, *Pagan Mysteries in the Renaissance*, London, 1958, 2nd ed. of 1967, pp. 78 ff., on the Platonic sources and Neoplatonic significance of these remarkable paintings.
7. Dante Alighieri, *Inferno*, early 14th cent., IX, 62-63.
8. Giovanni Boccaccio, *Genealogia Deorum Gentilium* ("Genealogy of the Pagan Gods"), manuscripts from the 1370s, many editions current in the sixteenth century.
9. Marsilio Ficino, *Opera Omnia*, ed. of Basle (1576), pp. 241 ff., p. 638.
10. Pierre de Ronsard, *Works*, ed. H. Vaganay (Paris), 1950, II, p. 997.
11. Goethe to Eckermann, transl. Richard Friedenthal, in *Goethe: His Life and Times*, London, 1965, p. 493.

12. See note 3 above.
13. Natale Conti, *Mythologiae* . . . ("Of Mythology . . ."), Venice, 1567 (an ed. cited for 1551 probably did not exist): in ed. of Venice, 1581, pp. 374-80.
14. See note 5 above.
15. Federico Ghisi, introd., D.P. Walker, ed., *Musique des Intermèdes de "La Pellegrina,"* Paris, 1962.
16. Vincenzo Cartari, *Le Imagini . . . de i Dei de gli Antichi* ("The Images of the Gods of the Ancients"), Venice, 1556.
17. Angelo Poliziano, *Orfeo*, performance at Mantua previously attributed to 1472, now most probably to 1478, the latest date possible being 1483.
18. See note 6 above.
19. Agostino Beccari, *Il Sacrificio d'Abramo* ("The Sacrifice of Abraham"), perf. Ferrara, 1554.
20. Torquato Tasso, *Aminta*, perf. and publ. Ferrara, 1573.
21. Giovanni Battista Guarini, *Il Pastor Fido* ("The Faithful Shepherd"), written in Ferrara in developing versions 1581-1590, prob. perf. Turin, 1585, publ. Venice 1590.
22. Pietro Bembo, *Prose della Volgar Lingua* ("Essays on the Vernacular Tongue"), Venice, 1525.
23. Gioseffe Zarlino, *Istituzioni*, Venice, 1558, IV, 32; *Tutte l'Opera*, I, Venice, 1589, p. 92; and compare Plato, *Republic*, Bk. III, Bk. X.
24. Girolamo Frescobaldi, *Toccate* ("Toccatas"), Rome, 1615-1616, preface, thus described them.
25. First found, to my knowledge, in the *Vocabulario* ("Dictionary") of the Accademici della Crusca, Venice, 1612.
26. Vincenzo Galilei, *Dialogo della Musica Antica, e Moderna*, Florence, 1581.
27. Girolamo Mei, letters ed. (with a most valuable introd.) by Claude Palisca, no place stated, 1960.
28. Orazio Vecchi, *Amfiparnasso*, perf. ? Modena, 1594, publ. Venice, 1597.
29. See C. V. Palisca, "The 'Camerata Fiorentina': a Reappraisal," *Studi Musicali*, Rome, 1972, pp. 203-36. This is a most valuable and important article.
30. In Giulio Caccini, *Nuove Musiche*, Florence, 1602.

# PART ONE

## Continuous Opera

Cᴇ✗✗ꜱꜱ

## The First Great Period: To 1700

The immediate cause of opera was an ideal which was stimulated by classical Greek drama but was not intended to imitate it. This ideal was a continuously unfolding "drama all in music" (*dramma tutto per musica*), of which the poetical structure follows the story, and the music follows the poetry, as flexibly and as faithfully as possible. This is music drama in the fullest sense.

In the earliest operas, the librettos are serious. The tension of the drama and the quality of the poetry are generally high. The main musical substance is recitative of a very fluid but melodious variety, merging readily into arioso, but using formal aria only to heighten the expression or to soften the sentiment where something in the natural feelings of the drama calls for it—and then usually in quite simple forms, such as strophic verses each to the same or nearly the same music repeated. Choruses and ensembles, when present, are like part-songs or madrigals of the more lightly polyphonic sort. The orchestra is based on strings, both bowed and plucked, with some woodwind and occasionally brass (especially trumpets with drums); it was not allowed to obscure the singers or to distract from them by instrumental passages longer than short introductions or refrains (*ritornelli*) or dances (sometimes also sung).

**13**

Early in the seventeenth century, this high dramatic and poetical tension was for the most part greatly relaxed, as librettos came under the influence of popular spoken drama (especially the Spanish drama then very fashionable) and grew looser and more inconsequential—though far from uneventful. Comic scenes were introduced for Shakespearean contrast and richness; but comic operas were uncommon, until later reforms of the libretto disfavored comic scenes in serious operas. By the second half of the seventeenth century, less attention was being given to shaping out the drama in poetry and music, and more attention to meeting the growing demands of the great virtuoso singers and their audiences for fine singing on its own account. As the arias became more elaborate, the conventions for introducing them became more rigid, and the recitative connecting them became more perfunctory. There was a gradual transition from the flexible but concentrated ideal of early baroque opera, as in Monteverdi, toward the relatively standardized and diffuse ideal of late baroque opera, as in Handel.

Florence, the birthplace of opera, was soon rivaled by Mantua, and shortly afterward by Rome. The lead then passed to Venice; but there were many other centers in Italy and other countries by that time. On whatever soil, opera remained as characteristically Italian an idiom as it had begun, until fairly late in the seventeenth century, when Italian opera was just about to turn decisively away from its original ideal as drama continuously and flexibly unfolding in words and music. French opera originated from that Italian idiom, and carried forward that original ideal almost intact from Lully in the mid-baroque to Rameau in the late-baroque. While the Italian librettos became more formal than dramatic, with vocal supremacy as their main consideration, the French librettos were no less formal, but were composed for dramatic expressiveness, and were still mainly set to a variety of recitative as melodious and as eloquent as the earlier Italian recitative had ever been. This parting of the ways between Italian and French baroque opera was the earliest such parting in the history of the art.

We may broadly distinguish early baroque opera as continuous and flexible, but late baroque opera (other than French) as discontinuous and predetermined by vocal rather than dramatic considerations. On this broad view, the seventeenth century may be called the first great period of opera, and its primary species may be called *continuous opera*.

# 2

# The Earliest Operas

The final transition into opera came some years after the decline of Bardi's *Camerata*, and shortly after his departure for Rome in 1592. Bardi's younger contemporary and social rival, Jacopo Corsi, had a circle of his own, not called a *Camerata* and not part of Bardi's *Camerata*. As Bardi had brought Caccini from Rome and been his patron, so Corsi brought, also from Rome, the younger tenor and composer Jacopo Peri (1561-1633). It was under Bardi that Rinuccini had gained youthful fame by his Neoplatonic verses for the interludes of 1586 and especially of 1589. But it was for Corsi, around 1594, that Rinuccini drafted his pastoral drama *Dafne*, "to make a simple test of what the music of our age could do."[1] This was the initiative which brought the transition into opera.

## Peri and the First Opera

Like its model (Poliziano's *Orfeo*), Rinuccini's *Dafne* combines uniform blank verse, very suitable for recitative, with patterned stanzas, very suitable for arias and choruses. But as yet there was no such thing as recitative. There were only arias in recitative style, with which both Caccini and Peri were by then equally experienced. Rinuccini himself doubted whether any music of his age could unfold drama as he supposed Greek drama to have been unfolded; but Corsi, thinking otherwise, began an amateur attempt, which he handed over to his professional associate, the composer Peri. After prolonged revisions of both text and music, a historic first performance was given at Corsi's residence during the

Carnival early in 1598. This[2] is the date of the earliest opera. Only fragments of the music survive,[3] but they resemble the *Euridice* of Rinuccini and Peri two years later, which is demonstrably opera.

*Dafne* is a mythological opera. It begins well, with Apollo's defeat of a monstrous snake or dragon, the legendary Python. But having killed this monster with his great bow, Apollo is unwise enough to tease Cupid, the god of love, about *his* little bow, asking him (more pointedly than at first appears) whether he intends to "uncover his eyes or shoot in the dark." Cupid, foreseeably, takes instant vengeance by shooting Apollo. Now himself the victim, Apollo falls desperately in love with the nymph Dafne, who is herself out hunting with bow and arrows. She rejects him with the protest: "I am a mortal woman, not a goddess from heaven." He answers (again more pointedly than at first appears): "If such light glows in mortal beauty, heaven's no longer delights me." She prays for delivery, and is turned into a laurel tree. "Immortal as I am," he paradoxically laments, "I languish and I die." But then he has a saving thought: "Always will I make your leaves and branches a garland for my golden hair," and for the crowning of poets, whose patron deity Apollo is.

This is the plot of the earliest libretto. If we take it in the spirit of its times as a veil which half reveals in the very act of half concealing an inner meaning, we find one of those truths about human nature of which Ronsard spoke. For Apollo was not only the Greek god of poets and other artists, in his role as leader of the Nine Muses. He was also the god of the daylight sun: "everywhere the image of the divine truth and goodness," as Ficino[4] described it, and a common mythological symbol for the light of conscious human reason. When Apollo kills that monstrous Python, we know without needing to be told that it is a victory of light over darkness. But Greek mythology took the symbol a stage further. When the corpse of the Python was left to rot in a pit under Apollo's temple at Delphi, the rising fumes entered the body of his priestess, causing her to prophesy. The implication of this is that the underworld of the unconscious is not only dark but ambivalent, the source of our potential alike for destructiveness and for creativeness. And when Apollo asks here whether Cupid intends to "uncover his eyes or shoot in the dark," he is referring to Plato's allegory[5] of the earthly Venus, whose blindfolded son Cupid stands for sensual passion, and the heavenly Venus, whose son is another Cupid with open eyes, standing for that Socratic passion for inner truth which was the original meaning of "Platonic love." We see them both in Titian's famous Neoplatonic painting of Venus blindfolding the sensual Cupid, while listening intently to whatever it is that Cupid's other, open-eyed self is whispering into her further ear.[6] Cupid in Rinuccini's Neoplatonic libretto, it seems, has shot Apollo "in the dark," since for the time being he prefers Dafne's "mortal beauty" to "heaven's" beauty of the spirit. But then, by accepting his unavoidable frustration in the flesh, he gets back from her, under the symbolism of the laurel leaves with which poets are crowned, the inner value which he has been projecting outward onto her mortal beauty. So it was that Beatrice focused for Dante[7] all that was most feminine in his own creative personality; or Laura for Petrarch; or Fiammetta for Boccaccio; and it is indeed a familiar situation. The

Titian, *Venus Blindfolding Cupid*. Borghese Gallery, Rome.

gain is in conscious maturity, and it comes from accepting the outer frustration for the sake of the inner growth. That is the truth about human nature which Rinuccini half concealed and half revealed in this enchanting libretto for the earliest opera.

Neoplatonic librettos continued into the early seventeenth century; but in the Age of Reason, deliberate symbolism went somewhat out of fashion until its Romantic revival, culminating, for opera, in Wagner. Intuitive symbolism, on the other hand, is so inherent in our human imagination that more or less autonomous images will come in, whether invited or uninvited; and it is the very nature of opera to invite them. Thus it is that opera went on, as opera began, an art rich in fairy-tale suggestiveness.

## Cavalieri and His Borderline Opera

Emilio de' Cavalieri (1550–1602), a Roman nobleman, was brought to Florence in 1588 to be court director of entertainments (to the considerable annoyance of both Bardi and Corsi—but Corsi adapted himself to the situation better); and there he set to music three pastoral poems by his friend Laura Guidiccioni. Two were performed in 1591 and one in 1594. They are lost, but we have evidence that they were sung in short arias throughout, not in recitative, and that they were not regarded as anticipating the first actual opera, which was *Dafne*.[8] But in 1600 Cavalieri returned to Rome for his stage work, *La Rappresentazione di Anima, e di Corpo* ("The Drama of the Soul and the Body").[9] There are large elements here both of the morality play and of the courtly interludes. There is a spoken prologue telling us (Neoplatonically) that we merely think we desire mortal beauty, whereas what we really desire is the lasting happiness that only heavenly delights can offer. But there is also some genuine recitative, in which the Soul receives good advice from Intellect, Counsel, and Guardian Angel. Pleasure and her Companions are disrobed to show inward rottenness (this is a distortion of the authentic Neoplatonic doctrine by which earthly pleasure is a valid though not final stage). There are some lively opposing choruses of damned souls and saved souls, testifying respectively to their eternal punishment and eternal blessedness. The preface gives instructions for full staging, with costumes, acting, and dancing. This is therefore not an oratorio. It is not an undoubted opera, since there is barely enough unfolding of situation and character. But if we do give it the benefit of the doubt, as probably we should, then Cavalieri's little work is the earliest opera to survive complete in both words and music.

## Opera at Court

The marriage in Florence of Henry IV of France (represented by proxy) to Maria de' Medici in 1600 marked the entry of opera into the highest society. For one banquet, an entertainment (we might call it a floor show) was prepared which, though it was not opera, was a good example of that fanciful society play-acting that was part of the background of opera.[10] It was flatteringly pretended that the guests were just a delightful mythological company, on whom Juno and Minerva had dropped in to discuss whether domestic virtue or warlike valor came first, or both at once, when so gentle a bride and so gallant a bridegroom were being united. Next evening, on October 6, Corsi presented to a small but distinguished audience Peri's second opera, *Euridice*,[11] on a libretto by Rinuccini deliberately modeled on Poliziano's *Orfeo*. But to suit a "time of so much gaiety," as he apologetically explained in his preface, Rinuccini changed the tragic ending and made all end happily. This leaves very little tension in the drama, and no growth of character. The prologue is an aria in recitative style; there are other arias of some lyrical charm, and some choruses and dances well placed for further contrast; but the main substance of the opera lies in open-ended recitative of the melodious, early variety, freely alternating with that in-between texture known as arioso. It is all beautifully fitted to the words, but Peri took few liberties to show off his music for its own sake. Within this strict limitation, the little opera is expressive and eloquent. Caccini refused to let his pupils sing in it except on condition of composing himself some of the choruses and the entire (but small) part of Euridice. This he did; but nevertheless, it is Peri's opera.

On October 7 an open rehearsal was held, and on October 9 the performance took place of an opera by Caccini, with some choruses contributed by three other composers. This is *Il Rapimento di Cefalo* ("The Apotheosis of Cephalus") on a colorful Neoplatonic libretto by Chiabrera.[12] The celebrated stage engineer

Apollo's battle with the Python, from Bardi's interlude of 1589. The stage dragon may have reappeared later in Peri's *Dafne*.

Buontalenti provided lavish stage-changes and flying-machines. The cost was astronomical, the audience numbered nearly four thousand, the style was like a showy "interlude," but there is real drama to which the music (unfortunately for the most part lost) undoubtedly contributed in the true manner of opera. The immediate impression was sensational; but there were no subsequent performances, as there were of Peri's *Euridice* (one as late as 1616 in Bologna).

Next Caccini composed in haste a completely serious opera, his *Euridice*. He used the same libretto by Rinuccini which Peri had used, and his score is as similar to Peri's as it could be without actually borrowing the same notes. Caccini managed to get his *Euridice* published in Florence in 1601, three months after the first performance but one or two months before the publication of Peri's *Euridice*. On the strength of this, and of his own prior works in the reciting style (but they were not opera), Caccini tried to claim the credit for having originated opera. This claim was and still is widely believed, but it is not true. Corsi, Rinuccini, and Peri were the pioneering team of opera.

## Notes

1. Ottavio Rinuccini, *La Dafne*, Florence, 1600.

2. Usually given as 1597. This is equally correct, but is misleading unless it is explained that 1597 is Florentine Old Style dating, for which 1598 is the modern rendering. Until 1750, the Florentines began their New Year on March 25 instead of January 1 (as we all do now), and were therefore still calling it 1597 when most other people were already calling it 1598 (but there were other Old Style datings in some other places and at different times, for which see A. Giry, *Manuel de Diplomatique*, Paris, 1894, pp. 83-314).

3. William Porter, "Peri and Corsi's *Dafne:* Some New Discoveries and Observations," *Journal of the American Musicological Society*, XVIII, 2 (1965), 170-96.

4. Marsilio Ficino, *Opera Omnia*, ed. of Basle, 1576, p. 119.

5. Plato, *Symposium*.

6. See note 6, chapter 1.

7. Dante Alighieri, *Vita Nuova* ("New Life"), probably completed by 1300, publ. Florence, 1576.

8. See Pietro de' Bardi's letter written to Giovanni Battista Doni in answer to his request: it was dated December 16, 1634; it is available in Angelo Solerti, *Le Origini del Melodramma*, Turin, 1903, pp. 143–47, or in Engl. transl. by Oliver Strunk, *Source Readings in Music History*, New York, 1950, pp. 363–66. See Doni's own Roman *Tratto della Musica Scenica* ("Treatise on Stage Music") of about 1635, ed. A. F. Gori in his *Trattati di Musica* ("Treatises on Music"), publ. Florence, 1763, II, Ch. ix, pp. 22 ff., and available in Solerti's *Origini*. Doni's evidence in the matter seems really quite conclusive.

9. Emilio de' Cavalieri, *La Rappresentazione di Anima, e di Corpo . . . per Recitar Cantando* ("to recite singing"), on a libretto by Agostino Manni, perf. Rome, Feb. 1600, at the Oratorio della Vallicella; publ. Rome, 1600.

10. Emilio de' Cavalieri, *Dialogo di Giunone e Minerva*, perf. Florence, 1600.

11. Jacopo Peri, *Euridice*, perf. Florence, Feb. 1600, publ. Florence, 1600 (Florentine Old Style, i.e., 1601 modern-style dating), on a libretto by Ottavio Rinuccini, also publ. Florence, 1600.

12. Music lost except for samples by Caccini in his *Nuove Musiche*, Florence, 1602.

# 3

# The Spread of Opera

The first outward spread of the new art of opera was to Mantua, a dukedom of considerable power and affluence, and for long in more or less friendly rivalry with Florence, leading to a considerable exchange of artists. One noble Mantuan who spent over ten years in Florence in the service of Cosimo de' Medici, composing madrigals and music especially for interludes, was Alessandro Striggio the elder. He was present at the celebrated Florentine interludes of 1589, with their conspicuously Neoplatonic scenarios arranged by Bardi under Cavalieri's supervision and mainly to poetry by Rinuccini. One "Alessandrino" played in the orchestra; and this "little Alexander," the son of the great man, was Alessandro Striggio the younger, librettist of the first great Mantuan opera twenty years later, in 1607: *Orfeo* ("Orpheus"), of which the music is by Claudio Monteverdi (1567-1643).

In 1600, not only was the Duke of Mantua present at those resplendent celebrations in Florence which included Peri's *Euridice* (available in print from 1601) and Caccini's *Rapimento di Cefalo:* he lent the Duke of Florence his most distinguished singer, the tenor Francesco Rasi, for the occasion. In 1607, it was the Grand Duke of Florence who in turn lent a noted tenor[1] of his own, Giovanni Gualberto Magli, to the Duke of Mantua, for Monteverdi's *Orfeo;* and the Duke of Mantua, who was present at many rehearsals, particularly appreciated his singing. Monteverdi, though born in Cremona, served from his early manhood in Mantua, where he was promoted master of the chapel (*maestro di cappella*) and made a citizen in 1602; for the first half of his career, therefore, he ranks as a Mantuan composer, with a steady output of madrigals and church music, and two great operas, to his credit. When Duke Vincenzo Gonzaga died in 1612, the succeeding Duke Francesco dismissed Monteverdi, the second half of whose career began in 1613, as a Venetian composer of the utmost renown.

Neither Mantua, nor Monteverdi at Mantua, developed opera independently. But what Florence and Peri originated, Mantua and Monteverdi more firmly established. Early opera in Mantua was of the same kind as early opera in Florence: Peri's kind (and thereafter Caccini's kind). The difference is solely in the genius. At the age of forty, Monteverdi was in his rising prime, a craftsman of high skill and experience in the style of the "modern" madrigalists—but not previously in the reciting style, of which he nevertheless made his *Orfeo* in 1607 the best example of opera so far composed.[2] The recitative has a longer arch, a stronger tension, a richer eloquence; the ensembles and choruses (many of them danced), the orchestral introductions and interludes and accompanying melodies are more brilliant and more affecting; the music has more beauty of its own to add, while doing no less faithful service to the words.

Striggio the Mantuan, like Rinuccini the Florentine whom he evidently knew and followed, made use of that same familiar Neoplatonic image of the clear daylight sky, ruled by Apollo as god of the sun, to suggest reason and consciousness, and of the dark night and the hateful clouds, and the yet darker underworld, to suggest unreason and unconsciousness. As published separately in Mantua in 1607, the poem not only has Euridice lost a second time, but Orpheus torn to pieces in the traditional tragic ending. As altered (probably by Striggio himself, since there is no falling off or change of style) for Monteverdi's score, the tragic ending is softened by having Orpheus taken to heaven instead by his father Apollo; but we shall see that this is not altogether an evasion, but rather another Neoplatonic metaphor for the same mythological implication.

## The Genius of Monteverdi

*Orfeo* has a short but radiant introduction (called *Toccata*) all on the chord of C major (written), which sounds in (concert) D major because mutes are requested which raise the trumpets by one tone. "All the instruments" are to play: two each are listed of harpsichords, chamber organs, archlutes (three occur in the score itself); one regals (portable reed organ resembling a tiny harmonium); one large double harp; ten normal strings of the violin family together with two tiny kits, and five viols; a high recorder; four trombones (five occur in the score); two cornetti (small wooden horns); three muted trumpets, and one (clarino) trumpet played high, with drums not mentioned but customarily present. It was a typical orchestra as used for late Renaissance and early baroque interludes—but probably not a typical orchestra for early seventeenth-century opera.

Next La Musica, music personified, most appropriately sings a prologue in which she promises to be with us movingly in scenes from this moving fable. Like Peri's prologue in his *Euridice*, and others of the period, this prologue is in the texture of recitative but the structure of a strophic aria, with instrumental introduction and refrain (ritornello): for each verse of the words, the melody repeats almost the same, above the same bass. That is to say, it is an aria in recitative style. But it is here that we may begin to notice Monteverdi's outstanding craftsmanship. La Musica makes conspicuous use of a fragment of melody, a mere descending scale; but we have heard it already. It came, together with a similar ascending scale, in that brilliant orchestral introduction (*Toccata*) which begins the opera. So far, they hardly appear to be themes, but merely common material such as Peri's or Caccini's recitative might show, to say nothing of contemporary madrigals. It is only later on that we may realize with what deliberate persistence they are being used throughout the opera, and with what unifying effect.

EXAMPLE 1    Monteverdi, *Orfeo:* ascending and descending scale-like passage as unifying theme, (a) introduction; (b) prologue, first verse with instrumental refrain; (c) Act I, opening recitative of shepherd; (d) chorus; (e) from Orpheus' first words; (f) from Euridice's first words. (Other instances are numerous. Figured bass realizations are mine.)

The purpose of Act I is to build up that pastoral fantasy of simple joys and sorrows, modest ambitions and tranquil happiness, on which poets have projected our unconscious yearnings for the supposed bliss of our own childhood and the yet remoter childhood of our race. Here are nymphs and shepherds rejoicing that their gifted leader Orpheus is as happy as he had before been miserable. And so the chorus calls propitiously on Hymen, the god of marriage: "may your burning torch be like a rising sun" and keep away "the shadows of suffering and grief." A shepherdess takes up this familiar Neoplatonic metaphor, asking the Muses to "tear away the dark veil of every cloud."

Orpheus at once confirms the same poetic theme, asking the sun, who is "the life of the world," and "sees all things," if ever he saw a happier lover; and as he turns to his Euridice, she answers him as happily. Yet her melody spans an interval which is not happy, but the most uneasy in all our traditional tonality: the tritone of three whole tones (D to G sharp here), dividing the octave ambivalently in the middle. It was a not uncommon interval in very early opera when extreme grief was to be expressed. But what has grief to do with Euridice's first words of happiness? Grief has nothing to do with her words here; but grief is going to come into her story soon enough. The irony thus prepared in the music is not sprung in the drama until, in the next act, the idyll is shattered by a messenger announcing the death of Euridice. But then, indeed, we begin to hear that grievous tritone again, not once but often, both in that sad scene, and later again in the opera when Euridice dies her second death. The hint of prophetic uneasiness in the music here is a small touch; but it is a touch of operatic genius. Only opera could have accomplished it.

EXAMPLE 2    Monteverdi, *Orfeo:* the tritone interval of grief, (a) Act I, ironically to happy words on Euridice's entry; (b) Act II, descending scale, then tritone to tragic words as the messenger describes the death of Euridice; (c) Act IV, as Orpheus is about to look back and lose Euridice for the second time; (d) the same scene, as Euridice dies her second death—and notice that here the descending-scale theme first combines in bars 1-2 with the tritone D-G sharp, on a most excruciating turn of the harmony; (e) the same scene, as Orpheus tries in vain to follow her; (f) Act V, as he realizes that he will never see her in the flesh again. (Figured bass realizations are mine.)

(d) **Euridice**

Ahi_____ vis - ta trop-po dol - ce  e trop-po a-mar - a
*Ah,_____ sight\_\_ too sweet\_\_  and\_ too bit - ter*

(e) **Orpheus**

Ma    chi me'l neg' ohi - me?    So - gno,ò va - neg - gio?
*But    who de - nies it me?    Dream, or de - lu - sion?*

(f) **Orpheus**

Si non ve - drò più ma - i    de l'a - ma - ta Eu - ri -
*So shall I see no more    the sweet eyes of my*

di - ce i dol - ci ra - i
*loved Eu - ri - di - ce_____*

In Act II, the poetry first delights us with a lyrical succession of stanzas, each of four lines, and rhyming on the simple and graceful scheme *abba:* first rhyme, second rhyme, second rhyme, first rhyme. The lines for Orpheus have eight syllables; the lines for shepherds or the chorus have seven syllables. When Orpheus sings, his music adds a further touch of elegance; for he repeats the first two lines of each stanza after the second two lines. The scheme of this is *aba:* a miniature da capo aria of first couplet, second couplet, first couplet. But now, when least we expect it, the blow falls. At one moment, there is a shepherd in lilting, triple-time C major, celebrating "so happy a day." At the next moment, a messenger has run in; the C bass has been wrenched to C sharp (of a 6-3 A major triad) for the most simple yet poignant of modulations (see Ex. 2b); the poetry has slumped into sudden heaviness; and Orpheus learns that his beloved Euridice is dead.

> Ahi caso acerbo! ahi fato empio e crudele!
> ahi stelle ingiuriose, ahi cielo avaro!
>
> Ah bitter chance! Ah pitiless and cruel fate!
> Ah stars injurious, ah covetous heaven!

The meter of these two lines in the Italian is one which is very usual for those portions of an early opera libretto carrying dialogue and action: eleven-syllable lines having much the effect of English blank verse (as in Shakespeare). But here, each line of this sombre couplet packs into its eleven-syllable meter no less than eighteen actual syllables. This is done by the normal and legitimate poetical device of elision: two syllables, not separated by a consonant (the *h* of *ahi* does not rate as a consonant), are scanned as one; but they nevertheless weigh heavier than usual, and slow down the pace. Two or even three elisions in a line of eleven metrical syllables would not be unduly straining this normal resource: but *seven* elisions, to pack in *eighteen* actual syllables, is a virtuoso effect of rare intensity. The lines are so weighted down that they can hardly move, and they are set to equally gruelling music (Ex. 2b). Again we see a double technique of words and music in drama, which only opera possesses.

There has been a surge of strings, a sparkle of lutes and harpsichords, a double-bass to give sonorous support. Out they all go at this moment of ill omen, and only a small chamber organ and a single lute carry on the sparse accompaniment. It is a quietness more poignant than any noisy violence of grief. But the harmonies are grievous, with that terrible tritone growing more prominent all through, and other harsh intervals making the melody jagged and the chords distressing. Orpheus cannot yet take it in, and the music shows it by scarcely rational modulations, or rather side-slips: E major to G minor; E flat major to E major; and E flat major to A major, straight across the tritone interval.

Then the messenger settles to her long narrative of how Euridice, bitten by the snake in the grass, "grew pale, and the light faded from her eyes with which she put the sun to shame"; and so, calling "Orpheus, Orpheus" (E major), she breathed a heavy sigh (G minor), and died. Orpheus knows it now, and sings a

EXAMPLE 3    Monteverdi, *Orfeo*, Act II, harmonic side-slips for the bewilderment of Orpheus on first hearing of Euridice's death.

heartfelt recitative, first rising by the ascending scale to a peak of high resolve; then falling again by the descending scale as he tells us of this resolve, which is: "if verses have any power, to go unharmed to the deepest caverns, and having softened the heart of the king of the shadows," to bring his Euridice back again; or else stay with her in death. "Farewell earth, farewell sky and sun," he laments; and down he goes, while the shepherds restore the music to rational balance in their formal though grievous finale.

Trombones had long been associated with scenes in the underworld (they still were in Mozart's *Don Giovanni*); and trombones, with silvery cornettos and that snarling little near-harmonium, the regals, greet Orpheus on his descent at the start of Act III. We may be sure that the change of scene was impressively staged: underworld scenes were a gift to the Baroque producer. The allegorical figure of Hope has guided Orpheus "to this sad and dark kingdom where the rays of the sun have never reached" in search of "those happy lights," Euridice's eyes, "which alone bring day to my eyes." Now he reads over the stone gateway Dante's famous line: "Abandon hope all ye who enter here." But Music, as she promised in the Prologue, is still with us, as Orpheus sings the central aria of this central Act III, *Possente Spirto*, "Powerful spirit and terrible divinity without whom no passage is made to the other shore." The powerful spirit is Charon, ferryman of the river Styx; and Orpheus lulls him to sleep, if not to compliance, with the utmost of his legendary virtuosity as poet and musician.

The poetry is in Dante's own meter, that simple but exquisite *terza rima* of three-line stanzas (rhyming *aba, bcb, cdc,* up to a concluding four-line *yzyz*). The music repeats with variations, over an almost unvaried bass, for all six stanzas (other than the fifth); and there are refrains for different instruments (violins, cornettos, double harp), which also accompany their respective stanzas. The complexity and brilliance of the song, ending with simplicity as if from the heart to the heart, contribute integrally to the drama; for without the power of his music, Orpheus could not have got past Charon, the guardian of the underworld. As soon as Charon drops off to sleep, Orpheus jumps into the boat, and over he goes.

More of the same underworld music; and we find ourselves for Act IV in the palace of Pluto (Hades) and his queen Proserpina (Persephone). She is pleading with him on behalf of Orpheus: "if ever you drew the sweetness of love from these eyes (*luci*, lights)," to let Euridice return. And Pluto assents: "but before he draws his feet from this abyss, let him never turn to her his eager eyes (*lumi*, lights)," or she will be lost to him again forever. Nevertheless, Orpheus does turn round, and she is lost to him again forever. "What hidden power," he asks in vain, "draws me against my will to the hateful light?" And we hear his anguished feelings in the music as it outlines again that anguished tritone from D to G sharp, exacerbated here by passing through a constricting diminished third, B flat to G sharp, on the way: for which see Ex. 2e. But the orchestra, after the manner of opera, makes quite another comment on the situation—a healing comment, with a fine new Symphony in seven real parts through the most rational of modulations, touching on chords of A major, D minor, G major, C major, and F major; then smoothly through A minor and, with a moment of the dominant E major, back to the tonic A major again. A five-part chorus of spirits, in orderly counterpoint, describes "virtue, a ray of celestial beauty, that merit of the soul in which the sun itself finds value," as alone enduring.

For Act V, we are back in those pastoral glades where Orpheus found so much happiness and so much grief; and we are listening again to that first instrumental ritornello, as if to assure us that the beginning will not be lost in the end. Orpheus is still in his state of temporary distraction, with harsh and bitter music once more expressing it in harmonic side-slips reminiscent of his previous grief and Euridice's. But his healing begins when he calls Euridice "my soul (*anima mea*)," and promises: "to you I dedicate my lyre and my song, as before I offered my burning spirit in sacrifice on the altar of my heart." This recalls Conti's Neoplatonic explanation, in 1567, that Euridice is "that soul (*animam*) which is married to Orpheus as to the body."[3] It seems that Orpheus, like Apollo in Rinuccini's *Dafne*, is having to learn that his beloved, Euridice the woman, has been carrying the projected image of his own soul, his feminine component. By looking round while still within the underworld (which hints mythologically at his own unconscious) he lost the woman, but regained that part of himself to which his lyre and his song really belong. As if in answer, his father Apollo "descends singing." Since "no joy down here endures," Apollo suggests, "if you wish to enjoy immortal life, come with me to heaven which invites you." But Orpheus still hesitates: "Shall I never again see the sweet radiance of my beloved Euridice?" And Apollo answers, as Dante himself thinking of his Beatrice might have answered: "You will look with love upon her fair semblance in the sun and the stars." With that, they break into a duet of perfect accord; the cloud machine carries them grandly up; the chorus comments approvingly; and with a danced Morisco to end all happily, this masterpiece of very early opera concludes.

There was a brilliant sequel in Mantua when, for the wedding of the hereditary prince in 1608, an immense temporary theater was erected, holding some four- to five thousand spectators. Early in the year came the *Dafne* of Marco da Gagliano (1582-1643), a young Florentine composer of rising prominence, on the original libretto by the Florentine poet Rinuccini; publication of the score was in the same year, in Florence. The style resembles Monteverdi, who brought Mantua still more fame in May of this same year 1608, with his *Arianna* ("Ariadne"), on a new libretto by Rinuccini which was published in that year in Mantua, Florence and Venice, and which survives; but the music, to our special regret, is lost except for the superlative recitative (with lost choral interjections) known as "Ariadne's Lament."

Back in Florence, Gagliano went into the lead after becoming chapel-master (*maestro di cappella*) to the Grand Duke in 1611. He did not eclipse Caccini or Peri; but he was the more versatile professional. He showed his admiration for Peri by including some music of Peri's in two of his own successful operas, of which *La Flora* shows his mastery of what was by then (1628) already a somewhat old-fashioned ideal of opera.[4] The preface to the libretto of his lost sacred opera, *La Regina Sant' Orsolo* ("The Queen Saint Ursula") of 1625, put "true and glorious Christian deeds" above "the empty tales of the pagans": an open attack on Neoplatonic symbolism.[5] And how much further could the original Florentine ideal of opera be relaxed than in Francesca Caccini's *Liberazione di Ruggiero* ("Rescue of Roger") of 1625, which after a good start ends up as a ballet on horseback?[6]

## Rome

The family connections of Caccini, Peri and Cavalieri all linked early opera with Rome; and it was Roman opera which next came to the front. The chief patrons in Florence and Mantua were the reigning dukes; in Rome, they were the princes of the Church, the great cardinals and popes, at this time vastly wealthy, and mostly with a taste for secular entertainment to match. Spectacularly extravagant stage-craft dominated opera even more than elsewhere: when those worthy cardinals lived it up, they lived it up. And madrigal-like ensembles or choruses in many parts, together with ballets, persisted as they did not elsewhere (except for Vienna and later Paris). Early Roman opera was showy opera.

Though not actually known to have been performed in Rome, Stefano Landi's *La Morte d'Orfeo* ("The Death of Orpheus") of 1619 has something of this showiness, combining genuine recitative, fine ensembles, comic relief, and a big, festive ending; the libretto (now thought to be possibly by Francesco Poni) retains a few Neoplatonic touches, but little of the old Florentine seriousness.[7] The first demonstrably Roman opera is *L'Aretusa*, by Filippo Vitali (d. 1653), a Florentine with Roman connections. We learn from the preface that it was performed at the Corsini palace in 1620, and that it claimed to have introduced the reciting style to Rome.[8] There is much recitative of only moderate interest, some two-part ensemble, and a full chorus or ensemble (*coro*) at the end of each act; the final scene is a long ballet (*ballo*) in which solo interjections diversify a big choral ending of considerable effectiveness. Then in 1626 there came a rather belatedly Neoplatonic opera, *La Catena d'Adone* ("The Chain of Adonis"), on a libretto by O. Tronsarelli. The music is by Domenico Mazzocchi, one of the best seventeenth-century composers of the still-continuing polyphonic madrigals, so that there are some outstanding ensembles in this admirable score, as well as much excellent recitative, and a construction so solid that it reminds us of Monteverdi.[9] Falsirena is a Circe-like enchantress who seduces the hero under the false shape of Venus, until confounded by the true Venus who redeems him. An *allegoria* at the end of the score recalls Plato's *Symposium* (see p. 16) by explaining that the false Venus stands for "feeling overcome by sense," whereas the true Venus brings us back "to heavenly delights." There is enough typically Roman spectacle in all this, but also a not so typical seriousness of purpose.

In 1632, the wealthy and cultivated Barberini family, who produced many noted ecclesiastics, had ready for inauguration a large and newly prepared (but dismountable) theater in their immense palace by the Four Fountains at Rome. The choice fell on an opera half sacred, half comic: *Il S. Alessio* ("Saint Alexis"), of which the composer was Stefano Landi, and the librettist, Giulio Rospigliosi, was that powerful statesman and cultured poet who became cardinal and pope (in 1677, as Clement IX).[10] The hero's adventures are edifying, the supporting characters are solidly serious, the comic personages are amusingly earthy; but the recitative, though quite expressive, is a little overshadowed by the usual Roman abundance of ensembles, choruses and dances, together with much spectacular stage machinery and change of scene. The same librettist wrote a comic text for *Chi Soffre, Speri,* jointly composed by Vergilio Mazzocchi (brother of Domenico) and Marco Marazzoli: an early comic opera, though probably not the earliest.[11] Of two performances in the Barberini palace, the first was in 1637; the second, in 1639, had not only the English poet Milton in the audience, but Mazarin, who had been forming an enthusiasm for opera since Cardinal Antonio Barberini employed him in 1632, and who later carried this enthusiasm to France with historic consequences. The comic dialogue is in lively recitative; but it is rather the mood than the idiom which shows the difference. There is necessarily a certain relaxation of the style when comic elements begin to enter into opera. But one element of artificiality was on the increase: the growing popularity, presently amounting almost to a monopoly in heroic roles, of the castrato virtuosos whose high voices were retained, but at adult power, by previous castration in childhood. The historic phonograph recordings[12] of the last of the long line, Alessandro Moreschi (1858-1922), demonstrate a massive and dramatic declamation which goes far to justify the Baroque preference. He sounds anything but effeminate. The best of the castratos were also notable for their broader culture. There is, for example, a late but beautiful pastoral opera almost in the original Florentine tradition, of which both words and music are by the distinguished castrato Loreto Vittori,[13] his *Galatea* of 1639.

But Roman opera by then was more apt to rely on crude spectacle, around which both words and music had to move, as in Luigi Rossi's *Il Palazzo Incantato* ("The Enchanted Palace") performed at the Barberini palace in Rome in 1642. The plot, taken from Ariosto, tells of that same seductive witchcraft and heroic rescue to which Neoplatonists habitually gave such healing symbolism; but it is so thrown into confusion here in order to provide opportunities for stage machinery and changes of scene that, according to one French observer,[14] it ended by becoming "exceedingly boring."[15]   Yet there is good music in the score, and Luigi Rossi is justly known as a superb composer of chamber cantatas. His only other opera was his *Orfeo*, brought to Paris in 1647 by Mazarin in his abortive attempt to acclimatize Italian opera there.[16] The librettist, Francesco Buti, so courted the Parisian taste with choruses, dances, and scene changes that the myth goes for nothing, and the music, for all its moments of magic and radiance, cannot quite hang together, and did not carry conviction. The time for opera in Paris was still a generation away.

But the time for early Roman opera was running out. Before the middle of the seventeenth century, the leadership in opera had already passed from Rome to Venice, where the second and more dazzling half of Monteverdi's career was richly spent.

## *Venice*

In 1613, Monteverdi was appointed master of the chapel at St. Mark's, Venice, the most prestigious of all Italian musical positions, where for thirty years he remained almost continuously productive in secular and sacred vocal music. Up to 1630, his operas were mounted in Mantua and Parma; but these, and his Venetian operas of the next few years, are without exception lost. One of them, *La Finta Pazza Licori* ("The Pretended Madwoman Licoris"), intended for Mantua, was on an apparently comic libretto by Giulio Strozzi; but neither text nor score survives, and it is not even certain that there was any performance.

When Venice did take up an interest in opera, matters moved faster than anywhere. It had for some time been a habit of Venetian artistocrats to admit a paying public to the plays professionally acted in their private theaters. One such, the Tron family theater (*Teatro Tron di San Cassiano*, i.e., in the parish of San Cassiano) had been disastrously damaged by fire in 1629, but was eventually rebuilt. Two impresarios were brought from Rome to mount a suitably impressive performance for its reopening in 1637: the composer Francesco Manelli, and his partner the poet Ferrari, who was also the business manager. They put on, not a play, but an opera in the Roman style: their *Andromeda*[17] of 1637. The stage machinery was deliberately economical, but the novelty so caught on that upward of a dozen opera houses opened (though not all stayed open at the same time) in seventeenth-century Venice, largely to cater to the vast tourist trade during the Carnival season. Their capital cost came from the big families, though they might be put out to commercial managers; the tastes of the paying audience on the floor, or even of the fashionable renters of the boxes, cannot have been greatly reflected in the style or the repertory, which were much as in other places. Composers of opera were everywhere well in touch with one another; and it was date rather than place which made the greatest difference in style. The taste for spectacle, only a little modified by economy, came from Rome. The taste for big ensembles and choruses, with extensive dancing and ballets, did not come, perhaps being too expensive except at the imperial court of Vienna and presently under the absolute monarchy in France.

The orchestra for the Venetian operas has not been established with certainty, but it may, at least in some instances, have been larger and more varied in its use of instruments than is revealed by the surviving manuscripts. These are in many cases no more than rough working copies left with many of the details to be filled out in rehearsal; they were not published, as many earlier operas and some contemporary Roman operas were. The vocal solo parts and the instrumental bass parts are likely to be shown complete or nearly so. The words are roughly underlaid, and a few bass figurings; some vocal ornamentation may need to be added, and all necessary expression marks; the bass line has to be realized more or less in performance. Instrumental introductions and recurring ritornellos appear usually on four or five staves; no instruments are specified, but strings are intended, though not necessarily strings alone. Sometimes staves are left blank; sometimes only the bass line is filled in, or not even that; sometimes the mere word "ritornello" or "ballo" is inserted, leaving it to us to supply the music needed. There are instructions in early seventeenth-century treatises[18] for working out a sort of half-improvised orchestral counterpoint of many instruments, and these may have retained some influence for a time. Horns, cornettos, trumpets (with kettle-drums assumed), flutes, recorders, oboes, bassoons, regals, chamber-organs, harpsichords, lutes, and strings all get mentioned occasionally in manuscripts of Venetian operas, and were, very possibly, more often used than mentioned.[19] The colorful orchestra of the courtly interludes and of Monteverdi's *Orfeo* does seem to have declined in opera, especially on tour, and filled out again by slow degrees only at the end of the seventeenth century with the approach of the second great period of opera. Clearly the forty instruments "of all sorts" noticed by the Parisian journal *Mercure Galant* at the Venetian performance in 1679 of Pallavicino's *Nerone* were for a special occasion; yet there is a spacious and public quality about most Venetian operas, given as they often were in large theaters with orchestra pits of ample size. Undoubtedly the solo singers came first, and in their recitative were supported only by small groups of instruments (sometimes called the "symphony" in contrast to the full orchestra); but other passages seem to require and may sometimes have been performed with a stronger and more varied orchestra than the scores depict.

Venice led in opera from Monteverdi's last works and Cavalli's first, through the transitional works of Pallavicino and Legrenzi, after which other centers took on as much or more importance. Opera meanwhile gained in popularity what it lost in intensity, as its original Neoplatonic symbolism gave place to more individual though still thoroughly operatic characters and situations. Monteverdi's last two operas show different stages in this gradual change.

Monteverdi's *Il ritorno d'Ulisse in patria* ("The return of Ulysses to his country"), performed at the Venice Carnival of 1640, is on a libretto taken by Giacomo Badoaro from Books XIII-XXIII of Homer's *Odyssey*.[20] There in Homer, the gods and goddesses whose strife sways the fortunes of their human favorites stand for relatively unsophisticated projections of our own warring impulses. Here, with Badoaro, there is almost too much sophistication, with not quited enough of the recent Neoplatonic conviction left to sustain the allegorical prologue. But as soon as Penelope and her faithful nurse come on stage to grieve for Ulysses (Odysseus), now ten years gone at the siege of Troy and another ten on his homeward wandering, we are in the grip of the old legend, its ancient spell deeply at work again. "Return, return, return, oh return, Ulysses" is Penelope's melting refrain; and in the next scene, return he does, though with no one left to help him but his inner guardian, the goddes Minerva (Athene). She disguises him as a decrepit old beggar to confront the three dangerous suitors who are in possession of his home and in pressing siege of his wife Penelope. But Penelope is resisting them still.

There is a passage of splendidly operatic construction as each suitor in turn displays his vocal virtuosity, with the common refrain: "love, then!" She has a balancing refrain: "I do not wish to love." Iro, a stutterer treated with rather heartless comedy, thinks to win easy honor by wrestling with the disguised Ulysses; the hilarious amusement of the suitors over his discomfiting has a dramatic irony which is not lost on us. Their turn will soon come. For now Penelope consents to marry the suitor who can bend the great bow of Ulysses, "or rather the bow of Love which must pierce my heart": a Neoplatonic reference to Ulysses' own true manhood, alone strong enough to do that deed, as both she and we perhaps foreknow. Three times a suitor fails, to three symmetrical recitatives and ritornellos. But then Ulysses, with Minerva above in symbolical support, strings his own bow and shoots the suitors down.

The awaited union of Ulysses with Penelope is delayed by a counsel and reconciliation of the gods whose enmity has been protracting his troubles this past ten years; thereafter, Penelope herself needs time to admit that this is indeed her own husband returned; for it is a big moment in their story, and must not be hurried. But now as his disguise little by little drops away from him, and with it the deeper strangeness of his twenty years' absence, their union finds its fulfillment in a rapt duet.

Whatever was advanced in the *Ulysses* became consolidated, only two years later, in Monteverdi's last opera *L'Incoronazione di Poppea* ("The Coronation of Poppea") of 1642, to an early example of a historical libretto, by Giovanni Businello.[21] The chief characters, the Emperor Nero, Ottavia his legal wife and Empress, Seneca his old tutor and adviser, Poppea his successfully designing mistress, are all drawn from the pages of Tacitus and Suetonius. Now Businello was assuredly not ignorant of those great Roman historians; yet he took liberties with his characters which change their entire impact on our feelings. During the Middle Ages and the Renaissance, historical figures such as even Paris and Helen perhaps once were, and certainly Anthony and Cleopatra or Nero and Poppea, were so poetically glamorized that they became in effect mythological images; and so Businello has made use of them.

History relates that Nero's mother, Agrippina, seduced and married the Emperor Claudius, whose daughter Ottavia she then got married off to Nero.

*L'Incoronazione di Poppea*, Act II. New York City Opera.

This she did in order to make Nero the heir, in place of the legitimate heir, Britannicus. Next, to expedite the succession, she had Claudius poisoned. Nero in his turn was seduced by Poppea, a woman psychologically after his mother's stamp, and evidently attractive to him because she was a woman after his mother's stamp. For Suetonius reports that Nero would have made his mother his mistress, too, if he had not been forcibly prevented. Agrippina then took up Britannicus again in jealous compensation, until Nero had him poisoned and her imprisoned. In 58 A.D., Poppea, having got Nero to create her his empress after divorcing Ottavia, made doubly sure by having Nero murder Ottavia, and for good measure, Agrippina too. Seneca meanwhile retired comfortably on his probably quite ill-gotten gains at court; only when, in 65 A.D., he joined an overt conspiracy against Nero's life was he also murdered. In 68 A.D., Nero was finally overthrown, comitting suicide just in time to escape execution, at the ripe old age of thirty-one.

Presented historically, how could this bunch of criminal lunatics command our sympathy? But in the opera, they are not presented historically. After another somewhat perfunctorily allegorical prologue, two comic soldiers guard Poppea's house, thus warning her husband Ottone, just back from a journey, that Nero is with her. Out come the lovers, agreeably romanticized. There is presently some sentimental duetting from a pair of young servants, and a faithful old nurse to sing Poppea a lullaby: both traditional features, much continued later in opera. Poppea does then have Seneca removed for getting in her way; and he, as the noble old counsellor he is in the opera, sings most movingly, to brief interjections from his friends, of his desire to die in spite of their appeals. Ottone is supernaturally prevented by Love (Amor) in person from murdering Poppea; but no one takes this very seriously, and Nero spares him with the magnanimity obligatory for victorious tyrants in Baroque opera, merely banishing him in the acceptable company of his accomplice Drusilla. Ottavia laments her own banishment to make way for Poppea, whose coronation as Nero's wife and empress is celebrated in their concluding duet: a passage[22] of such serene and haunting beauty that we can no more feel shocked at their still quite substantial misdeeds than we feel shocked at the brutal incidents in a fairy tale.

The reason is that their story has been told as if it were a fairy tale. When the two children in Grimms' tale No. 6 have to be brutally murdered before (but this is not previously known) they and Faithful John can be brought back to life again, we are not shocked, because our intuitions sense the healing symbolism beneath the naive images. Businello's images are not naive. We are meant to enjoy the obvious sensual union, but also to pick up the Neoplatonic undertones of that royal or sacred marriage which in many myths and ritual initiations symbolizes an inner reconciliation of our masculine with our feminine components. Because our deepest intuitions say yes to this, we feel none of the disapproval which so much callousness and cruelty would call for in the outside world, where in any case it would be too guilt-laden to yield so serene a happiness. Our intuitions also say yes to overcoming, as this young couple has symbolically overcome, the inhibiting aspect of parental authority. And finally, all the world loves a lover. This is opera at its best, and *Poppea* is one of the best of early operas.

EXAMPLE 4    Monteverdi, *L'Incoronazione di Poppea:* the serene love-duet climaxing the sensuous opera (realization mine).

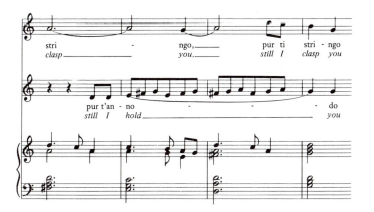

stri - ngo,_____ pur ti stri - ngo
clasp_____ you,_____ still I clasp you

pur t'an - no - - - do
still I hold_____ you

# After Monteverdi

When Monteverdi died in the next year, 1643, opera had reached a form which it substantially retained until the transition into the second great period was well established: a form flexible in construction, popular in content, and even when taken outside Italy, Italian in style.

As early as 1627, Heinrich Schütz (1585-1672), the greatest of Monteverdi's foreign disciples and the greatest composer of his generation in Germany, had an opera performed at Torgau on an adaptation by the distinguished German poet, Martin Opitz, of Rinuccini's first and original libretto, *Dafne*.[23] To our regret, the music is lost; but we should certainly expect it to have been in the reciting style. We have next, at Nuremberg perhaps in 1644, an interesting attempt at a pastoral with German words after the Italian model: *Seelewig*,[24] composed by Sigmund Theophil Staden (1607-1655). But the Thirty Years' War postponed further progress.

In the imperial capital at Vienna, opera was strongly supported; but it was opera in the prevailing Italian style, whether by Italians or by natives; and the only local feature was an ostentatious display with choruses and ballets. In England, the Italian reciting style was successfully imitated quite early in the seventeenth century by Nicholas Lanier (1588-1666) and a few others, both as chamber cantata and in some of the dramatized court masques derived from earlier Italian and current French influences; but there the Civil Wars intervened. An abortive initiative was taken in London in 1656 with Sir William D'Avenant's Italianate *Siege of Rhodes;* the music by Henry Lawes, Henry Cooke, Matthew Locke, Charles Coleman, and George Hudson, is lost, but it was carried all through, with recitative for the dialogue. No firm tradition of English opera took root at the time. In France, opera took root only with Lully, from 1673.

In Italy, Monteverdi's successor was Francesco Cavalli (1602–1676),[25] a singer and later an organist at St. Mark's, actually under Monteverdi; his first operas were successfully performed before his master died. In 1668, Cavalli was eventually appointed to Monteverdi's old post as master of the chapel at St. Mark's. He was a less conscientious craftsman, though cunning enough; his keen sense of theater and his wonderful gift for melody make him, might we say, the Bellini of the seventeenth century. Of some thirty-five operas attributable to Cavalli, twenty-seven survive.[26] The first was *Le Nozze di Teti e di Peleo* ("The Marriage of Thetis and Peleus") of 1639; the last of which a performance is known was *Coriolano* ("Coriolanus") of 1669; the last, not performed, was his *Massenzio* of 1673. An excellent specimen available for study is *L'Ormindo*, of 1644: a chivalric tale of disguises and misunderstandings ending in magnanimity and reconciliation, in which two princely young couples are allowed to get themselves into some very amusing as well as sentimental situations, and the angry old tyrant turns out to have a very human heart. It is all no end of a dramatic tangle, but the music follows every twist with felicitous and appropriate invention, and the result in spite of all defects is very good opera indeed.[27]

There are choruses in some of Cavalli's earlier operas, and again his *Ercole Amante* ("Hercules in Love") which was performed in Paris in 1662; but this was commissioned by Mazarin for the French court, where choruses and dances had always been fashionable in the court ballets (but Lully composed the dances for this production). Like Monteverdi in his later operas, Cavalli made the main substance of his music a very fine and flexible recitative, merging easily into arioso and back again, with aria not very different nor distinct, so that the whole flows smoothly and accommodatingly in the proper manner of continuous opera.

The nearest rival to Cavalli's reputation in mid-seventeenth century opera was a considerably younger man, Antonio (christened Pietro) Cesti (1623-1669). This restless, wandering musician of a composer spent alternating periods in Rome, in Venice, in Innsbruck, in Vienna, and in Florence, where he died. He was a famous composer of chamber (mainly solo) cantatas, of that wonderful school of which Giacomo Carissimi and Luigi Rossi were leaders. Sensitive melody, in alternating recitative and aria, is the mark of this school: the words are exquisitely set, with almost flawless attention to their sense and their sound; yet we may feel that the chief attention went not so much to the individual words as to the soaring melodic arch, shaped and moulded from one end of a long phrase to the other. Certainly the words are well served, but no longer quite in the old detailed manner.

Unlike Carissimi (who may possibly have written one or two lost operas) and Luigi Rossi (who wrote only the two mentioned above), Cesti gained an equal fame in chamber cantata and in opera. Most of Cesti's operas are in a style hardly changed from Cavalli's, except for a little added tension in the harmony, and an occasional running bass part which momentarily anticipates the coming transition. Cesti's operas for the imperial court in Vienna, in particular his well-known but partly lost festival opera of 1667, *Il Pomo d'Oro* ("The Golden Apple"), employ somewhat lavish orchestral and choral forces, without in other ways being notably exceptional.[28]

## *Notes*

1. Apparently for the name part, though Rasi may have taken this: both were virtuoso tenors; the frequent statement that Magli was a castrato seems to be a fairly modern guess, since there is no contemporary evidence cited that this was so, and the part is certainly in the tenor clef. See also *Musical Times*, May, 1977, p. 393, letter from Tim Carter and David Butchart.
2. First performed at the Carnival in Mantua in 1607, probably on February 24; twice repeated shortly after at Mantua; other probable performances in Cremona, Florence, Milan, and Turin. Publ. Venice 1609 and 1615; libretto publ. Mantua, 1607.
3. Natale Conti, *Mythologiae*, ed. of Venice, 1581, pp. 505 ff.
4. Marco de Gagliano, *La Flora*, on a libretto by Andrea Salvadori, publ. and perf., Florence, 1628.
5. Libretto by Andrea Salvadori, publ. Florence, 1625 (first performed as *Santa Orsola, Vergine e Martire* at Florence in 1624).
6. Publ. Florence, 1625. Libretto by F. Saracinelli, also publ. Florence, 1625.
7. Publ. Venice, 1619. Libretto is no longer believed to be by the composer; nor is this now thought to be the first of the Roman school of opera.
8. Publ. Rome, 1620.
9. Publ. Rome, 1626.
10. Publ. Rome, 1634.
11. Neither score nor libretto was published, but both survive in ms., and there is an *Argomento et Allegoria* ("Plot and Allegory"), publ. 1639, in the Library of Congress, Washington, D.C.
12. On G and T 547776-7, made in 1902-1903.
13. Publ. Rome, 1639.
14. M. de Lionne, letter to Mazarin, February 27, 1642.
15. The opera was published neither in score nor libretto, but several mss. survive.
16. Also unpublished, except for an *abrégé* ("summary") of the libretto in 1647.
17. Libretto publ. Venice, 1637.
18. Contemporary instructions from Agazzari in 1607, Praetorius in 1618/19, Doni in about 1635, and Pietro della Valle in 1640 will be found quoted and discussed in Robert Donington, *The Interpretation of Early Music: New Version*, London, 1974, pp. 171-72, 606-09.
19. See Gloria Rose, "Agazzari and the Improvising Orchestra," *Journal of the American Musicological Society*, Vol. XVIII, No. 3 (1965); and Robert Donington, *The Interpretation of Early Music: New Version*, London, 1974, App. IV.
20. Not originally published. The performance at Venice in 1641 is now known not to have been the first. A performance (thought to be the second) at Bologna, 1640, is also known. Monteverdi's authorship is now accepted by most musicologists.
21. Libretto publ. Venice, 1656.
22. Though perfectly in the style of Monteverdi and fully worthy of him, this duet is of disputed authorship: see A. Chiarelli, "L'Incoronazione di Poppea e Il Nerone: Problemi di Filologia Testuale," *Rivista Italiana di Musicologia*, IX (1974), 117. In itself the music must incline us to Monteverdi, but the question cannot be dismissed.
23. Libretto publ. 1627.
24. Publ. in Harsdörffer, *Frauenzimmer Gesprechspiele*, IV, 1644.
25. Born Caletti-Bruno, baptized Pietro Francesco; but renamed, as was customary, after the patron responsible for his education, when he also seems to have dropped the name Pietro.
26. See T. Walker "Gli Errori . . .," *Atti della Tavola Rotunda Venezia e il Melodramma nel Seicento* (1972), Florence, 1975.
27. Perf. Venice, 1644. The libretto is by Giovanni Faustini; publ. Venice, 1644.
28. Libretto by F. Sbarra, publ. 1667 and 1668.

# 4

# The Parting of the Ways

It was in the second half of the seventeenth century, while the original ideal of drama continuously and flexibly unfolding in words and music was losing its hold on Italian opera, that French opera emerged to take over that ideal. The reciting style had been introduced to France by Caccini himself, on a celebrated visit to Paris in 1604 with his family, who were also singers. This, together with de Nyert's visit to Rome in 1633, brought into fashion a French imitation; but it was much less flexible and much less eloquent, hardly departing from the simple songs (*chansons*) and court airs (*airs de cour*) familiar in ballets and elsewhere. Particularly since the remarkable *Ballet Comique de la Royne* in 1581, court ballets had flourished whenever they were not interrupted by civil dissension. Some of these were little more than social balls in costume; but the most elaborate of them were staged with grandiose spectacle, scene changes, and machinery. There was a plot of sufficient continuity to provide at least a loose framework for the action. French and sometimes Italian poetry was recited, both in speech and in song, but to melody resembling unpretentious airs rather than true recitative. Such drama as occurs can hardly be said to be unfolded in the music. Under the partial influence of that pedantically measured music inherited from the theories of the Pleiad, the choruses and airs are rather solidly symmetrical; but the dances are both lively and theatrical. They are arranged in a bold succession of "entries" culminating in a "grand entry," after which the evening might close with general dancing for the entire aristocratic assembly.

Though they were not opera, these costly entertainments were the background against which Italian opera was introduced by Mazarin, that inscrutable cardinal who served his apprenticeship at the Barberini palace when opera was first being cultivated in Rome. As chief French minister with little interruption from the death of Richelieu in 1634 to his own death in 1661, Mazarin combined business with pleasure by importing Italian singers, machinists, and operas to distract his French enemies from politics, as he hoped, while indulging his friends, his employers, and himself in his own genuine passion for the art. There was "an Italian play in the Great Hall and a ballet danced by several noblemen of the Court," wrote the *Gazette de France* for March 4, 1645, of which the great castrato Atto Melani explained to his regular employer back in Italy that "we have at last recited the opera"; adding that "I succeeded beyond my wishes," while "Signora Checca" (who was a very celebrated soprano) "acquitted herself as well as it was in her power to do." We seem to catch the authentic aroma of operatic vanity in this casual letter of 10th March, 1645.

On December 14 of 1645, a great impression was made by the performance in Paris of a new version of Sacrati's *Finta Pazza* ("The Feigned Madwoman") with its scenery and stage machinery by the already famous Torelli, of which the impact on French stage spectacle was of historic significance. In 1646, Cavalli's *Egisto* was produced; in 1647, Luigi Rossi's *Orfeo;* in 1654, Carlo Caproli's ballet-like *Nozze di Teti e Peleo* ("Marriage of Thetis and Pelius"). For the marriage of Louis XIV to the Infanta of Spain in 1660, Cavalli was with difficulty persuaded to come to Paris to oversee his *Ercole Amante* ("Hercules in Love"). Vigarini the elder, now quite aged but very famous as a stage designer and machinist, was engaged not only on new machines but a new theater, none of it anywhere near ready in time; and Cavalli's six-year-old *Serse* ("Xerxes") was modestly performed that year instead. New music for the ballets was composed by that rising young newcomer, Lully, presently the founder of French opera: he got more praise than Cavalli, which hardly soothed the old composer's anger at the perpetual delays. When, in 1662, *Ercole Amante* was at last produced, the acoustics of the new theater proved intolerable; and in so far as the music could be heard at all, it was again Lully's ballets which aroused enthusiasm. Cavalli returned to Italy in high discontent; Lully (a naturalized Frenchman since 1661, in which year Mazarin himself had died), remained in possession of the field.

Jean-Baptiste Lully (1632-1687) was born of humble parents in Florence (of all historical ironies); he was brought to France at about the age of fourteen as a sort of exotic page-boy, and shortly got himself transferred to the court of young Louis XIV as a violinist, a dancer, and soon a composer of ballets. He did not strictly originate French opera, for which Michel de la Guerre (c. 1605-1679) claimed precedence with a sung pastoral, *Le Triomphe de l'Amour* ("The Triumph of Love") first produced with scenery in Paris in 1657. So did Robert Cambert (c. 1628-1677) for a sung pastoral, untitled, but known as the pastoral of Issy, where it was performed in 1659; the libretto is by Pierre Perrin, the music again being lost. The same pair produced other works, including *Pomone* (perf. Paris, 1671), a longer pastoral of which the prologue and first act survive, and which inaugurated the Royal Academy of Opera, a privilege granted by the king to Perrin in 1669 for the exclusive performance of opera in France.

Meanwhile, from 1663, Lully, making it his astute business to be more French than the French, had been composing incidental music of great charm and prominence for the musical comedies (*comédie-ballets*) of the great dramatist Molière (the glorious *Bourgeois Gentilhomme* is still in the repertory of his old company, known since 1680 as the *Comédie Française*). Perrin's enterprise having become bankrupt in 1672, Lully bought the surrender of his privilege quite honestly, though very shrewdly, for hard cash. The king confirmed Lully in an even more closely defined monopoly of French opera, with other rights, which Lully earned by creating a national style of opera, and by composing an opera a year until his death in 1687.

## The French Opera of Lully

The librettist who (except for the brief period when he was in disgrace) wrote the texts for all of Lully's operas was Philippe Quinault (1636-1688): a talented member of that classical school of French drama led in tragedy by Corneille and Racine, and in comedy by Molière. We do not look in the work of this school for that rich outpouring of warmth and spontaneity which Shakespeare brings to his characters, but for a more poised and calculated exposure of our human passions, presented as consistent types rather than as wayward individuals. Such types may be depicted with an intensity all the more focused for its formal discipline and verbal precision. No living person has ever been so uniformly of one piece, for good or for bad, as the characters set up in the French classical drama; but characteristics which in varying proportions occur in all living people are shown there in simple concentration, and if we mentally put the entire cast together, we have a study of human character in the round. This was Quinault's method; and although he could not transcend it as the great masters did, he was an accomplished craftsman and an adaptable collaborator. Corneille was a better poet, but a worse librettist, as was seen when during Quinault's disgrace he briefly collaborated with Lully. Had Quinault been greater in poetry, he might have been less adaptable to music. And Lully, who might not have been (as Verdi was) equal to Shakespearean diversity, was well suited by Quinault's straightforward type-casting. For like Handel, Lully had a gift for the obvious, amounting to genius, and over and over again could do the seemingly predictable thing with really quite unpredictable imagination.

We miss in Quinault that deep awareness which the Neoplatonic librettists at the origins of opera had so well known how to reveal, in the very act of concealing it, in their mythological images. Yet so long as mythological images are retained substantially intact, some of their intrinsic significance is also retained. There is much fairy-tale substance in Quinault's librettos which is good and suitable substance for music and for opera. We today may find them far too long; but they are good theater, well constructed, and in poetry whose very conventionality leaves all the freer scope to the composer.

For such conventional poetry, Lully developed a genuinely French variety of reciting style. He had studied the spoken declamation at the conventional theater, then at a peak of classical stylization and expressive brilliance. He had formed the closest acquaintanceship with the Italian operas brought to Paris by Mazarin, having himself composed some of the ballet music for them. He had much other experience, vocal as well as instrumental, in the court ballets, and in the musical comedies with Molière. From all this, Lully learned to compose a melodious recitative as finely shaped to the individual rhythms and sonorities of the French language as had ever been shaped to the Italian. It retained its arioso tunefulness, as the later Italian recitative did not. It used a more complex notation, with changes of time signature less found in Italian recitative, but in spite of appearances, some at least of those changes affect (for French recitative) only the length and pulse of the bar, and not (as they may do in other contexts) the unit of measurement.[1] The arias are song-like, mostly simple and expressive rather than ornate or brilliant. The core of the orchestra is five-part strings with lute and harpsichord continuo.

The French overture was taken over from the Italian overture as it then often was: slow, fast, slow (the Italian later became fast, slow, fast). As Lully developed the French overture, the slow opening section is of a massive pulse, enlivened by dotted notes (over-dotted in performance) and rushing scales (delayed and speeded in performance); the fast section in two repeated parts is lightly fugal, soon relaxing into mere sparkle and brilliance; the returning slow section (optional) may be replaced or followed by dances, or we may be taken immediately into the first scene of the Prologue. By strict convention, the long Prologue flatters the king with a mixture of aria, recitative, chorus, and dancing, celebrating his latest exploits under the transparent disguise of some mythological or chivalric situation. There are then five acts, also long, in which to unfold this situation or some sequel to it, while actually suggesting, on a well-established pattern, the agreeable pretenses and wishful thinking (rather than the harsh realities) of current French court life. Ample provision is made for the stage machines and scene changes, the choruses, the ballets, and the prolonged divertissement (especially near the end of the last act) which French taste required. A happy ending was ordinarily expected, where necessary by supernatural intervention. It was not a realistic formula, even as opera goes; but it worked excellently for almost a century before Gluck brought it back into the main stream by basing on it the reforms which he was trying to introduce into the Italian opera of that later day.

## A Chivalric Fantasy

A good example of Quinault and Lully in collaboration is their *Amadis*[2] of 1684. The main characters were originally drawn from a Celtic cycle of romances in which Amadis was a typically mythological princeling, illegitimate, exposed at birth, but rescued to become the conqueror of kings and wizards and the winner of an English princess encountered on a magic island. In the reworked chivalric version as adapted here, a French overture takes us straight into an enchanted forest of no particular time or place, but with pastoral inhabitants just waking from a magic sleep. A benevolent enchantress, Urgande, and her consort, Alquif, alternate, in arioso duet, with a full chorus of their attendant spirits, to tell us that "when Amadis was lost, we were compelled by sadness to conceal ourselves in these groves. A spell of deep enchantment made our eyes to close until fortune restored the fate of the world to one" (meaningful looks toward Louis XIV in the audience) "who shall be still more renowned, still more glorious." Dancing to show their pleasure, as "the statutes who support the pavilion" (faint creaking of machinery) "carry it up in flight," the chorus proceed "it is he" (Amadis? Louis?) "who has taught us the true way to rule"; and so, as "the Loves and the Joys fly" through the air, the leisurely divertissement and the fulsome flattery unfold together.

Act I opens with a no less leisurely and typical discussion of *l'amour* and *la gloire,* love and glory: the typical preoccupations of serious French baroque opera. "I love, alas," sings Amadis; "that is enough to make me unhappy." There is, however, a more particular reason. Amadis loves Oriane, who is also unhappy because she believes that Amadis is unfaithful. Florestan is not yet unhappy, loving as he does Corisande who loves him in return: but they are soon going to be, and meanwhile he assures her rather ominously that "if I had loved glory less, you would not have loved me so much."

Oriane, lost by now in more senses than one, wanders through the forest declaiming in bitter recitative that her hero Amadis, who should be coming to her rescue, is following another. Twice her anger breaks out into heightened indignation; and twice her music heightens with it into furious arioso. In another part of the same forest, Amadis sings his famous air, "Dense Wood" (*Bois Épais*), complaining that he is not unfaithful, only misunderstood. We may well be meant to recall those yet more famous lines with which Dante began his *Divine Comedy:* "In the middle of the journey of our life I found myself in a dark wood [*selva oscura*], for the straight way was lost."

The plot thickens yet further when Corisande, lost in the same part of the wood as Amadis, laments that her Florestan, though she does not think him deliberately unfaithful, has allowed himself to be tricked by a pretended damsel in distress into the power of an opposite pair of magicians: the malevolent enchanter and enchantress, Arcaläus and Arcabonne. Glory indeed! Now Corisande and Amadis approach each other, still singing very movingly by turns, until they meet in astonishment, and Amadis resolves on glorious rescue. Prompt to the cue, Arcaläus steps out to oppose him in a declamatory exchange of ferocious energy. Then in swinging six-eight Arcaläus invokes a ballet of infernal demons. They menace Amadis in a pounding four-four rhythm, but he fights them off intrepidly until some of the demons take on the cunning disguise of nymphs. "What defense can courage make," they sing, "when beauty makes the attack?" None, it seems; for when one of them takes on Oriane's shape, Amadis falls straight under the illusion, and follows her bemusedly into captivity. No illusions are so powerful as those into which we wish to fall. Amadis could not have been deceived if he had not been drawn back into one of those regressive fantasies of childhood bliss and comforting irresponsibility for which the pastoral convention stands. He is caught, in short, through the same self-deceptive weakness as Florestan whom he was so sure of rescuing.

We soon see a dungeon where half the chorus enter into the action as jailors, and the other half as their prisoners, among them Florestan and Corisande: united now, but in misfortune. Arcabonne, the malevolent enchantress, announces her newest victim: Amadis himself, the slayer, as she now tells us, of her brother, whose ghost she magically invokes to a five-part orchestration fully worthy of the sinister occasion. In an aria of somber power, the ghost rebukes her for betraying him. We next see why; for she recognizes in Amadis the mysterious stranger who once saved her life and inspired her love, so that she now feels impelled to spare him and, at his request, to let her prisoners go free. They go off rejoicing in song and dance; but Amadis is fiercely retained, and thrust into a magic trance by Arcaläus, who plays on her jealousy of Oriane to renew her hatred. Next Oriane is shown Amadis apparently dead, and she faints away. But all this display of dark power seems to constellate the counter-power of light; for with a glory of orchestra and spectacle, Urgande, Alquif, and their train appear from an elaborate machine, and she sings the remarkable words: "I rule by my laws Hell, Earth and Sea; without anyone knowing where I am, I journey through the world, and I know the secrets which the Gods have not shown yet to any eyes but mine. Take care to know Urgande: know and accept." There is only one force within us for which symbolically such claims are valid, and this is that deeper self which carries our true life's purpose, and which allows us to prosper in so far as we can intuitively know and accept it. Urgande restores the lovers with her magic wand, and the duet with which they greet each other is vintage Lully. Quinault was no Neoplatonist, however, and that was as far as his purely poetic insight was able to take him. The rest of the opera (and there is a great deal more of it) is mere spectacle, rejoicing and divertissement, with a danced and partly sung chaconne of vast proportions to frame a grand finale.

EXAMPLE 5 Lully, *Amadis:* (a) slow opening of French overture, as notated (b) as performed; (c) quick continuation; (d) duet recalling overture; (e) free continuation (then repeated by chorus); (f) French recitative (flexible, and virtually unornamented); (g) French aria (liable to ornamentation, as here suggested); (h) French chorus (symmetrical but expressive).

**Fairly quick**

(c)

(d) **Urgande**

Ah! j'en - tends un bruit qui nous pres - se
*Ah! I hear a noise which now calls us*

**Alquif**

Ah! j'en - tends un bruit qui nous pres - se
*Ah! I hear a noise which now calls us*

**Strings**

(e) **Urgande**

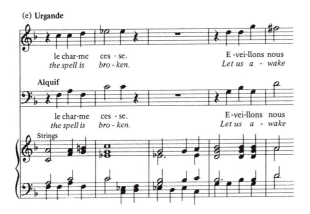

le char-me ces - se. E -vei-llons nous
*the spell is bro - ken. Let us a - wake*

**Alquif**

le char-me ces - se. E -vei-llons nous
*the spell is bro - ken. Let us a - wake*

**Strings**

(f) **(Very flexible tempo)**
**Oriane**

L'é-clat de tant de gloire a-vait jus-qu'à ce jour E-blou-i mon â-me cré
*The show of so much glo - ry daz-zled my weak soul. Till to-day his bril-liance de-*

**Continuo**

46

du - le.      Ah!_____   Les plus grands hé-ros ne font pas  grand    scru - ple  d'une
ceived   me.    Ah!_____   But the great-est he - ro  has  no  great-est    scru - ple  to

in - fi - dé - li - té  d'a - mour
*keep from in-fi-de - li - ty*

(etc. Then:)

Quick, and pressing on

Jus - te dé - pit  bri - sez, bri - sez ma    chaî - ne,   Jus - te dé -
*Right - eous__ an - ger,   an - ger break my    bond - age,  right - eous__*

(poco rit.)          (softer and slower)

pit bri - sez, bri - sez ma chaî - ne,  j'al - lais fi - nir mes tris - tes jours
*an - ger,   an - ger,  break my bond - age,  I mean to   end my wretch - ed days*

## Germany and England

There was an early attempt at national opera in Germany, particularly in Hamburg from 1678 onward. Here, both Italian and French operas were presented, in the original languages or (wholly or partly) in German translations or adaptations; and there were also German operas imitated from both these styles, separately or in combination. The German composer Johann Sigismund Kusser (1660-1727), a lifelong traveler who spent some eight of his earlier years in Paris under the influence of Lully's operas, directed the Hamburg opera from 1694 to 1696, presenting there a wide range of his own and other works. It was a time of French fashions in keyboard and orchestral music; but in opera, the French influence was partial and transient; the native German element was not yet very assured or durable; and there were many Italian composers active in Germany such as Agostino Steffani (1654-1728), who got a taste for French overtures and French ballets at Paris from 1678 to 1679, combining these with German counterpoint and innate melodiousness, and spending more of his working life at Munich and Hanover than ever he did in Italy. The Italian influence thereafter prevailed; and this first bid for a national German opera had already lost its impetus some years before the Hamburg opera shut down in 1738.

In England, the restoration of Charles II to the throne in 1660 brought over many of the French tastes which he had acquired during his long exile at the French court. He reorganized his own court music in the French manner, appointing a very inferior French composer, Louis Grabu (dates unknown), to be the master of his music. In 1674, Cambert's *Ariane* and his *Pomone* were produced in London probably with alterations by Grabu. Dryden's one libretto for opera, an inept and undramatic work, *Albion and Albanus,* was composed by Grabu in the style but without the genius of Lully, and when performed in London in 1685, it met deservedly with failure.[3] There were many plays with incidental music and some masques, including a version by Shadwell (with music partly by Matthew Locke) of Molière's *Psyche* (originally with music by Lully); this was performed in London, probably in 1674. But only two other English works of this period are really operas. Both were under the double influence of Italianate recitative as already known in England, and of Lully's style, as it was then becoming known.

John Blow (1649-1708), one of the best musicians at the restored court of Charles II, was the composer of the miniature but inspired *Venus and Adonis,* of about 1684. In its manuscripts it is described as a masque, for which it certainly passed at the time; but since there is some development of character, and since this development unfolds as much in the music as in the words, it is in effect a small but genuine opera. The overture is French; the recitative is astonishingly free and eloquent, based on the early Italian idiom but modified by a wayward passion so English that perhaps only Blow or Purcell could have composed it so; the choruses are like Lully, but intensified to a power of feeling derived from the long English tradition of great choral music, and even from the English madrigals of an earlier time. Cupid amuses us, and must have still more amused the original audience of courtiers, by pointed sallies about their amorous inconstancy; the young singer herself was an illegitimate daughter of Charles II, and her mother, Moll Davies, was in the role of Venus. Sounds of huntsmen are heard; but Adonis is for once strangely reluctant to join them. Yet he yields to Venus's insistence, while a very masque-like scene entertains us as a chorus of young Cupids is taught how to make amorous trouble among the susceptible, and worse trouble still among those who think themselves unsusceptible. But Venus has premonitions of tragedy; and soon Adonis is brought back, mortally wounded by that deadly boar who seems to stand mythologically for a nagging woman's most destructive component. She swings, however, into genuine grief, as her woman's heart responds; and from there to the end, the opera moves through arioso-like recitative of the wildest expressiveness to a brief but melting final chorus (but it was instrumentally accompanied and may legitimately be spaced out with ritornellos), the form of which might have come from Lully, but never these haunting harmonies.[4]

Henry Purcell (1659-1695) was actually a pupil of John Blow. He wrote much excellent theater music; but his only true opera is *Dido and Aeneas,* performed in London in 1689. This is extremely similar in musical style to Blow's *Venus and Adonis,* but the libretto, by Nahum Tate, is much inferior, since the character of

The witches plot in *Dido and Aeneas*. Act II. The Mini-Met (Metropolitan Opera Company).

Aeneas is conventional and does not grow, while the character of Dido grows only in the deepening of her grief at the end when Aeneas leaves her at the call of duty. But this is growth enough, since the music expressing it is so magnificent. There is an unusually arresting overture, French in form but very much of Purcell's individuality. Aeneas, flying from the sack of Troy and a storm at sea, has been sheltered by Dido, Queen of Carthage. Both are evidently smitten with mutual attraction, and the Queen's counselor urges a dynastic alliance, concerning which the Queen nevertheless expresses deep forebodings. Masque here takes over from opera, as a chorus of witches plans to destroy these prospects of happiness by sending a spurious Mercury to warn Aeneas off; since the gods (as is very plain in Virgil) really do wish him to move onward in order to found Rome in Italy, the witches and the spurious Mercury are dramatically neither necessary nor convincing. Aeneas makes vacillating excuses and seems momentarily unsure of his decision; but Dido will have none of him now, and sends him contemptuously off. She means to kill herself, and sings that famous lament on a brief repeating ground bass which redeems the conclusion as opera of the highest rank. This form of lament had long been traditional in early Italian opera, but Purcell, as he so often did, made over the borrowed form into the most personal of idioms. A chorus of lamenting attendants has, as in Blow, the last sad word.[5]

EXAMPLE 6   Purcell, *Dido and Aeneas*, brief English recitative and start of Dido's lament.

Purcell died prematurely in 1695, and Blow seems to have lost interest in opera. In 1706, the vast success in London of Antonio Bononcini's *Il Trionfo di Camilla* ("The Triumph of Camilla") led to an almost insensate fashion for Italian opera, which Handel's operatic career in London, from his *Rinaldo* of 1711 onward, confirmed. Under these circumstances, national English opera, though not discontinued, fell far behind.

## Italian Opera in Transition

The transition in Italian opera was just beginning with Antonio Cesti (see p. 38). Then came Giovanni Legrenzi (1626-1690), a Venetian composer of great enterprise; Carlo Pallavicino (1630-1688), whose career also began in Venice but continued in Dresden, where he became one of the leading Italian expatriates so influential in Germany; Bernardo Pasquini (1637-1710), who was born in Florence but established himself firmly and successfully in Rome, where he was of conspicuous importance; and Alessandro Stradella (1644-1682), a restless character of many posts and many wanderings, who was baptized (and therefore presumably born) in Rome (October 4, 1664), became entangled with prominent women and their protectors in several places, and was murdered by a jealous rival, at the age of thirty-eight, in Genoa.

During this transition, recitative and aria grew somewhat more distinct, and were less apt to blend into an intermediate arioso. Recitative began to lose its early tunefulness, and to settle into melodic and harmonic formulas, particularly at cadences; arias became longer and grander, with more brilliant and concerto-like accompaniment, often with an obligato flute, trumpet, or other instrument, and with energetic basses which may stride along in persistent eighth notes. The "motto beginning" came into fashion: here the voice starts with a brief motto-like phrase, and after a few bars for instruments repeats it and goes on. The continuo (figured bass) accompaniment settled toward the subsequently standard keyboard with bass instrument, but an increasing proportion of arias were given full orchestral accompaniment. Ensembles, other than duets, declined, and only Vienna and Paris much favored choruses and dances. Orchestral introductions and interludes made a more resplendent contribution; but the subsequent monopoly of the vocal structure by alternating recitatives and *da capo* arias (whose beginning repeats after a middle section) was already building up.

In Legrenzi's fine *Totila*, performed in Venice in 1677, the recitative is still very flexible and inclined to arioso, while the arias display much of the advanced virtuoso impressiveness, and the chorus only sings, at the end, a mere five measures of *viva la pace, viva Roma* ("long live peace, long live Rome"). But in Pasquini's *L'Artido*, performed in Rome in 1678, the recitatives are much more distinct from the arias, many of which are da capo and often with motto beginnings. A short introductory Sinfonia in the older style leads to a big strophic aria on a ground bass, the verses separated by an identical ritornello (again somewhat on the older pattern); after which comes a passage of recitative, and then a long and impressive accompanied motto aria in the advanced manner, which repeats entire; but there is only a hint of a middle section, so that the da capo pattern is not really developed here. Yet the general style of the work is unmistakably different from before; and while the transition into the second great period of opera is not yet concluded, it has, by the time of this extremely interesting Roman opera of the last quarter of the seventeenth century, made considerable progress.

## Notes

1. See Robert Donington, *The Interpretation of Early Music: New Version*, London, 1974, pp. 643-50.
2. Perf. and publ. Paris, 1684.
3. Libretto by John Dryden, publ. London, 1685. Score publ. London, 1687.
4. No original publication.
5. No original publication.

# PART TWO
## Number Opera

ᒉᔍᔭᐧᔑᖋ

## The Second Great Period: To 1775

Italian serious opera (*opera seria*) of the eighteenth century moved far from the original Florentine ideal of opera as drama continuously and flexibly unfolding in words and music. Instead of the drama conditioning the poetry, and the poetry conditioning the music, all three were conditioned by a predetermined convention. According to this convention, the drama must be based on a more than human superiority of virtue, expressed in poetry of monumental dignity, and forwarded expeditiously in recitative which is often perfunctory and mostly "dry" (*secco*) in the technical sense of being accompanied only by bass and harpsichord. The main musical substance lies not in the recitative but in the arias. The orchestra kept its core of strings and continuo; but flutes and oboes (though often with the same players doubling) and bassoons were now standard; trumpets and drums were frequently introduced (and horns at times); and virtuoso obligato parts for flute, trumpet, solo violin, or other melodic instrument became a regular feature both in the introductions (longer now) and in the refrains (*ritornelli*) and the accompaniment of arias. But many arias, too, were accompanied only by a continuo of melodic bass instrument and harpsichord. Almost all arias are da capo ("from the beginning") arias, where one emotion is first treated at length, next considered from another angle, and then repeated virtually unaltered, no matter how undramatically this leisurely construction may often interrupt the action. Simple, song-like arias (sometimes called *arietta*—"little aria"—or *cavatina*, in fact only in one section without middle section or da capo repeat, or *cavata*, in fact only a brief arioso at the end of a recitative) are very rare in opera at this period, though common subsequently. Each scene or sequence builds up to a big da capo "exit aria," taking the character off-stage to increase the applause whether or not this is dramatically appropriate. On this method, the feelings of the characters are given every opportunity for vocal expression, but the dramatic continuity is correspondingly weakened. The "number" is the effective unit of construction. This is not music drama in the fullest sense.

The elements of comedy which had so enlivened serious Italian opera in the seventeenth century were almost eliminated by the eighteenth century. As if in compensation, Italian comic opera (*opera buffa*) acquired greater independence as a distinct category. Here, too, convention ruled, but less rigidly. Stock situations and stock characters were usual at first; but instead of impossible virtue or villainy, they were limited to equally impossible farce and earthiness. For all their crude vitality, the stock figures of so much baroque comedy are no more human portraits in the round than are their solemn opposites. However, there was a progressive refinement in both the texts and the music of eighteenth-century comic opera. As its main characters became less farcical, and more sentimental, so they acquired a more genuinely human individuality. Before the end of the century, this more human characterization spread over into serious opera.

The recitative of Italian comic opera does not differ from its serious counterpart. Except in the so-called "patter arias," in which the words go so fast that they can barely be fitted in, with very breathless and humorous effect. Many comic arias are of the formal da capo pattern, but other patterns are also frequent, and there is no obligation to take a character off-stage after an "exit aria" regardless of the dramatic probabilities. But all the mannerisms of serious opera may be ludicrously parodied, especially in comic operas which are themselves parodies of serious operas; for most fashionable successes evoked this dubious attention, often in several versions.

The greater flexibility of the comic convention permitted one especially important development in operatic construction. The climax of each act, especially the last, came to be built up from a succession of scenes, with solos, duets, larger ensembles, and (eventually) choruses, into a cumulative finale. The area of continuity thus established was gradually extended, until the entire opera came to some degree within its influence. As this influence also spread over into serious opera, together with the tendency toward more human characterization, something, although not all, of the original Florentine ideal of continuous and flexible opera returned.

Meanwhile, French serious opera (*tragédie lyrique*) still aimed rather at dramatic eloquence than at vocal brilliance. Some especially elaborate French airs (called for unknown reasons *ariettes*, "little airs") showed the influence of the Italian virtuosity. But the main musical substance still lay not in the airs but in the extensive and melodious recitative. Though French opera had neither the brevity nor the concentration of the earliest operas, and though the proportion of dances for which dramatic pretexts had to be found in it was always high, it remained a purposeful and flexible drama in music. French baroque opera is continuous opera.

French comic opera was a post-baroque development, imitated from Italian comic opera as brought to Paris by visiting companies in the middle of the eighteenth century. There was a native background of spoken comedy with incidental music, both crude (as in *vaudeville*) and sophisticated (as in Molière and Lully). As a result of this background, the dialogue of *opéra comique* (even when its subjects became as much serious as comical) was always spoken, whereas the dialogue of *opera buffa* (of which the subjects were similarly widened) was always in recitative. The airs of French comic opera, as of French serious opera, reflect some of the Italian vocal virtuosity, but without moving very far from their traditional simplicity.

In Germany, popular comedy with incidental music provided a similar background, from which comic opera with spoken dialogue (*Singspiel*) derived under the influence of French comic opera, when this was introduced to Vienna shortly after the middle of the eighteenth century. In England, "ballad opera" (at first comical but later sentimental), with spoken dialogue, had considerable success while remaining relatively unsophisticated. In Spain, the Italian influence on the popular comedies with incidental music had produced some genuine opera quite early in the seventeenth century; and by the eighteenth century there was a varied range of more or less operatic entertainments (*zarzuela*) on pastoral, heroic, comical, or mingled subjects, mainly with spoken dialogue but sometimes with recitative, in which the Italian elements rather than the native elements prevailed.

The centers of late baroque opera were widespread, and for the most part in close touch with one another. Venice yielded its international preeminence. Naples inherited from Venice the outstanding prestige with foreign visitors, but was not otherwise in the lead except to some extent in comic opera. Venice, Florence, Bologna, Rome, Vienna, and other centers in Italy and elsewhere shared in the advancement of Italian opera; French opera was centered on Paris, but performed and partly imitated in Italy in Parma, and in Germany in Hamburg and Stuttgart.

Thus the eighteenth century, which began with divergence, ended with cross-fertilization. There was some considerable reconciliation between the Italian vocal brilliance and the French dramatic eloquence, and also between the extremes of affectation in serious opera and of exaggeration in comic opera. If we regard Gluck as having forwarded and Mozart as having confirmed the resulting transition from late baroque opera to classical opera, about the first three quarters of the eighteenth century may be called the second great period of opera; and its characteristic species is that commonly called *number opera*.

# 5

## Serious and Comic

Like opera itself, number opera emerged from the thoughts of poets rather than of musicians. The French poetic drama of the seventeenth century was classical in form and rational in content. Its Italian admirers founded the Arcadian Academy in Rome in 1692. Here reforms of drama were initiated, which included the librettos for opera. Apostolo Zeno (1668-1750) became the most prominent reformer of the libretto in that generation; and in the next generation Pietro Metastasio (1698-1782) was a yet more elegant and graceful poet whose mastery of his own rather stilted but theatrically effective species of drama was unsurpassed.

We see here an extreme reaction against the disorderly complexity and frequent obscurity of the mid-seventeenth century librettos. The cast was ordinarily reduced to some six to eight characters, each representing one virtue or one vice in an exclusive concentration such as never happens in ordinary life. But as ingredients in ordinary people, we recognize the types well enough, and on the stage they have all the power of their superhuman consistency. Each has his own single motive or ruling principle, such as loyalty or patriotism, envy or ambition—or at the most his single obsession, such as a conflict between honor and interest, or duty and inclination. Love, as the universal passion, is always included, often as one side of the inner conflict. A happy ending after protracted suspense is almost invariable. Tyrants still turn magnanimous after victory; and perhaps this rather sympathetic convention derives from an intuition that we do all have baser qualities for which we need to forgive ourselves.

Comic relief is almost excluded. Only superior servants are admitted, for sharing confidences which we can overhear. Glamorized history or chivalry is preferred to the more open forms of mythology. Except in a special class of "magic operas," supernatural interventions and miraculous stage machines were, used, if at all, mainly in final scenes. The three "unities" of subject, time, and place (misleadingly attributed to Aristotle) were more or less broadly respected. Dialogue and action in mainly "dry" recitative lead to long and mainly "accompanied" arias, almost invariably da capo, with a slightly contrasted middle section returning to the opening section "from the beginning"—unchanged except for slight ornamental variations left to the singers to improvise. The big "exit aria" to which each scene builds up may take the singer off-stage with dramatic appropriateness, or it may break inappropriately into the continuity. No singer must be given more than one exit aria of the same kind (brilliant, tender, imposing, etc.), nor can more than two arias of the same kind occur in succession. Arias were allotted to each singer in proportion to his importance (not so much in the opera as in operatic politics outside); and so was the indulgence with which his own frequent excesses of florid ornamentation might be received.

Almost all heroes, and a few villains, were soprano or alto castratos; tenor heroes were very rare. Tenor villains were not unknown, but basses were usual; wise old sages were also generally basses. In the absence of a fashionable castrato, a woman might sing the part of a hero, and a few such parts were actually composed for a woman's voice. Heroines were sopranos, mezzo-sopranos, or even contraltos; they were sometimes, but not often, sung by castratos. But in France, where castratos were little liked, heroines and villainesses were normally sopranos, heroes tenors, and villains and sages basses.

Italian serious opera of the eighteenth century became more than ever stylized through this preference for high voices. It is so natural to associate high voices with femininity and low voices with masculinity that we feel, when the vocal range is kept so consistently high, as if we were in some strange world of disembodied spirit—as in the symbolical sense perhaps we are; and perhaps the Age of Reason felt more at ease with passion on these diluted terms. It is disastrous both musically and stylistically to transpose male castrato parts an octave down for tenors or baritones; much the best substitutes are male counter-tenors if they are strong enough, and female sopranos and mezzo-sopranos if they are not.

Choruses or ensembles for several voices are rare and brief, and chiefly though not wholly reserved for spectacular endings, particularly when stage machinery was to be employed. Duets are relatively common. Instrumental interludes, with or without dancing, either required some pretext in the plot, or else serve to give time and emphasis for stately entries or other stage movements. The overture, however, follows its own set forms: where the French overture (consolidated by Lully on early Italian models) goes slow, fast, optional slow, the Italian overture (consolidated by Alessandro Scarlatti) goes fast, slow, fast. There was not usually much if any musical or dramatic connection between the overture and the body of the opera until French influence was brought to bear in its turn, as the ways of opera reunited later in the eighteenth century; but Monteverdi's *Orfeo* was a subtle precedent, and Cesti's *Pomo d'Oro* a more obvious one.

# The Transition into Number Opera

The greatest of the composers who carried Italian opera into its second period, as number opera, was Alessandro Scarlatti (1660-1725). Over 800 of his fine chamber cantatas are now known to survive, while of 114 operas probably composed by him, not many more than half appear to survive. Scarlatti was born in Palermo, and began his operatic career in Rome. He spent some twenty years in Naples, but decided in 1702 that conditions of taste there did not allow him to do himself full justice. He thereafter composed some of the finest of his operas for Prince Ferdinando de' Medici of Florence, either there or while again in Rome, where in 1706 he was elected to the Arcadian Academy at the same time as Corelli and Pasquini. In 1707 Scarlatti was in Venice, producing his masterly *Mitridate Eupatore.* By 1709 (or possibly not till 1713) Scarlatti was back in Naples, but he kept his Roman connection with some of the best of his later operas; he died in Naples in 1725.

We can no longer regard Scarlatti as the founder of a "Neapolitan" school of opera. He taught very little in Naples, nor was there any serious opera in Naples which was distinct from what was going on in many other operatic centers just as soon and just as extensively. Scarlatti did not even create his best work for Naples. Scarlatti's earlier operas remain in the transitional style of the Venetian Legrenzi, the Roman Pasquini, and the roving Stradella. Even after the turn of the century, in Rome in 1708, Scarlatti's *Il Figlio delle Selve* ("The Son of the Woods"), on a libretto by C. S. Capace, has a French-style overture (*ouvertura*) passing into transitional-style recitative, and arias of which only some are da capo, and most are fairly short, together with duets, ensembles, and ballet in fairly high proportions; there is some brilliant, concerto-like orchestration, and a moderate separation of recitative and aria. All this is on the boundaries of number opera, yet not altogether into it. Ten years later, however, in Rome in 1718, Scarlatti's *Il Telemaco* ("Telemachus"), also on a libretto by C. S. Capace, is altogether number opera, the recitative (including some orchestrally accompanied recitative) being very distinct from the big (and altogether orchestrally accompanied) arias. There are a fair number of duets, but a larger ensemble only at the end; and there is a great deal of exciting, concerto-like work for the orchestra throughout, including trumpets and horns. In short, this is an opera very much of the second great period, and composed very much like a Handel opera. The style became extraordinarily widespread at the hands both of the Italians and of their imitators. The Venetian Antonio Vivaldi (c. 1675-1741) was typical rather than outstanding in this field. His present fame and his greatness lie in his brilliant instrumental music; but he also composed many serious operas, some on librettos by Zeno and by Metastasio, and with much success until he grew to be somewhat out of fashion by contrast with the younger generation.

The form of overture Scarlatti's preference for which did much to associate it with Italian opera, namely the Italian overture (going fast, slow, fast), had many precedents in mid-seventeenth century opera, especially for the introduction (*sinfonia*) before the second and third acts. Scarlatti helped to develop it, as Lully developed the French overture (going slow, fast, optional slow); but many serious number operas in the Italian style were given French overtures rather than Italian.

We see this conspicuously in that important and interesting school of opera, partly native and partly imported, which Kusser greatly developed and which, early in the eighteenth century, still flourished at Hamburg under Kusser's reputed pupil, Reinhard Keiser (1674-1739), an erratic but talented and prolific composer of operas blended from German, Italian, and French idioms; and this range of tastes was also represented there by the general repertory. A yet more talented and prolific composer active in opera at Hamburg was Georg Philipp Telemann (1681-1767), who studied Lully's scores and was a leading German exponent of French idioms in his own voluminous instrumental music. His exact contemporary Johann Mattheson (1681-1764), though now better remembered as a musicologist of vast prolixity, was also involved both as a performer and as a composer in Hamburg opera.

These men were the models, the friends, the rivals, and the colleagues of George Frederick Handel (1685-1759) as a young man, at the peak of the Hamburg opera, before its gradual decline to its eventual closing in 1738. Here it was that Handel served his first apprenticeship, and had his first opera *Almira* performed in 1705. But in 1706, Handel contrived to get to Italy, where he learned his trade as a composer of Italian opera (modified only by his solid German craftsmanship and his preference for French overtures) to such good effect that, already in 1707, Florence performed his *Rodrigo,* and in 1709 his *Agrippina,* with conspicuous success. In 1710, Handel returned to Germany an established composer, as musical director (*Kapellmeister*) to the Elector of Hanover. Later in 1710 Handel reached London as a visitor, where his *Rinaldo* (rushed together on a libretto produced in equal haste for him by Giacomo Rossi) was performed in February of 1711, also with spectacular success. Handel returned to Hanover, but was back in London on a further leave of absence in 1712, protracting it until the Elector ironically caught up with him in 1714 by becoming King George I of England. George I showed his good will, however, by confirming and increasing the court pension already granted to Handel by Queen Anne, and by further supporting his operatic career. Italian opera was in full London fashion; and Handel contributed to it a long succession of Italianate operas, until after many vicissitudes this remarkable episode in English musical life ended, and Handel embarked on a new but closely related career as the founder of English oratorio. In 1762, Thomas Augustine Arne (1710-1778) translated into English a libretto by Metastasio, and set it in the Italian manner, including recitatives, with some success, as *Artaxerxes.* But Arne, Charles Dibdin (1745-1814), William Shield (1748-1829), Stephen Storace (1763-1796), and Henry Rowley Bishop (1786-1855), though they kept English opera alive with considerable talent, did almost all their work in forms so marginally operatic that they had no real impact on the main stream.

# Italian Serious Opera

The immense vitality which could be imparted to serious Italian opera at its best may be seen in Handel's *Giulio Cesare* ("Julius Caesar"), on a libretto by N.F. Haym, and performed in London in 1724. There is (as commonly with Handel) a French overture. It is for strings, oboes, and basses (including, by convention, many bassoons, and of course, the regular continuo harpsichord or harpsichords). The slow opening movement calls for over-dotting. The succeeding fast movement needs crisp performance. This goes straight into a "chorus" (*coro*) for which the names of six of the original soloists (two on each of the lower two out of four voices, SATB) are indicated: an ensemble, therefore, rather than a full chorus; but with parts for four horns added to the orchestra for power and brilliance. Victorious Caesar, a contralto castrato, is being welcomed to the Nile, and returns thanks in a bravura aria, accompanied by the orchestra without the horns (but it is not a da capo aria, merely showing a fermata for an improvised cadenza). Then during his courteous recitative with Cornelia and Sextus, wife and son of the defeated Pompey, a gruesome interruption occurs: the Egyptian general Achillas enters with the severed head of Pompey, whom he has had murdered with the treacherous intention of pleasing Caesar. But it does not please Caesar: it provokes him to a furious exit aria. He leaves Cornelia on stage to sing a da capo aria of lamenting, and Sextus one of manly vengeance.

So far the action has been sure and swift, the recitative intensely felt, and the arias musically fine and dramatically convincing. Certainly this is number opera; but librettist and composer have been carrying us along with irresistible momentum. Now comes a change of mood as that archetypal seductress, Cleopatra, Queen of Egypt, her brother Ptolemy, King of Egypt, and her confidential companion Nirenus meet to plan a policy of mischief. Cleopatra, disguised as a supposedly wronged servant of herself under the name of Lidia, visits Caesar, who is at once attracted to her, but instead of pursuing his advantage, sings an exit aria and exits. Soon Cleopatra, after what would be her conventional exit aria, is unconventionally prevented from making her exit by Nirenus, who has seen Cornelia approaching; and Cleopatra, still pretending to be Lidia, accosts her conspiratorially. But left alone, Cleopatra achieves both an exit aria (singing Carmen-like of her own desires, presumably for Caesar) and an exit; by which time we may well be getting something of that bemused feeling inseparable, it seems, even from the best of late baroque operas. From the ensuing recitative between Ptolemy, Caesar, and Achillas (largely conducted in asides) we merely gather that they neither love nor trust each other as much as they pretend; and Caesar, left alone, compares himself, in a much-used species of da capo aria known as a "simile aria," to the prey sought by a cunning huntsman, on which pretext Handel provides him with an elaborate and splendid horn obbligato. He exits, and Act I soon concludes with a tearful da capo duet between Sextus (the top part, since he is a soprano castrato) and his mother (who is a female contralto).

Act II combines drama and divertissement in a spectacular vision, contrived by Cleopatra, of Parnassus, Virtue and the nine Muses, to an orchestra enchantingly colored with a harp, a lute, and a viola da gamba. The same ravishing orchestration continues as Cleopatra sings the most langorous of da capo arias, into which an utterly captivated Caesar inserts four measures of astonished recitative *before* the da capo return: Handel not only at his most unconventional, but also at his most inspired.

EXAMPLE 7    Handel, *Giulio Cesare*, II, 2 (a) Sinfonia (vocal interjections exceptional—notice the telescoped cadence); (b) recitative (later Italianate); (c) introduction (with exceptionally interposed recitative) to (d) aria (having exceptionally interposed recitative before da capo repeat).

su - on che me ra - pi - sce? A - vrà di sel-ce il cor che non lan - gui - sce
*sound-ing which so en-chants me? That heart would be of flint which did not lan-guish*

Gui - lio, che mi - ri? E quan - do con a - bis - so di
*Ju - lius, what see I? And have then with such in - fi - nite*

lu - ce sce - se-ro i Nu - mi in ter - ra?
*ra - diance, have then the gods come to earth?*

Then "as Caesar runs toward Cleopatra, Parnassus closes, and the scene changes back as it was at first"; but Nirenus promises to bring the infatuated conqueror into the company of the supposed Lidia, whom Caesar has hardly known whether to take for fact or phantom. Nirenus not only hints that "Lidia is kind," but that she will lead Caesar to Cleopatra, which for the moment does not seem particularly to interest him. But as the tangled plot unfurls, through disguise and conspiracy and treachery and an attempted assassination of Caesar which frightens Cleopatra into revealing her true identity to him, we begin to see how it will all end; and sure enough, by the final scene we have Caesar in the customary role of the magnanimous victor united with Cleopatra as his glamorous consort, and giving us very much the same profound and irrational satisfaction as Nero and Poppea at the end of Businello's and Monteverdi's *Poppea*, almost a century of eventful operatic history earlier. That ends with the celebrated duet (see p. 36); this ends with another "chorus" for an ensemble of soloists (two to each of four parts) with full orchestra and the four horns, thus balancing the radiant opening with as radiant a close.[1]

Of Handel's many contemporary rivals, Carl Heinrich Graun (1704-1759) established his reputation as a composer of Italian opera so successfully that in 1740 he was invited by Frederick II to Berlin, where he built up a repertory almost exclusively of his own works, occasionally bringing in a work of Hasse, or collaborating tactfully in a joint composition with the versatile and music-loving monarch himself. Johann Adolph Hasse (1699-1783) was yet more eminent, another German-born composer, like Handel Italian-trained, and perhaps a still more typical representative of the Italian serious number opera. Hasse began, as a raw though talented apprentice at Hamburg under the influence of Keiser, with a setting of a libretto by Zeno and Pariati: *Antioco* ("Antiochus"), performed at Brunswick in 1721. Hasse next studied in Naples, it seems rather unsympathetically, with Nicola Antonio Porpora (1686-1768); then sympathetically though quite briefly with the aged Alessandro Scarlatti. Hasse began a long series of successful operas, the first of which to have its libretto by Metastasio was *Ezio*, performed in Naples in 1730. Hasse went to Venice in late 1729 or early 1730, then to Dresden. His wife, the soprano Faustina Bordini, was a further asset to the company there; but they both (together or apart) traveled widely in pursuit of their international careers. Hasse became Metastasio's most admired composer; he had the famous librettist's own personal advice in composing Metastasio's favorite and much-revised libretto, *Attilio Regolo* ("King Attila"); this was performed in Dresden in 1750. Sooner or later Hasse composed almost all of Metastasio's librettos, the last work of both of them being *Ruggiero* in 1771. Their entire convention of opera was being challenged by then; and indeed they had not done much to change it for half a century. But they ended with still unrivaled reputations. Their style of serious opera (*opera seria*) could really go very little further.

## Italian Comic Opera

Comic parts on the baroque stage were mainly though not wholly reserved for the lower orders. Such parts are found early and often, not only in the relatively few comic operas, but in many serious operas of the first great period, until they were largely though not completely excluded from serious operas of the second great period, through the influence of Zeno and of Metastasio. But as interludes between the acts of an opera, or as postludes after the opera, comic scenes flourished still, as well as a rapid expansion of comic operas in their own right. All this came under the general name of comic opera (*opera buffa*).

There was an old background everywhere of farces and skits with frivolous spoken dialogue and catchy tunes, mostly borrowed from topical ballads and court airs, out of which grew entertainments more or less near to without quite being opera. A very successful and influential example was the so-called *Beggar's*

*Opera*, performed at London in 1728, with its earthy humor, its political satire, its parody of serious opera, and its medley of tunes from all manner of sources (even from serious opera) brought together (rather than composed) by John Cristopher Pepusch (1667-1752) on a very lively text by John Gay. Similar entertainments, ranging from largely improvised sketches with song and dance to quite dramatic presentations, might go by the name of vaudeville (*vaudeville*) in France or singing-play (*Singspiel*) in Germany. In so far as they were dramas (and *The Beggar's Opera* has certainly its moments of drama), they are spoken drama with incidental music, which was not even, for the most part, specially composed. Yet the satire and the parody and the catchy melody were all ingredients in comic opera as it reshaped itself during the eighteenth century.

Other ingredients (deriving ultimately from such sources as the classical Latin of Plautus and his Greek originals) had coalesced from the start of the baroque period into a traditional set of stock characters and situations: this was called the drama of the arts (*commedia dell' arte*), art being doubtless required to improvise dialogue on the mere framework of its written scenarios. Both in its crude originals and in its dramatic and operatic refinements, the audience always loved it, recognizing in it the universal types of their own human desires and weakness. Yet these types are, of course, no more literally lifelike than the types of serious opera. They are merely exaggerated on the grosser instead of on the nobler side of human nature.

The refinement of comic opera got more attention after its virtual exclusion from serious opera than ever it had while it was allowed to enter there. There was a renewed upsurge of comic interludes, not only between (and sometimes after) the acts of a serious opera, but performed independently. This was an Italian initiative, and Naples took a large though by no means exclusive share in it. By the middle of the century, however, the Italian comedians almost continuously present in Paris had brought it to France, with remarkable consequences for comic opera there and elsewhere.

Just as Zeno and Metastasio stood out among the many reformers of serious librettos, so the Venetian Carlo Goldoni (1707-1793) and to a lesser extent the Neapolitan Francesco Cerlone (c. 1730 to c. 1812) stood out among the many reformers (including their own imitators) of comic librettos. Goldoni (himself a member of the Arcadian Academy at Rome) was a playwright inspired by the example of Molière primarily to plays and secondarily to librettos, in which truth and naturalism (but a very stylized kind of naturalism) should refine the stock characters and situations of the *commedia dell' arte*. For this purpose, Goldoni reduced the improvisation and extended the written text; restrained the grossness of the lower characters; and introduced characters higher in the social scale, whose parts became not so much comical as sentimental, often in quite a serious way. Cerlone, who was of less literary importance, added a taste (perhaps of Spanish origin) for magic, fairy tale, and supernatural fantasy.

Thus the new direction for comic opera was not laughter alone, but tears and laughter mingled, together with a touch of fantasy; and we can see how, some distance further along in that direction, there developed historically such an

*opera buffa* as Mozart's *Don Giovanni*, and such a *Singspiel* as his *Magic Flute*.
But the new turning point in the middle of the eighteenth century was unexpected. It was caused, in France, by a sudden enthusiasm for the performances
in Paris in 1752 to 1753 of the Italian comedians, and in particular of an exceptionally charming little two-scene Neapolitan comic interlude, twenty years old
by then: Pergolesi's *La Serva Padrona* ("The Servant Mistress").[2]

The text (by G. A. Federico) is of the slightest, but it is full of punch from start
to finish; the plot is never in any doubt or obscurity; the honors go to homely wit
and determination, not to rank or dignity; there is just enough sentimental
appeal to save the joke from harshness. The music is impetuous and genuinely
comical; but it too is sufficiently "galant" and sentimental to be agreeably
touching. There are only two singing characters: the pert young maid-servant
Serpina (soprano) and her stubbornly bachelor master Uberto (bass); there is a
third character, Uberto's man-servant Vespone, "who does not speak." The
overture (*sinfonia*) in Italian form (fast, slow, fast) is brief but energetic; it is
believed to have been written by another composer after Pergolesi's death. An
"introduction" next has Uberto caught to the life in a miniature aria (not da capo);
and the situation is then presented at once in the ensuing recitative, as he
grumbles over this servant whom he has treated like a daughter and who has
grown so proud that "the servant will finally become the mistress" (a prophetic
statement and meant to be so taken). Serpina, as if in confirmation, offers, in the
very presence of the master, to teach Vespone manners. She keeps addressing
him though he makes no answers; but he plays up with plenty of comical mime,
till Uberto breaks into a mock-bravura, da capo aria (but being comic, he does not
have to exit after it). More sparring between maid and master; more appeals to

Eighteenth-century stage design for *La Serva Padrona*.

the stooging Vespone; and then she comes out with an imperious da capo aria on the theme of "be quiet, stop talking, Serpina wants it so," which leaves us in no doubt about her character either. Neither character is in the least a subtle one: each represents a type, rather than an individual; but they are certainly a relief after the impeccable types of contemporary serious opera, showing us as they do the other side of the human coin. They return to their quarrelling in quick-fire recitative, and end the "first intermezzo" with a duet which unites them fervently in a clash of wills.

EXAMPLE 8    Pergolesi, *La Serva Padrona*, (a) Italian overture (not by Pergolesi); (b) duet ending "first intermezzo."

In the "second intermezzo," Serpina deploys a simple but sufficient intrigue, with Vespone pretending to be a soldier in the simple but apparently sufficient disguise of a false moustache: for intrigue and disguise were habitual recourses of serious opera, and therefore fair game for parody in comic opera. The intrigue is that Serpina pretends she has decided to marry this dangerously choleric soldier, with a dowry to be provided, of course, by Uberto; and each stage in this monstrous proposal is reinforced by Vespone's miming a pretense of violence barely restrained, until (after Serpina and Uberto have each again sung one apposite aria, hers progressive, his da capo), Uberto from a mixture of miserliness, fear, and perfectly human jealousy throws in his hand with a firm offer; Serpina accepts him with the happy cry, "and truly the servant becomes the mistress"; Vespone removes his false moustache to Uberto's dumbfounded amazement but hardly ours; Uberto begins to feel he likes it after all; and with a sudden turn into a rather touching sentiment (typical of this developing kind of not wholly comic opera), they sing another quite long duet to balance the first. But they are united this time by happiness.

And this was the well-turned little masterpiece which, though making no special impact at its first performance in Paris in 1746, found the moment ripe upon its return performance in 1752. It brought down not only the house but the country too. The moment was ripe because of that mounting passion for the simple and the unpretentious which the French Encyclopedists Diderot, D'Alembert, and Jean-Jacques Rousseau were cultivating, on the fallacious but influential misunderstanding that the evils of humanity grow only from an overlay of civilized sophistication. *The Servant Mistress* became a token of that supposedly natural character and situation found deficient in French serious opera (*tragédie lyrique*), chiefly because it had never been attempted there. And so began the War of the Comedians (*guerre des buffons*, from Italian *buffone*, "comedian"), that wordy battle of pamphlets which was neither the first nor the last in the long conflict between partisans of French and Italian music. The Italian manner took further impetus in 1752 from Jean-Jacques Rousseau's naive and sentimental but highly popular *Le Devin du Village* ("The Country Diviner"), on his own libretto. The natural virtue of a simple village girl foils the lecherous intentions of a sinister aristocrat, and unites her in the end with her village lover. The dialogue is composed in undistinguished Italianate recitative; the airs are in mildly vivacious French melody such as had long served (whether borrowed or, less often, composed) for a wide variety of French spoken comedies with sung lyrics. Rousseau's naive libretto and his innocent musicianship were soon improved upon; his dialogue in recitative was quietly dropped. Spoken dialogue continued to be the French convention right down to the culmination of *opéra comique* in Bizet's *Carmen;* whereas dialogue in recitative continued to be the Italian convention right down to the culmination of *opera buffa* in Verdi's *Falstaff.* But in most respects, the art of opera, though still finding room for great variety, returned after the late baroque period toward a more uniform condition than it had shown during the previous parting of the ways.

*Notes*

1. Nicola Haym's libretto, in its all too typical complication, is taken with adaptations from G.F. Bussani's *Giulio Cesare in Egitto*, first composed by Antonio Sartorio for Venice in 1677. So foreign an art was serious opera in England during the first half of the eighteenth century.
2. Perf. Naples, 1733, as the intermezzi between the acts of Pergolesi's serious opera *Il Prigonier Superbo* ("The Proud Prisoner"). The Paris performance of 1746 had an overture by G.A. Paganelli; that of 1752 had an overture by Telemann.

# 6

# The Rejoining of the Ways

Number opera was rooted in the reforms of Zeno and Metastasio. Now the younger composers began a reform of that reform, under the growing influence of French serious opera. This was still very much as Lully had left it at his death in 1687. Pascal Colasse (1649-1709) achieved a certain individuality in his *Thétis et Pélée* of 1689. Da capo arias in Italian style were cultivated by André Campra (1660-1744), who was, however, less significant for his serious operas than for having set a new fashion in light opera-ballet with his *L'Europe Galante* of 1697. Marin Marais (1656-1728) made something of a sensation in 1706 with a big orchestral storm scene in his *Alcyone;* but this is a fine, expressive and very French opera throughout. With Jean-Philippe Rameau (1683-1764), the range of the harmony has grown a little wider, especially in diminished sevenths and other altered chords; but no more so than was to be expected from the prevailing trend of the times. The instrumentation is likewise rather more varied, and the orchestral tone painting more extensive. On these grounds, Rameau was accused by conservative colleagues, after his first performed opera in 1733, *Hippolyte et Aricie*, of having debased the pure inheritance of Lully with unduly Italian extravagancies. He quite properly denied this, proclaiming his fidelity (though not servility) to the ideals of Lully; and when in 1752 the old quarrel between supporters of French and Italian music broke out into a new war of pamphlets, Rameau himself came under attack as being, on the contrary, too conservatively French. His own best-known operas had been composed by then: *Castor et Pollux* of 1737; *Dardanus* of 1739; and *Zoroastre* of 1749. Conservative Rameau was not, since he absorbed much valuable Italian influence. But French he was, renewing with calculated virtuosity what Lully had achieved with simpler means, but perhaps on balance with deeper feeling: that French serious opera which was still, unlike the Italian, essentially continuous opera.

It was Rameau's even more than Lully's operas which, when heard abroad or by visitors to Paris, contributed toward rejoining Italian and French serious opera. Thus Nicola Jommelli (1714-1774), though he displayed some youthful boldness at various Italian centers in making his recitatives more richly musical and his arias more dramatically adaptable, went much further (without ever losing his avowed admiration for Metastasio and Hasse) while at Stuttgart from 1756-1769; for there, French tastes and French opera were in fashion, and there from 1760, the French dancer and reformer of dancing, Jean-Georges Noverre (1727-1810), was seeking in ballet for the same kind of human expressiveness and drama as did Gluck in opera, and achieving an international reputation with his challenging *Letters on Dance and Ballets*.[1] Jommelli shows the influence of Rameau in overtures connected directly or indirectly with the opening scene; in orchestral and choral storms, battles, temple rituals, and other stirring episodes; in numerous and prominent ballets; in more fluid recitative, arioso, and aria (accompanied less by continuo only and more by full orchestration); and by more forward action in the arias with less suspense of the drama. In 1765, Jommelli was actually warned by Metastasio to trust the moving purity of song rather than distract from it by too much orchestral beauty. But Jommelli by then had learned from his German environment at Stuttgart a certain richness of orchestral texture and a certain boldness of harmonic progression, just as he had learned from his experience there of French opera a certain dramatic force and flexibility. Such freedom of words and music was beyond the scope of either Metastasio or Hasse. The reform of Italian serious number opera had gone some way already with Jommelli.

This same expansion and relaxation of Italian serious opera through French influence was taken farther by Tommaso Traëtta (1727-1779). He, too, gained early success at some traditional Italian centers of opera before experiencing French opera in strength, as the result of a prestigious appointment under the Duke of Parma, then a Spanish principality of French artistic leanings. There was a French director of opera at Parma, du Tillet, who regularly mounted the operas of Rameau; and some of the originally French librettos set by Rameau were set again in Italian translation by Traëtta. The dramatization of the arias achieved by Traëtta brought many formal modifications, such as extending the middle section, and shortening the da capo repeat of the first section; occasionally a brief passage of recitative comes within the aria itself (see Ex. 7, p. 64, for a case of this in Handel's *Giulio Cesare*).

How seriously Traëtta's reforms were taken at the time may be judged from the explicit approval given to him by the noted critic and reformer Francesco Algarotti, in his influential little *Essay on Opera* (*Saggio sopra l'Opera in Musica*), which was published, at a place unstated, in 1755. The purpose of the reforms is there plainly stated to be the subordination of all purely musical beauty, including vocal beauty, to the requirements of the drama, in the manner of the earliest operas. In theory, this brings us back full cycle to the original Florentine ideal; but it was, of course, very differently expressed in practice. There was no return to the seamless, tuneful recitative of the earliest operas. There was at most some modification and relaxation, which was encouraged by current French opera, of Italian number opera.

## Gluck and the Reform of Opera

Christoph Willibald Gluck (1714-1787) gained the greatest credit for the reform of Italian number opera; but neither the credit nor the reform can be accepted quite at face value. In Prague, Vienna, and Milan, Gluck first learned the conventional form of serious Italian opera. His career began with *Artaserse* in 1741, *Demetrio* in 1742, and *Demofoonte*, also in 1742, all of them on librettos by Metastasio, and in music nearer to the tradition of Hasse than to the approaching reforms of Jommelli and Traëtta. Throughout his career, sixteen out of Gluck's thirty Italian operas were on librettos by Metastasio, whose ideal of opera Gluck must evidently have continued to respect even after he had departed from it in the relatively few works, composed at different times, which constitute his "reform operas." And in these, the novelty is only Gluck's in part. Much of it is drawn from the ideas of Algarotti and the scores of Jommelli and Traëtta, as well as from Gluck's first reforming librettist, Ranieri Calzabigi (1714-1795).

In 1745, Gluck passed through Paris, and may already have received there an impression of the continuous French serious opera of Rameau which certainly became crucial for him in his reform operas a dozen years and more afterward. He then stayed in London into 1746, receiving more of an impression from Handel (particularly Handel's choruses) than Handel seems to have received from him. If Handel really said that Gluck knew no more counterpoint than his cook (an operatic bass, as it happened), we can only agree that Gluck never was a technically resourceful composer, but one who touches us, at his best, through simple expressiveness of melody and harmony.

Back in Vienna, Gluck made in 1750 a financially advantageous marriage, which perhaps emboldened him to greater unconventionality. In 1754, he was made an official court composer; and in 1755 he was put in charge of a series of French comic operas, by the recently appointed imperial director of theaters. This was Count Giacomo Durazzo, who led a discreet but formidable opposition to the still powerful poet laureate, Metastasio. Durazzo sent operas by Gluck to Paris, and was sent from Paris by Favart some comic operas (on Favart's librettos), which Gluck adapted to the local requirements in Vienna so energetically that he ended by replacing most or all of their French airs by others in the same style of his own composing (as usual in French comic opera, the dialogue was spoken). Gluck certainly learned much from the French tunefulness of melody and vitality of drama thus brought to his attention.

Upon this potentially explosive situation, there arrived in Vienna in 1761, after seven years in Paris, that already somewhat notorious poet, critic, and adven-

Orpheus moves the Furies to pity by his singing, *Orfeo ed Euridice*, Act II. Metropolitan Opera Company.

turer, Calzabigi. As critic, Calzabigi went out of his way to flatter Metastasio; as poet, he gave Gluck not only the first of his reform librettos, but some very French-inspired and anti-Metastasian advice upon how to compose it. This was subsequently acknowledged by Gluck in generous terms; and we may notice, once again, the impetus for an operatic innovation coming from the poet rather than from the composer.

The first reform opera by Calzabigi and Gluck is *Orfeo ed Euridice* ("Orpheus and Euridice"),[2] performed in Vienna in 1762. After an uncommonly cheerful overture in C major, the curtain rises upon the tomb of Euridice, whose tragic death is not enacted, but assumed as a recent happening. Except for the overture, there is nothing to acquaint us dramatically with the previous happiness against which we might experience the contrast of the present tragedy, as there had been in Rinuccini and in Striggio. We are taken straight into a grieving chorus in C minor, simple and homophonic like Rameau and Lully, but like them eloquent in its simplicity. Orpheus (a castrato alto) three times sings over this chorus the name of his beloved Euridice: not a novel device, but used here with great certainty and expressiveness. Orpheus in brief recitative asks for a last tribute of flowers, and after these have been bestowed on the tomb in a suitable dance, the chorus resumes, but is dismissed by Orpheus. He embarks on a touching aria in rondo form, the refrains being, unconventionally, matching passages of recitative, but tuneful like arioso, and orchestrally accompanied. Amor, the god of love, responds by telling him to win Euridice back from the underworld by the power of his harmonious lyre. After a considerable scene of mingled dialogue and aria, during which Amor reports that the gods will require of him the traditional test of not looking back, Orpheus closes the first act with an appropriately exultant aria, continuously developed without formal recapitulation, but with much conventional floridity which the dramatic situation here amply justifies.

The second act is conducted essentially in choruses and ballet, as Orpheus is confronted by the assembled Furies, but persuades them by brief samples of his legendary singing to let him pass, upon which they indulge themselves in some far-from-brief dancing and pantomime. This part of the underworld proves to be surprisingly agreeable; and once again, we miss that much more dramatic and realistic contrast between the daylight world above and the dark underworld below, with which the earlier librettos of Rinuccini and of Striggio made such significant play. A chorus of happy spirits duly produces Euridice, and there is much beautiful singing about the brightness and serenity of those blessed realms; but while we enjoy it musically, we are not gripped dramatically, since we are given no sense of character in growth by trial or suffering.

The third act shows us the return journey; but such trial as Orpheus now undergoes really consists of his being nagged persistently by Euridice, in spite of his quite sufficient explanations, until he can stand no more of it and gives into her by looking back despite himself. That does nothing for his character, and not much for our sympathies as she dies again. There follows, however, the most famous and heart-melting of all Gluck's melodies, a somewhat free and flexible da capo aria beginning in the Italian *Che farò senza Euridice, dove andrò senza il mio ben?* ("What shall I do without Euridice, where go without my love?") and in the subsequent French version prepared for performance in Paris in 1774, *J'ai perdu mon Eurydice, rien n'égale mon malheur* ("I have lost my Euridice, nothing equals my misfortune"). But though the tune is heart-melting, it is not particularly sad, with its C major tonality and its easy lilt. The contemporary French critic Boyé[3] maliciously remarked that the same tune would go even better to the words: *J'ai trouvé mon Euridice, rien n'égale mon bonheur* ("I have found my Euridice, nothing equals my good fortune"). Gluck had not Mozart's gift, nor Wagner's, of conveying musically a precise character or situation or feeling; he just conveys feeling in general. But that is itself a wonderful gift, and it is chiefly by moments such as this, not altogether common in his operas but very moving when they do occur, that Gluck earned his small but secure place in the modern repertory.

It is Gluck's sensibility, not his theory, which carried him however intermittently to greatness. He shows it here by recalling plainly (though not for certain deliberately) the music of the grievous scene at the start of the opera, which much more expectedly is in C minor, but with otherwise just the same melodic opening shape.

EXAMPLE 9    Gluck, *Orfeo ed Euridice*, melodic contour (a) at start of Act I; (b) Euridice momentarily in III, 1; (c) in *Che faro senza Euridice*, III, 1.

With no further preparation, Orpheus announces in nine bars of recitative, eight of arioso, and three more of recitative his immediate intention of killing himself to rejoin Euridice, but is promptly prevented by Amor. In the brief dialogue which follows, Amor explains that he requires no further proof of Orpheus' constancy, and restores Euridice to him once more alive. But Orpheus' constancy has never for a moment been in question. It is for any sign of growth of character and understanding, any increase in consciousness and maturity, that we still look in vain. The opera dissolves into agreeable divertissement, with choruses and dances in plenty but nothing in either words or music to satisfy the deeper values of the myth. Compared with Rinuccini, for all his compromising ending, and still more with Striggio, who did not really compromise at all, Calzabigi made shallow work of it; and Gluck seemingly desired no more.

In Gluck's dedication to his next reform opera (not his next opera), his *Alceste* ("Alcestis") of 1767, we read that the vanity of singers must be restrained, the music "serving the poetry" by "following the situation of the story without delaying the action or burying it under a worthless excess of ornamentation"; without the undramatic repeats of da capo arias; with recitative and aria brought closer to one another, and instrumentation serving only the dramatic purpose; with overtures musically relevant; and altogether with music directed to the "beautiful simplicity" of human feeling.[4] Much of the substance of this is to be found already in Jommelli and Traëtta; none of it was consistently observed by Gluck, even in his reform operas; and all of it amounts essentially to giving Italian number opera some of the expressive liberty and theatrical immediacy which Gluck had learned, above all, from the continuous French opera of Rameau.

Gluck now repaid his debt to the French by conquering half of Paris in April of 1774 with a more uniformly excellent opera, on a libretto greatly superior, by Le Blanc du Roullet after Racine's masterly adaptation of Euripides: *Iphigénie en Aulide* ("Iphigenia in Aulis"). In spite of his own stated principles, there are borrowings of music from earlier works (and thus originally to different words); there are ballets without dramatic necessity; there are da capo repetitions not furthering the action; there are many deliberate concessions to French taste; moreover, there is both Italianate dry recitative and French tuneful recitative. But in overall effect, it is the mobile French quality rather than the static Italian quality which prevails. In August, 1774, a French version of Gluck's *Orfeo* was produced at Paris, with a tenor hero replacing the original castrato (unacceptable to French taste), and many changes made by Gluck in the score to suit this altered tessitura. In February, 1775, *Iphigénie en Aulide* returned with extensive revisions and additions, including whole passages lifted from other works by Gluck. In 1776, a French version of *Alceste* followed. But meanwhile, the unconquered half of Paris struck back by setting up the moderately talented Niccolò Piccinni (1728-1800) as a rival to Gluck, in a further war of pamphlets which neither champion encouraged, and which did not survive the manifest success in 1779 of Gluck's finest opera both for words and for music: *Iphigénie en Tauride* ("Iphigenia in Tauris"), on a libretto by Nicolas-François Guillard adapted directly from Euripides.

Unlike many French adaptations from the classics, Guillard's libretto allowed the genius of Euripides to hold the stage undistracted by added complications of plot or of extra characters. There is a swiftness of action and an immediacy of feeling which were evidently very much to Gluck's liking. He took advantage of so excellent a libretto in music which also moves swiftly and surely, full of dramatic insight and effective contrast. The overture is an orchestral storm which sets the mood for the opening scene, and passes directly into it, as Iphigenia relates a terrifying dream to a chorus of supporting priestesses. Into the barbaric kingdom of Thoas, there are brought two Greek prisoners, to the fearful glee of the barbarians in fierce dance and chorus. Orestes is brother to Iphigenia (but neither yet knows it); he has recently murdered his own mother, Clytemnestra, the adulterous murderess of his father, Agamemnon, and is paying for this unnatural though mythologically significant act with an inner torment outwardly represented by the legendary Furies: Pylades is his friend and companion: one of them must die in sacrifice at Iphigenia's hand to appease the superstitious fear of Thoas over the storm; each wishes to save the other; but for the moment Orestes has all he can do to contend with his own guilt and agitation, represented in the orchestra by an agitated accompaniment on the violas even as he tells himself with unconvincing calm that he is really perfectly all right—a good stroke of theater and of music too.

EXAMPLE 10   Gluck, *Iphigénie en Tauride*, Act II, the false calm of Orestes contradicted by the revealing agitation of the violas.

The opera is very protracted; but the climax comes swiftly when Orestes, just as Iphigenia's sacrificial knife is raised to strike him, reveals by a few seemingly inadvertent words that he is her brother. At this moment of consternation, a most timely party arrives to the rescue. Thoas the barbarian king is killed in the confusion, and a happy ending follows. And here, too, concludes Gluck's intermittent but sincere attempt at reforming serious opera. With failing health, he lost not so much the wish as the power to adventure further.

## The Transition Toward Classical Opera

Comic opera was also in transition. Thus we find Baldassare Galuppi (1706-1785) achieving an international reputation with *Il Filosofo di Campagna* ("The Country Philosopher"), first performed in Venice in 1754. His librettist was the celebrated Carlo Goldoni (1707-1793), a leading reformer of comic drama. Niccolò Piccinni (1728-1800) became almost as famous with *La Buona Figliuola* ("The Good-Natured Girl"), first performed in Rome in 1760; and this, too, was on a libretto by Goldoni. From 1761 Goldoni settled in Paris. From 1766, Piccinni also settled in Paris, where his gifts in comic opera were much appreciated. His serious operas there were a blend of Italian tunefulness with French dramatic quality, largely through the influence of his rival Gluck. Piccinni's *Didon* (1783) is a fine example of the style; it is on a libretto by Marmontel, a French reformer whose influence in comic opera became joined with that of Goldoni and of Charles-Simon Favart (1710-1792). And here we notice an element of romantic expressiveness entering into the very origins of classical opera. An early example is *Le Déserteur* ("The Deserter"), which was performed in Paris in 1769. The composer was Pierre-Alexandre Monsigny (1729-1817), who was an admirer of Pergolesi's *La Serva Padrona* and one of the leaders of the new French comic opera; his music is appealing in an immediate way, although not profound, and he had much influence on the emerging style. The librettist of *Le Déserteur* was Jean-Michel Sedaine (1719-1797), then coming greatly into fashion. There is a hero, Alexis, who is not comic either in his person or in his situation; for he is imprisoned and under unjust sentence of death. He has a companion in prison, Montaucel, who is both comic and drunken. He also has a beloved, Louise, who at the last possible moment, after a final act of accumulating suspense, contrives his pardon by the king himself. It was a novel and attractive mixture of ingredients, and started a vogue, of which a still more fashionable example was *Richard Coeur-de-Lion* ("Richard Lion-Heart"), performed in Paris in 1784. This was also on a libretto by Sedaine. The composer was André Ernest Modeste Grétry (1741-1813), a Belgian who was training in Rome when a score by Monsigny turned his enthusiasm to French comic opera; and from 1767, Grétry like so many others settled in Paris, where he composed some successful serious operas, but more numerous and yet more successful comic operas.

King Richard is languishing in captivity, but is at last discovered by his faithful minstrel Blondel, who sings an imitation troubadour melody (used throughout almost like a Wagnerian leading-motive) which is supposed to have been composed by the king for his beloved long ago. In a famous scene of great theatrical effectiveness, made possible by a new form of stage illumination, the king appears at dawn in growing sunshine, while Blondel appears in shadow outside the moat. Both are visible to the audience, but neither to each other. Blondel sings the first verse; the king in astonishment returns the second verse; both swing into harmonious duet. With much spectacle and ballet (since this is French opera) the castle is stormed and the king is rescued. What the music lacks in depth, it makes up for in naive energy and excitement. Having spoken dialogue, the form is technically *opéra comique*; but the treatment is substantially romantic, and led to a long line of such "rescue operas" of which the greatest, a generation later, was Beethoven's *Fidelio*. It is to the classical operas of Mozart and Beethoven, often with strongly romantic leanings, that we have next to turn.[5]

## Notes

1. Jean-Georges Noverre, *Lettres sur la Danse et les Ballets*, Stuttgart and Lyons, 1760.
2. The French version, in a translation and adaptation by Moline, was given at the Paris *Opéra* in 1774. In changing Orpheus from a castrato soprano to a normal tenor, Gluck made substantial changes in the layout of the score.
3. Quoted gleefully by the celebrated but conservative Viennese critic Hanslick (Wagner's opponent) in his brilliant essay *Vom Musikalisch-Schönen* ("The Beautiful in Music"), Leipzig, 1854, transl., ed. G. Cohen, New York, 1957, p. 32.
4. Gluck's dedication to his *Alceste* will be found in English translation by Eric Blom in O. Strunk's *Source Readings in Music History*, New York, 1950, pp. 673-75. On pp. 657-72 a long extract is given from Algarotti's *Essay on Opera*, of 1755, which makes an interesting comparison.
5. From this point, details of publication are seldom in doubt, and will not be noted, except for special reason. They can readily be found in the usual books of reference.

# PART THREE
## Scene Opera

ᏁᎦᎤᎦᏉᏍᏂ

## The Third Great Period: To 1850

The last quarter of the eighteenth century and the first half of the nineteenth brought the divergent styles and categories of opera increasingly into contact, and renewed still more of the original ideal of opera as drama continuously and flexibly unfolding in words and music. Unlike the Florentine pioneers, and unlike Gluck, Mozart held the theory that "in opera, the poetry must in all ways be the obedient servant of the music."[1] In practice, however, Mozart went farther than any composer since Monteverdi had yet gone to balance the dramatic, the poetical, and the musical elements of opera.

Now balance is of the essence of the classical style. It is not classical to avoid emotion. It is classical to contain emotion within an order and proportion which themselves contribute to the intensity of the experience. *Classical* and *romantic* are not only period terms; they are terms for complementary tendencies in all of us. But at some periods, and in some individuals, the one tendency or the other may be uppermost. Mozart in both respects was a classical composer. He wrote that "music, even in the most terrible situations, must never distress the ear, but must give pleasure to the hearer, or in other words, must never cease to be music."[2] Nevertheless, within this moderation there burns a radiance of feeling to which the early romantic operas shortly afterward were greatly indebted. Mozart combined the vocal fluency which he learned from Italian opera with the dramatic truth which in part he drew from French opera, and in still larger part from his own innate genius for thinking dramatically in music. Da Ponte, the best of his librettists, gave him texts in which serious emotion combines with comedy, and tears and laughter are not far apart. Mozart, with his genius for reconciling such different styles and categories, confirmed the new direction not only for classical opera, which he best represented, but also for early romantic opera, which grew out of it.

Classical and early romantic opera retained the set "numbers" of late baroque opera, but linked and dissolved them more continuously into longer scenes. The scene or sequence became the effective unit of construction. "Dry" (*secco*) recitative, supported only by bass and harpsichord, gave place increasingly to "accompanied" recitative, supported by orchestral figures and melodies to which the vocal declamation has to fit in stricter measure than is really proper to recitative. This brings recitative near to arioso; and arioso only needs a little more symmetry in the vocal melody and a little more conclusiveness in the cadences to become aria. Thus the distinction between recitative, arioso, and aria, which had been flexible in the continuous opera of the first great period, but more rigid in the number opera of the second great period, became once again more flexible. The arias themselves are more free and varied in their formal construction. Music drama in the fullest sense was brought much more nearly although not completely back by these developments.

The classical orchestra anticipated by Gluck and confirmed by Mozart resembled the baroque orchestra in resting on a firm foundation of bowed strings. The number of parts, which in some baroque scores may be as few as three or as many as five, settled to four as the normal situation, though the violas may often do no more than double the bass line, making once again three real parts. The continuo harpsichord remained by force of habit for instrumental music, where it became increasingly unnecessary and eventually obsolete in so far as the harmony was more fully sustained by written inner parts, especially chords on woodwind and horns. But for opera the continuo harpsichord remained necessary, since a large proportion of the recitative was still accompanied by harpsichord and cello only, while some arias were also still accompanied in this manner. Flutes, oboes, and bassoons remained a standard element, and were joined by clarinets, which were evolved early in the eighteenth century, but used only on very exceptional occasions in baroque music by Handel, Rameau, and others. When first brought regularly into the standard orchestra, the clarinets were played by oboists doubling on both instruments, so that they could not be used (though the flutes now could) at the same time as oboes. Mozart had a particular affection for clarinets, and in his later though not his earlier scores, could count on specialized players being available for them. The ordinary provision for the classical orchestra was double woodwind throughout. A pair of orchestral horns also became a standard provision by the middle of the eighteenth century (and by the end of it, in big opera houses, two pairs). The use of a pair of trumpets with their associated kettledrums, borrowed by long precedent from the military and ceremonial establishments, was taken over until, in classical times, at first in the theater and then in the concert hall, these once royal and military instruments acquired civilian status. Three trombones (alto, tenor, bass) could be introduced for any opera requiring them, but were not yet standard components of the regular orchestra, though they were beginning to be so around the end of the eighteenth century. The greatest difference, however, was not due to adding wind instruments, but to using them independently, as contrasting sonorities rather than mainly as doublings of lines already being played by the strings. The classical orchestra was a balance of instrumental sounds, not sustained throughout a movement or an aria as in much late baroque music, but alternating within a single passage for a variety of effects and gradations.

Paris became the preeminent center for opera. There the presence or popularity of Rossini, Bellini, Cherubini, Spontini, Weber, and Meyerbeer gave the French tradition an international quality, until in the second half of the nineteenth century, Verdi crossed this tradition with Italian serious opera, and Wagner discarded it in favor of German music drama to complete, in their different ways, the return to the original ideal of continuous and flexible opera. On this broad view, the last quarter of the eighteenth century and the first half of the nineteenth century may be called the third great period of opera, and its characteristic species was a development of number opera which may be distinguished as *scene opera*.

## Notes

1. Letter to his father, October 13, 1781.
2. Letter to his father, September 26, 1781.

# 7

# Mozart, the Central Point

The genius of Wolfgang Amadeus Mozart (1756-1791) appeared just half way down the four hundred years which cover up to now the history of opera. He was a central figure not only in this matter of date, but also in bringing to a focus all those tendencies toward a union of styles and categories which marked his time. His father, Leopold Mozart, was a violinist and teacher of considerable distinction, who nurtured his precocious gifts with every advantage of early professional training. As a child prodigy, Mozart was taken through many great cities where opera of all current varieties was being performed. Vienna, Paris, and London were among them, and in Italy Bologna (where the celebrated Padre Martini bestowed on him much praise and a little counterpoint) and Rome. There were later journeys, including a return to Paris by way of Mannheim in 1777-1778. In 1781, Mozart was attending most of the rehearsals for the Vienna revival of Gluck's *Iphigenia en Tauride;* and from about the same date, there was a mutual exchange of admiration and influence between Mozart and his rather older and very famous contemporary, Haydn. The vocal brilliance of Italian opera, the dramatic eloquence of French opera, the suggestive innovations of Gluck, the rich orchestration and symphonic development of the German composers of the Mannheim school, and finally the sympathetic example of Haydn, were all in turn assimilated into Mozart's own incomparable resourcefulness.

Already between the remarkable ages of twelve and fourteen Mozart had achieved *La Finta Semplice* ("The Feigned Simpleton"), a passable *opera buffa* on words adapted from Goldoni; *Bastien and Bastienne,* a charming little German *Singspiel* on words adapted from an *opéra comique* by Favart after Rousseau's *Le Devin du Village;* and *Mithridate*, an *opera seria* on words adapted by V.A. Cigna-Santi from Racine, which for all its inevitable immaturity gives considerable indications of the dramatic power to come. This power is evident in Mozart's first important opera, *Idomeneo*, an *opera seria* on words adapted by Giambatista Varesco from a French libretto (a *tragédie lyrique* by Antoine Dachet already composed by Campra), which was given a splendid performance in Munich in 1781. This is a late and outstanding though not quite typical example of a form already near to decline. As with Gluck (himself one of Mozart's models), there is much French influence. This shows in the use of intensely dramatic choruses; in the vivid scenes with descriptive instrumentation; in the march and ballet music; and in an overture of great solemnity and full sonority, certain themes of which recur in the accompaniments of subsequent recitative and aria. The King of Crete, Idomeneo, having been caught by the sea-god Poseidon in a furious (and furiously orchestrated) storm as he returns from the siege of Troy, vows—like Jephtha—to sacrifice the first person he meets on his safe return. He meets his own son Idamente: a confrontation from which Poseidon eventually releases them, after Idamente in person has overcome a sea-monster—but on condition that Idamente shall take his father's place on the throne, perhaps in token of the ongoing future.

By the time of *Die Entführung aus dem Serail* ("The Abduction from the Seraglio"), a *Singspiel* performed in Vienna in 1782, Mozart had gained the confidence to have his librettist, Stephanie, amplify its conventional, mock-Turkish scenario "just as I want it,"[1] giving Osmin as the villain a more distinctive part and Belmonte as the hero a more persuasive one. Other characters are less strongly drawn; but the music throughout does much to sharpen the lines, especially by uniting the main characters in ensembles whose easy counterpoint retains even as it contrasts their musical distinctness. The finale to the second act is a particularly strong example of Mozart's skill in constructing a big scene from a succession of recitatives, arias, ensembles, and choruses. The plot opens with the heroine, Konstanza, in the power of the Pasha Selim (a speaking part), whose chamberlain Osmin is in parallel pursuit of her maid Blondchen. The hero, Belmonte, is brought in, disguised, by his resourceful servant, Pedrillo, who is in love with Blondchen. Their attempted flight having been foiled by Osmin, they are first condemned but then forgiven by Selim, although Belmonte proves to be the son of an old enemy. Nevertheless Selim allows Belmonte to marry Konstanza whom he loves himself. In this he doubly shows the magnanimity still habitual among operatic tyrants.

Mozart's full stature was reached with his greatly deepened *opera buffa*, at once a comedy and a drama to touch the heart, *Le Nozze di Figaro* ("The Marriage of Figaro"), which was performed in Vienna in 1786. The libretto, by Lorenzo Da Ponte, adapted a socially challenging play by Beaumarchais—the second of three in which Figaro, that quick-witted man of the people, stands for natural right against aristocratic oppressiveness. In Da Ponte's text, however, and still more in Mozart's music, the emphasis shifts from social commentary to human reconciliation. We begin in pointed comedy but end in chastened feeling, because the music does.

The overture to *Figaro* has the customary Italian vitality, but at a strangely intensified pressure. The unison string eighth-notes and wind harmonies of the first subject sweep on to a dominant modulation for a piquant second subject (at measure 59); so far, it is a regular sonata-form exposition. There are other keys for other subjects, in somewhat irregular abundance; but a bridge subject (m. 108) turns to reminiscence of the opening, and our expectation is aroused for a development section—which does not happen. Instead, we are taken (m. 139) straight into a shortened but sufficiently regular recapitulation and a coda. It is as if the action will not wait upon the normal proprieties. The impact of this sonata-form movement with abounding themes but no sonata-form development is unusual in the extreme, and prepares us for the unusual opera to follow.

There is nothing very unusual about the opening scene. The servant couple start it off in the ordinary vein of Italian comic opera, with their ready verbal sparring: quick and sharp on the side of Susanna; slower, but with mounting suspiciousness, on the side of Figaro, as her pert remarks get it through to him that she has been attracting the attention of the Count, and that she is more pleased about it than Figaro as her intended husband thinks she has any right to be. He will not put up with it! But since for all his independence he never for a moment doubts that he is a servant, his opposition will have to be by cleverness rather than by standing up to the Count as man to man. Actually, Susanna is the stronger character, like other young servant girls in *opera buffa* (we met one of them in *La Serva Padrona*). She is certainly pleased, and she would certainly like to make Figaro a little jealous, but she has no intention of slipping into the conventional role of aristocrat's mistress, and she will show herself a true woman later in the comedy. But for the present, comedy is all we see, as Bartolo and Marcellina bring in an older but not wiser generation of stock comic figures; and here comes the page-boy, Cherubino, seeking our sympathy for his youthful entanglement with Barbarina, the gardener's daughter. At last the Count arrives in person to throw Susanna into yet naiver confusion, and Figaro into yet more impotent rage and jealousy. The music so far has been both charming and amusing. But with Act II, there comes a change of mood.

We see for the first time the Countess, and hear in her poignant melody the human suffering which all this entertaining frivolity has been covering over. She sings of her unhappiness in a brief but profoundly moving cavatina (simple aria in one section), introduced and supported by an orchestral commentary in which contrasted pairs of clarinets, bassoons, and horns answer one another with all the flowing eloquence of her wounded feeling. And somehow we sense that the Count, who talks rather about his pride than about his passion, and who seems to be more in search of reassurance to his self-esteem than of satisfaction for any genuine desire, has not only upset his Countess. He has upset the symbolical balance of things. Their nobility of birth and rank has no value except as it stands symbolically for a nobility of the human spirit which in such circumstances their social inferiors still have the unsophisticated need to project onto them. In disregarding this, the Count with his compulsive vanity is acting out of role. For Susanna is not the Count's natural partner, as the Countess is; and the effect of his aberration is to bring the two women together across the social distinction.

Figaro, who has not much nobility natural or otherwise, now sings more openly of his reasonable fears. Cherubino sings with artless charm of the conflicting emotions which love has begun to thrust upon his inexperienced sensuality; and the Countess is not above some flutterings of rather more experienced response. Next the ingenious Figaro suggests a plot by which the Count may be caught in his turn. There is a particularly eventful finale to Act II, in which the advantage lies first on one side and then on another, faithfully reflected in the music, but ends in favor of the Count and his disreputable allies. Thereafter, the plots and the counterplots grow far more complicated still, with several of the stock situations of comic opera used to good effect; but somehow we no longer take it for unmixed comedy. We no longer doubt that the happiness of all the four main characters is at stake—real characters, these, in telling contrast to the stock figures who are not allowed to confuse our sympathies. Through every disguise and concealment and false assignment and hastily improvised mendacity, it is Mozart's music which keeps the characterization truthful and lucid, until the last surprises are sprung and the final reconciliations reached. The happy couples will quarrel again, without a doubt, and make up again; for that is the way of human marriages. But now there comes into the music a glow as of radiant

EXAMPLE 11    Mozart, *Le Nozze di Figaro*, the reconciliation shown by the music just before the end.

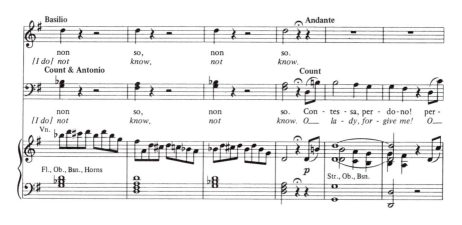

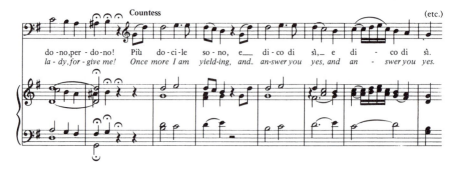

undermeanings deeper than the simple words, and perhaps having to do once more with that reconciliation of ourselves with ourselves on which not only our outer marriages but our inner contentment must eventually rest.

## The Hero with a Heart of Stone

In Prague next year, in 1787, Mozart followed up this deepened *opera buffa* with another, on a still more masterly libretto by Da Ponte, and still further enriched by ingredients blended in from *opera seria*. This is *Don Giovanni*, based on a traditional and much used story from early seventeenth-century Spain, and called a *dramma giocoso* or "playful drama." Some drama; some play. Where *Figaro* leads from verbal sparring through bewildering intrigue to final reconciliation, *Don Giovanni* plunges straight into violence and tragedy. The overture has a slow opening like a French overture, but is less stable in harmony or majestic in rhythm than the slow opening of a French overture would ordinarily have been. There is a gloom and mystery of shifting diminished sevenths which anticipates the first entry, freely, and the second entry more exactly, of that statue whose stoniness is going to confront Don Giovanni eventually. The second part of the overture is an energetic allegro, in sonata form like the overture to *Figaro*, except that here there is a normal development section, in which both the main subjects of the exposition are well worked out. At measure 277, what appears to be a concluding fanfare ends in a deceptive cadence, from which the opening portion of the second main subject changes the key from D major to F, for a direct transition into the first scene of the opera. The curtain rises on Leporello, a servant less ingenious and more cowardly than Figaro, but all the more useful in revealing something of the reverse side of the character whose obverse side makes so fine a show of it in the master. Leporello, who is like a shadow to Don Giovanni, starts by telling us that he would like to *be* the master, but hides quite unmasterfully when he hears someone coming. It is, however, Don Giovanni himself, pursued by his latest entanglement, Donna Anna. Partly in recitative or arioso, partly in ensemble, the scene moves swiftly on. Donna Anna goes off; her father the Commandant (*Commendatore*) comes on to challenge Don Giovanni, who is reluctant to fight him, but when the old man insists, kills him. Master and servant depart after a brief exchange in recitative; Anna and her betrothed Ottavio, a dull but worthy character, stumble on the corpse and swear vengeance in further recitative and arioso, leading to a substantial duet; and on this the eventful opening scene abruptly ends.

Who, then, is this Don Giovanni, this Don Juan of so many legends, plays, and operas? He is always presented as the very type of the man who forever seeks the affair of the heart which his own heartlessness puts forever beyond his reach. Such heartlessness is often the symptom of a man who, not having been loved enough in childhood, spends his life looking for the ideal mother he never had. But no sooner does some actual woman attract him, by reminding him of his mother's unattainable fascination, than she frightens him, by activating this genuinely dangerous fantasy in himself which is all the time draining him of his real manhood under the illusion of fulfilling it. Can we wonder that Don Giovanni runs away, as we have just seen him running away from Donna Anna?

And now, as he and Leporello are planning the next day's adventure, Donna Elvira comes into view. She is a woman; therefore Don Giovanni runs after her. But as soon as he recognizes her for a former mistress still in pursuit of him, he runs away again, leaving Leporello to sing to her that brutally amusing "catalogue aria" (I, 4): "fat or thin, tall for dignity, small for charm, old women for the list's sake, poor girl, rich girl, ugly girl, pretty girl, so long as she is in a skirt, you know what happens!" That is not desire; that is compulsion. Donna Elvira frightens Don Giovanni worse than anyone, not because she is more desirable, but because she is more real. She might really cut across his compulsion, and thus draw him into a real relationship from which he could not run away. He fights her off throughout the rest of the opera with a cruelty which gives us the measure of his fear.

We are next introduced to the betrothed peasant couple who, like Susanna and Figaro, form complementary opposites to the noble characters. They are Zerlina and Masetto. Zerlina, at once compulsively pursued by Don Giovanni, is warned off him by Donna Elvira in a short but extraordinarily concentrated and impressive aria (I, 8). He contrives to invite the entire peasantry to a party at his home in celebration of the forthcoming wedding. A prolonged and very elaborate finale builds up, culminating in a spectacular ball, to which Don Giovanni's enemies, Donna Anna and Don Ottavio, and his ambivalent friend, Donna Elvira, also get themselves invited in disguise. While host and guests group and regroup themselves, both vocally and theatrically, and while Don Giovanni does all he can to edge Zerlina away (as Masetto well can see), an orchestra strikes up on stage with a minuet, a second orchestra tunes up and takes over with a contredanse, and yet a third orchestra with a German dance: visible and musical symbols for the confusion in the action and the conflicting emotions in the actors' minds. Don Giovanni having now got Zerlina off-stage, her protesting screams are heard. In the confrontation which follows, there is a five-part chordal ensemble of Don Giovanni's accusers, with *sotto voce* (in an undertone) asides of anxious embarrassment from Don Giovanni and Leporello. The coda condenses the rhythm and whips up the excitement still further for the fall of the curtain, at the end of this long and impetuous first act.

The second act begins with a stock situation of *opera buffa*, as Don Giovanni changes clothes with Leporello. His plan is to serenade Donna Elvira's maid. When Donna Elvira herself appears on the balcony, without yet seeing him, she is singing heartrendingly of her undiminished love; and he answers heartlessly by pretending to welcome her back again. Now he slips away, leaving the reluctant Leporello (disguised as Don Giovanni), to continue paying court to her in his place. It is conventionally comedy; but we are hard put to take it for a joke. We, at least, feel for her, if he does not; and it is a tribute to the intuitive depth of understanding in Mozart's music that it warms us to her without altogether

The seduction of Zerlina, *Don Giovanni*, Act I. Metropolitan Opera Company.

letting us cool to him. We are with him in his difficulties, though not perhaps quite in the admiring spirit he might expect of us.

Rough farce takes over when Masetto and his peasants find Don Giovanni, still disguised as Leporello; he gets Masetto's weapons from him by pretending to join in the hunt, then beats him mercilessly and makes off, leaving Masetto to be comforted by Zerlina on the very womanly condition of never again being jealous of her as he has been over Don Giovanni. Their recitative is swift, her beautiful aria offers him her true heart, and we enjoy the *opéra comique* sentiment as much as we have been enjoying the *opera buffa* uproar. But there are mixed feelings again when Donna Elvira, reappearing with the disguised Leporello, is left alone by him; and then a complicated scene ensues in which Leporello has walked straight into the pursuing peasants. She pleads for her supposed Don Giovanni; he gets out of it by revealing himself as Leporello, to her pitiful distress. She ends the long scene with a recitative and aria of the most serious beauty, facing her new knowledge of Don Giovanni's deceitfulness, yet unable still to cease from loving him.

And now comes the confrontation to which Don Giovanni's inner (rather than his outer) difficulties have all along been leading him, dodge as he may. He is hiding, of all places, in the graveyard, where the stone statue of the Commandant stands, the moon shining brightly on it. As usual, the Don's thoughts are of women; and when Leporello finds him, he sings about his latest attempt, which turns out to have been upon Leporello's wife. This is too much even for that faithful shadow; and when Leporello is shocked, we may indeed feel shocked in sympathy. But Don Giovanni laughs. And the statue answers (to the accompaniment of those awesome trombones traditionally associated with the underworld): "Your laughter will end before the dawn!" "Who spoke?" cries Don Giovanni; and Leporello replies, "That must be some spirit from the other world, who knows you from the bottom." But what, at bottom, is Don Giovanni? We have already learned something of his stony heart. Now he shows his underlying courage. Through the mouth of his trembling henchman, he invites that stony statue to dine. With a nod, the statue accepts; and when Don Giovanni doubts the evidence of Leporello's eyes, the statue confirms it with a somber: "Yes!"

The climax is postponed as the bereaved Donna Anna in a brief interview puts off Don Ottavio, ostensibly on grounds of public propriety; but possibly she too is getting a little bored by his unremitting conventionality. Don Giovanni is hardly conventional, and has never yet bored anyone. Here he is at his supper table, entertained by another stage orchestra with operatic selections, one of which is from Mozart's own *Figaro*, as if to put Don Giovanni's womanizing into comparison with Count Almaviva's; and Leporello's dry comment is, "I know that a bit too well!" Donna Elvira breaks in to make a last appeal to Don Giovanni, not for herself now but begging him to repent and save himself. He has no thought of it; and Leporello gives the explanation which we know already: "He has a heart of stone." She leaves with a scream as she almost walks into the approaching statue; and Leporello as good as completes the connection by announcing: "The man of stone." We may spell it out by saying that what confronts Don Giovanni, at this terrifying moment of truth, is his own stoniness.

In myths or in dreams, it is often the spirit world of ghosts and ancestors which is the most solid, carrying as it does the full compelling force of our archetypal conditioning. The Commandant in the flesh was a rather unimpressive old buffer of a father-figure; but in marble, supported by his solemn trombones, he has become in more senses than one a man of substance. Refusing dinner on the somewhat Neoplatonic grounds that "they do not feed on mortal food who have eaten heavenly food," he invites Don Giovanni to eat with him instead, and holds out his hand. There is no more dodging; Don Giovanni takes it, and cannot let go. And now at last he feels. What he feels is a deathly coldness, such as he has always had, but did not know that he had. "Repent," sings the statue; "change your life." But for Don Giovanni to change his life merely to save his skin would be tantamount to not being himself, and that is the worst betrayal of all. Instead, he prefers the more radical alternative of letting life change him. Like other mythological heroes before him, he dares to go down into the underworld, for whatever transformation of character that devastating but not really at all uncommon human experience may bring. Most people find themselves in hell from time to time, and come out again not quite the same. And so Don Giovanni goes to hell, where he can at least be certain that he will not any longer be able to be cold.

EXAMPLE 12    Mozart, *Don Giovanni*, statue music at the start of the overture, heard also later, at appearances of the Man of Stone.

No sooner has Don Giovanni gone down than his pursuers arrive to draw the moral of his just fate, in an ensemble of six parts but no great solemnity. It is the traditional light ending for an *opera buffa;* and it somehow puts the whole story in its proper proportions, as a fairy tale to be taken perceptively, but not portentously. It is beautiful music, and sends us home, most appropriately for a "playful drama," in a happy mood.

In Vienna in 1790, there came *Così Fan Tutte* ("So Do They All"), Mozart's last *opera buffa,* on a polished but unfeeling libretto by Da Ponte, this time not based on a good earlier source. Two young men are persuaded by an older "philosopher" friend to test the fidelity of their prospective brides by feigning departure; by returning in disguise to court, successfully, each the other's partner; and then having to be reconciled to the original situation on the cynical reassurance that "so do they all." There is in mythology a "wise old man" often aided (like the "philosopher" here) by a young girl of native intuitiveness, and it would be possible to argue here that the outcome has been some slight gain in self-awareness; but it is only certain that we are hearing some of Mozart's most beautiful melodies, some of his most delightful instrumentation, and a remarkably high proportion of wonderful ensembles. It may be a shallow drama, but it is a lovely score, unusual in the extent to which heartless words are transcended by heartfelt music. The belated *opera seria, La Clemenza di Tito* ("The Magnanimity of Titus"), which Mozart prepared in great haste but with astonishing inspiration for performance in Prague on September 6, 1791, is on an old libretto by Metastasio slightly reworked by Caterino Mazzolà to include (untraditionally) some ensembles and choruses magnificently set, and is again notable for the orchestration (especially for flutes and clarinets) in such fine arias as that for

Sextus in I, 9, and for Vitellia in II, 23. As a belated flowering of a form by then almost wholly outdated—the *opera seria*—it is a wonderful achievement, which recent performances have proved to be still extremely well worth staging. But by then, Mozart had already almost finished his last and loveliest opera, *Die Zauberflöte* ("The Magic Flute") performed in Vienna on September 30, 1791. By December 5, 1791, Mozart was dead.

## Opera as Fairy Tale

*The Magic Flute* is a *Singspiel*, having spoken dialogue, a fairy-tale plot with hidden meanings, and some of the most enchantingly profound music that Mozart ever composed. The libretto is by Emanuel Schikaneder, with substantial assistance from Mozart and possibly some others,[2] and is concerned with the broad significance though not the innermost secrets of the Masonic order, into which Mozart was initiated in 1784 (a few weeks before Haydn), and Schikaneder in 1788. Fairy-tale pantomimes with stage marvels and magical scenarios, plentifully enlivened by incidental music, were currently fashionable in Vienna; and this was to be, at Schikaneder's suggestion, a "magic" opera. Material was taken more specifically from Cristoph Martin Wieland's recent collection of fairy tales, and from the Abbé Jean Terrason's fantastic historical novel of ancient Egypt, *Sethos*, published in Paris in 1731 and available in German translation from 1777-1778. Garbled as this supposedly Egyptian history was, it had interesting roots in the Neoplatonic symbolism of the sixteenth century, transmitted both by the Rosicrucians and the Freemasons. There is a link here with the origins of opera.

The overture begins, *adagio*, with a small leading-motive (or suggestive unit of musical material) which will be repeatedly found throughout the opera, giving it both a particular significance and a strong coherence by a method not at this period customary (it became so with Wagner). The essence of this motive is a simple triad—the three notes of a common chord. Here in the overture it appears as the common chord of E flat major in root position; the common chord (but for one note, identical) of C minor, also in root position; and again the common chord of E flat major, but in its first inversion, with its major third G as bass. Three chords, of three notes each, all proper (diatonic) to the key of E flat major which is the main key of the opera—that is the firm statement with which *The Magic Flute* opens, and to which it returns or refers at moments of similar significance throughout.

But what is this particular significance? We find it in the Masonic symbolism on which both the text and the score of *The Magic Flute* are based. Because three is the number of persons (all masculine) in the Holy Trinity, it had official associations with the realm of the spirit and became prominent in Masonic symbolism, besides being traditionally associated with the masculine principle as four is with the feminine principle. It stands here for initiation into the mysteries of the spirit. The triadic motive opens the opera in the crisp but majestic "double-dotted" rhythm in which a French overture was customarily performed (though not usually notated). The following fugal allegro is more solid than most French overtures, and is interrupted by a return (in the dominant) of the triadic motive. Strings and woodwind rest on a warm sonority of two E flat horns, two E flat trumpets with their customary kettledrums, and three trombones—not then so customary, but having special associations with the spirit world.

Prince Tamino, the hero, sings on the triadic motive, but in C minor, frightened as he is at the moment by a huge serpent standing presumably for some formidable inertia or obstacle within, so that he faints; but three ladies cut it into three pieces with three blows (heard in the music) of three silver spears. They have been sent by the Queen of the Night, an ambivalent mythological personification, but seen at first in her positive aspect as she starts Tamino off on his growth toward initiation. The hero's unheroic counterpart now arrives: Papageno, the Queen's bird catcher who himself is feathered, as if to suggest that instinct is also part of us and must not be left behind. The three ladies return to show Tamino a miniature portrait of Pamina, daughter to the Queen, and to offer him the triple prospect of "joy, honor, and glory" if he can rescue her from a "wicked demon." He greets the portrait as a "divine image," meaning that he recognizes not only his future bride, but also that quality in himself which Goethe called, in the famous last line of *Faust*, "the eternal feminine." A man has a feminine component which may show negatively, as irrational moodiness, or positively, as visionary creativeness, but which will swamp him less and serve him better as he gets into better intuitive communication with that side of himself; and this may be represented in a fairy tale as searching for a distressed heroine and rescuing her from a dragon, a witch, or an ogre, often gaining some hidden treasure on the way. A woman has a masculine component which may show negatively, as assertive false logic, or positively, as genuine intellect and order; and she too will need to integrate this less conscious side of herself so as to be not swamped but served by it. It is a mutual search, here presented as a shared initiation; for while Tamino and Pamina are certainly meant to find love and happiness together, they would not have to go through such testing adventures if they were not also meant to help focus for each other the complementary qualities whose union, within any man or any woman, makes for inner wholeness.

With a sound of thunder, the mountain opens to reveal the Queen of the Night in "star-flaming" glory, which like her birds connects her with the Great Mother of many manifestations, and suggests that state of nature in which we begin, but from which we have also to grow away, toward the more human state of maturer consciousness. That is the purpose of initiation; and now the Queen herself calls Tamino "my beloved son" to the notes of the triadic motive of initiation, asking him to trust her "mother's heart." Her "daughter" has been stolen away by a "wicked villain"; but we shall find that this is only one way of looking at it. All profound changes are apt to feel wrong at first. The Queen displays her fairy-tale quality by a dazzling display of coloratura vocalization. The mountain closes over her again, to more thunder; but her three ladies bring Tamino the "magic flute." It is of gold, the metal of the sun as silver is the metal of the moon. A flute is by tradition a symbol of manhood, and of the breath of the spirit; we hear later that this flute was given to the Queen, in trust for Tamino, by Sarastro, the High Priest of the Sun—the same whom she has just described as "wicked." Papageno, with his humbler limitations, gets a silver set of bells. Sarastro has three black slaves and a black overseer, Monostatos, who has just caught Pamina and is about to rape her. It seems that there are dark forces in Sarastro's camp, too; and no doubt he is ultimately as ambivalent as the Queen herself. But we only see his bright face directly in the opera. At this critical moment, Papageno appears; and as he has never seen a black man before, and Monostatos has never seen a feathered man, each takes the other for the devil, and runs away. Papageno, plucking up courage to return, recognizes Pamina from her portrait—now hanging around his neck as if to show how closely he is linked to Tamino, in search of whom they wander off together. Three bright spirit boys, holding silver palms as the three ladies held silver spears, encourage Tamino with an enchanting trio supported by warm trombones. Alone again, he approaches three great temple doors. On either side, he is turned back with chromatic distortions of the triadic chords. At the center door (and here the triads become diatonic) he is asked his business by an old priest, and answers: "to possess love and virtue." "Fine words," continues the priest; "but love and virtue do not guide you while death and vengeance inflame you." In language which recalls the old Neoplatonic search, Tamino asks: "Oh eternal night! When will you lessen? When will my eyes find the light?" An invisible chorus tells him that Pamina is alive; and Papageno returns with Pamina—but he misses them. They are caught by Monostatos and the three black slaves, until Papageno thinks of his silver bells, which send them dancing innocuously off-stage. The orchestra brings on Sarastro radiantly with trumpets and drums. A priestly chorus greets him with the C major triads, picked up in the orchestra as Pamina kneels to him and he explains that "a man must guide your heart"—which is not true outwardly, but may be in reference to her own masculine component. Tamino is now brought in by Monostatos, who instead of being rewarded for his unctuous pains gets punished for his wicked intentions. The chorus praise Sarastro "who rewards and punishes," and who next combines fatherly kindness and sternness by ordering the young couple "into our temple of probation," while chorus and orchestra announce the old Neoplatonic moral that virtue makes earth a paradise, and men like gods.

Act II opens without trumpets and drums, but there are horns and trombones and the darker coloring of a pair of Mozart's favorite tenor clarinets (basset horns). As a B flat triad is three times ceremonially repeated, the speaker calls Tamino "a prince," but Sarastro replies with Masonic humanism: "what is more, he is a man." The chorus pray to Isis and Osiris to help the young couple through their dangerous ordeal. And now it is night in the temple courtyard. Tamino and Papageno are left alone in the dark, as it thunders thrice and each time to Papageno's worse fright. On being told by the Speaker that "there is still time to go back," Tamino is resolute to go forward; Papageno is not resolute, but decides to take a chance on it when told by the Second Priest that a mate like himself, and named Papagena, waits for him. They are forbidden to break silence; for "this is the beginning of the testing time." Now the three ladies try (and this is part of the test) to warn them off the whole fateful enterprise; and what with Papageno predictably breaking silence and Tamino telling him not to, a fine quintet is presently built up. The music keeps touching on the triadic motive; but there are also harsh tritones and minor sevenths to convey the anxiety inseparable from these hazardous transitions. The two priestly voices consign the three ladies to hell, through a trap door, the sound of trombones confirming that this is where they properly belong. Then no sooner have Tamino and Papageno been veiled and led off than the scene changes to a garden, with Pamina asleep, and Monostatos creeping up on her again. But the poor fellow never does have much luck; the Queen of the Night herself rises through "the middle trap door" (of three!); gives Pamina a dagger "sharpened for Sarastro"; overrides Pamina's protests with another of her dazzling coloratura arias; and goes down as melodramatically as she came up. Monostatos, hopeful as ever, slips back and adroitly gets the dagger from Pamina. "Why are you trembling? At my black color, or at the murder you plan?" She starts in astonishment at his knowing that; but he has been listening all the time. As he threatens her once more, Sarastro appears from nowhere to hurl him back. Foiled again.

In all this fine fooling, there are recollections of another figure of Egyptian mythology who was no matter for laughing. This was Set, the dark brother of Osiris and his sister-wife Isis, who killed Osiris and Horus his son, and tried in vain to possess Isis for himself. The murdered deities were resurrected, but Set remained to represent that dark shadow of unreason which is the one real danger to our human race. In this present comic situation, Sarastro merely tells Monostatos that since his soul is as black as his face, he had better go away; but as he goes, he announces ominously that since he cannot have the daughter, he will try joining forces with the mother. After the next change of scene, Papageno remarks that he could do with a drink of water. A hobbling old woman brings it, announcing herself to his dismay as Papagena, Papageno's sweetheart; we may guess that it might be the water of life for him, but he cannot yet accept this and off she goes. The three boys promise that when the two male neophytes see them for a third time, joy will reward their courage. Meanwhile the boys return Tamino his flute and Papageno his bells, as well as conjuring up food and drink. Tamino flutes; Papageno eats. The flute brings back Pamina, but Tamino will not speak to her because of his instructions and Papageno cannot because his mouth is full. In her despair she sings a lovely aria before going off to seek peace through death.

Three drum signals thrice repeated summon our heroes to another scene, inside a pyramid, where a chorus sings of the rays of the sun which drive gloomy night away. Tamino and Pamina (found again and veiled) are dispatched separately for further trials. In the dark outside, Papageno is humorously let off, but told he will never arrive at heavenly delight. All he asks is a glass of wine, which appears magically, and has the sacramental effect of making him want to fly to the sun (which we now know that he cannot) and . . . and . . . (his bells tell him)

. . . to be blessed with a wife! As the orchestra lights up with the glitter of the glockenspiel, the ugly old woman comes tottering back. It is the traditional fairy-tale test of Beauty and the Beast, reversed. As soon as he accepts his seemingly repellent destiny, she turns into the beautiful, the adorable, the one and only Papagena. For the moment, however, she too is snatched away as yet another change of scene begins the long finale.

It is a garden, with the three boys, to whom Pamina enters. She is lost again; but they prevent her from suicide by telling her that Tamino loves her still. In the next scene, one mountain pours forth a waterfall, and another mountain pours forth fire. Tamino is confronted by two men in armor, who sing in octaves the tune though not the words of the chorale *Ach Gott, von Himmel sieh darein* ("Ah God, from Heaven Look Thou Down"), against a superb fugal counterpoint in the orchestra, with the trombones yet again sonorous in support. They warn him that the ordeal by fire, water, air, and earth for initiation into the mysteries of Isis can only be entered at the risk of death; when he assents, he is permitted to speak to Pamina as she comes in. Protected by his magic flute, they pass together through the fire and the water, while the wind howls (for air) and the thunder echoes through the caverns (for earth). It is not very specifically presented, no doubt so as to preserve the final Masonic secrets. But we have the second-century Neoplatonic account by Apuleius[3] of his initiation into the mysteries first of Isis, then of Osiris, and finally of some third and higher stage in relation to them both. He, too, passed through the four elements "close to the boundaries of death" and "saw the sun gleaming with bright splendor at the dead of night." This released him from his immature obsession with women, and confirmed his slow growth toward greater human consciousness, as his story narrates. He even mentioned a sacred flute player on the temple steps; and now, as we hear Tamino playing his magic flute, and he and Pamina together achieve their fourfold passage "through death's gloomy night," a door opens into a bright temple, and the chorus welcome them in with a decisive C major statement of the triadic motive.

But outside, Papageno is about to hang himself, yet keeps putting it off in the hope that someone, somehow, will come to the rescue in answer to his piping. Sure enough, the three boys appear to suggest he try his bells instead. And there at once stands Papagena, to sing with him their enchanting duet: "Pa-pa-pa-pa-Papageno-Papagena." Next the Queen of the Night and her three ladies conspire to marry Pamina to Monostatos for his support. But the full orchestra, with horns, trumpets, drums, trombones, and all, overwhelms the forces of darkness as in a blaze of light "the whole temple turns itself into a sun." Tamino and Pamina are there "in priestly garments," and "the three boys hold flowers." The conspirators confess themselves to be of "the eternal night"; and Sarastro proclaims night to be driven away "by the rays of the sun." The chorus yields the praise to Isis and Osiris, thus paying joint tribute to the eternal feminine and to the eternal masculine. For can we doubt that the sun acclaimed here by the initiates of Isis and Osiris is as Ficino[4] described it at the start of Renaissance Neoplatonism, "everywhere the image of the divine truth and goodness"? *The*

*Magic Flute* is an opera about initiation. And initiation, in plain human language, is about growth of character, through growth of consciousness. We can quite see why Wagner later regarded this strange and wonderful masterpiece as the true starting point of German opera.

EXAMPLE 13  Mozart, *Die Zauberflöte,* the triadic motive: (a) start of overture; (b) Tamino's first entry; (c) the Queen of the Night's first entry; (d) the opening of her big aria following; (e) chromatic for the wrong temple doors; (f) diatonic for the right temple door; (g) the chorus greets Sarastro; (h) Pamina submits to him; (i) as the priests' threefold chord; (j) the chorus of welcome; (k) with strengthened harmony in the final rejoicings.

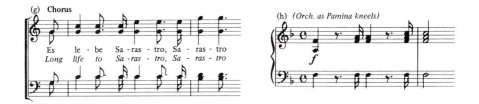

## Mozart's Contemporaries

Of Mozart's contemporaries in opera, the best known today (though not for his operas) is Franz Joseph Haydn (1732-1809). His life was mostly spent in some isolation, as resident composer at the country palace of Esterházy, and his quite numerous operas, both serious and comic, were not widely known at the time, nor have they since been established in our current repertory. They contain a great many passages and scenes of remarkable beauty and dramatic characterization. As wholes they fall short of Mozart's genius for unfolding drama in music. Nevertheless, some modern revivals of them have proved uncommonly enjoyable. The very lively *opera buffa* of 1773, *L'Infedeltà Delusa* ("The Disappointed Infidelity") is a particularly concise, lyrical, and warmhearted example.

Giovanni Paisiello (1740-1816) made his name in Naples, but was employed in St. Petersburg when he composed his most brilliant success, his comic opera of 1782 on a libretto after Beaumarchais, *Il Barbiere di Siviglia* ("The Barber of Seville"); he had a large number of comic operas and a smaller number of serious operas to his credit, and he comes perhaps closest to Mozart (whom he influenced) in melodic style and dramatic expressiveness. Domenico Cimarosa (1749-1801) was a very productive and talented composer, also close to Mozart in style; his most resounding success was his comic opera in Vienna in 1792, *Il Matrimonio Segreto* ("The Secret Marriage"). Antonio Salieri (1750-1825), who drew on texts by Metastasio, Goldoni, and Da Ponte, is important particularly as Gluck's most direct successor, recommended by Gluck to Paris as best able to represent his methods there, which Salieri did with a series of operas culminating in 1787 with *Tarare*; but Salieri was also long active in Vienna in direct rivalry with Mozart. When the Viennese, the Italian, and the French schools came yet closer in the early nineteenth century, romantic opera was the outcome; for this, we must turn first to Paris, and then to Germany.

## Notes

1. Letter to his father, September 26, 1781.
2. Johann Georg Metyler, known as Gieseke, may have contributed certain of the most serious scenes, though this cannot be proved; and some very superior persons of the Masonic order may also have been concerned at least in the general conception. So far as actual evidence takes us, Schikaneder was the librettist. The question is extremely well discussed by Jacques Chailley, in his unusual and interesting book, *La Flûte Enchantée*, Paris, 1968, pp. 17 ff.
3. Lucius Apuleius, *Metamorphoses* ("Transformations," commonly known as *The Golden Ass*), 2nd cent. A.D., XI, 23.
4. Marsilio Ficino, *Opera Omnia*, ed. of Basle, 1576, p. 119.

# 8

# Toward Romantic Opera

By the nineteenth century, Paris had become the most prestigious center of opera, where different styles and categories took on an increasingly international quality in common. At the national theater of the Academy of Music (the home of the Paris *Opéra*), there was *tragédie lyrique:* serious opera, of which the dialogue was required to be in recitative. At the theater known as the *Opéra-Comique* and other theaters, there was *opéra comique:* not only comic but also serious opera of which the dialogue was spoken. This structural distinction could be obliterated, however, merely by changing spoken dialogue into recitative. The work was then eligible for performance at the *Opéra*. Meanwhile, another distinction was emerging between *grand opéra* (grand opera in the sense of having very spectacular plots, music, and staging) and average opera. But this was only a difference of degree. The tendency was altogether toward greater ostentation. Moreover, the difference between French and Italian styles of recitative, arioso, and aria went on diminishing; while choruses were now used in all kinds of opera. The orchestra, though not much changed in its constitution, grew noisier in its scoring. Paris, in attracting composers of various nationalities, imposed on them many features designed to meet the fashionable taste for immediate effectiveness in the text and score, and for lavish display in the visual production. It was this tendency which did most to give Parisian opera its shared quality.

## The Rescue Opera

Many baroque operas had turned upon the rescue of bemused victims from enchanted palaces or gardens. This popular subject now took a new and still more fashionable direction, from the social and political developments connected with the French Revolution. Here the victims of wrongful imprisonment must be rescued not from enchantment but from a tyrant's prison or an enemy's castle. A pioneering specimen in 1784 was Grétry's *Richard Coeur-de-Lion*, already mentioned. In 1793, Jean-François Lesueur (1760-1837) explored in *La Caverne* the romantic attraction of a chivalrous, brigand chieftain, anticipating Bellini or early Verdi. Étienne Nicolas Méhul (1763-1817) was most successful with serious subjects having the spoken dialogue of *opéra comique* but the musical texture of *tragédie lyrique*. Another such work was the *Médée* ("Medea") of Luigi Cherubini (1760-1842), a Florentine with a fine reputation in both serious and comic Italian opera before he settled in Paris in 1788. But *Médée* was not so successful in Paris in 1797 as it became in Berlin in 1800. Cherubini's most influential works were rescue operas, of which *Les Deux Journées* ("The Two Days"), first performed in Paris in 1800, was one of the sources of Beethoven's *Fidelio:* the greatest although not in all ways the most successful (and certainly not the most typical) of rescue operas.

The *Fidelio* of Beethoven (1770-1827) is on a German text which was derived from a French text by the same librettist as *Les Deux Journées*, Jean Nicolas Bouilly. The first performance of *Fidelio* in Vienna in 1805 had little success; a second version in 1806 was quickly withdrawn; another version, substantially different, appeared in 1814, and this is as we now know the opera. Despite earlier teaching and advice from Salieri, Beethoven never became an altogether felicitous composer for the human voice; and he, who made of instrumental music so eventful a drama, did not take so naturally to drama unfolding in both words and music.

The overture for the final version of 1814 begins with an impetuous allegro phrase in which three mounting triads resemble, both in shape and in scoring, the famous triadic motive with which Mozart's *Magic Flute* had so memorably begun. After a few bars of adagio, these triads are heard again, followed by the adagio at greater length. Then (m. 47) a normal sonata-form allegro opens, with a quiet second subject (m. 82), violently interrupted (m. 98); but quiet again into a regular development section (m. 118) having fragmentary references to the triadic opening. This leads to a somewhat modified but basically regular recapitulation (m. 147); and that in turn brings back the triadic opening (m. 230), the brief adagio continuation (m. 234), and a presto coda (m. 248) which tightens the dotted rhythm of the triadic opening to a tenser excitement. But unlike *The Magic Flute*, there is in *Fidelio* no recurrence of the triadic opening as a leading motive unifying the whole opera.

We are taken at once into a situation proper to comic opera, with the porter of a castle, Jaquino, pleading with his beloved, Marzellina, the daughter of the good-hearted old jailor, Rocco. It turns out that a somewhat complicated state of affairs has arisen. For Marzellina has been losing her heart (and this is what Jaquino is in course of perceiving) to a young newcomer under the name of Fidelio ("the faithful one"). But this Fidelio, although appearing as a man, is actually Leonora, the faithful wife of the noble Florestan whom she believes, correctly as it turns out, is imprisoned here out of envious ambition by his designing enemy, Pizarro. Leonora means to find Florestan and rescue him if she can. For this is a "rescue opera," of which the nobility appealed to Beethoven, but the conventional element of comedy gave him great difficulty. Much of the first act shows some awkwardness. One remarkable quartet (I, 3) for Marzellina, Leonora, Jaquino, and Rocco has all four parts in canon, and is a beautiful though unexpected inspiration in such a context. But when Leonora sings to herself of her wifely loyalty, she has a long accompanied recitative and a freely da capo aria to which Beethoven brought the most moving intensity. There is intense drama, too, in the magnificent, mainly choral finale to Act I, where Rocco has been persuaded by Leonora to allow the common prisoners briefly into the open courtyard. Their dazed greeting to the "warm light of the sun" is moving both on a literal and on a symbolical level, especially to those who know (as Beethoven did truly know) what it is to feel imprisoned in the spirit. Of course we look for Florestan among the crowd, and so does Leonora; but he is not there. Pizarro brutally commands them underground again.

Act II has a brief orchestral introduction, revealing to us that despair to which Florestan, in the deepest dungeon, is now very near. This becomes the accompaniment of his grievous recitative, out of which grows a wonderful aria in two sections—his great vocal utterance of the opera. He seems still steadfast, but grim; then with a prophetic vision of Leonora coming to his rescue, he rises to a strange exaltation of hope. He faints from weakness; the orchestra takes up again. We have been told, but he has not, that the benevolent minister Fernando has certain suspicions which he is coming to investigate in person. A trumpeter is watching for him on the ramparts; Pizarro, to avoid discovery, will have to dispose of Florestan promptly; and down comes Rocco, with Leonora as his assistant, to open up an old cistern in the dungeon floor as a secret grave. And so at last she is within sight of her desperately ill-used husband. Rocco seems as heavy-hearted as Leonora, as they talk, at first in speech across the orchestra. This is technically melodrama, for a time a fashionable method even for entire works, but somewhat incongruous and ineffectual here. Pizarro next comes down, drawing his own dagger to make certain of the murder; Leonora stands between him and Florestan and reveals her true self to the astonishment of all of them; at the critical moment, she pulls out a pistol; and most memorably and operatically the distant trumpet rings out.

A very long and weighty overture, discarded by Beethoven and known as Leonora No. III, is now sometimes played during the change of scenery; but having no proper part in the drama here, it throws it somewhat out of balance. When next the curtain rises, to our great relief we are in the open once more, as Don Fernando orders punishment for Pizarro and liberty for the prisoners. Leonora and Florestan voice their joyful reunion in a duet (II, 15) which looks forward to the Ninth Symphony with its Hymn to Joy; Marzellina overcomes the shock of discovery and rejoins her Jaquino; and with chorus and ensemble, the great finale builds up, more than ever in that same mood of triumph won from adversity by courageous greatness of spirit. For in 1802 Beethoven[1] described the bitter loneliness and suicidal despair to which his growing deafness (and still more the tensions of his own driven personality) had brought him, around his thirtieth year. He described, too, his courageous resolve to overcome his adversity for the sake of his creativeness. In 1803, he broke through with his Third Symphony into the confident brilliance of his "middle period." Sketches of *Fidelio* were already being made. Beethoven seems to have identified himself with his imprisoned Florestan, and with Leonora—the woman who could enact the man's role when the man could not. He seems to have sensed that his own rescue could only come through his own feminine and faithful Muse. It did.

EXAMPLE 14    Beethoven, *Fidelio*, (a) opening of overture like opening of Mozart's *Magic Flute*; (b) Florestan's courage at the start of Act II.

# The Approach to Grand Opera

During the middle years of the nineteenth century, grand opera reached its height in Paris. A strong impulse in this direction was given by Gasparo Spontini (1774-1851), whose reputation for Italian opera was already considerable when he reached Paris in 1803, and there in 1807, under the patronage of the Empress Josephine, produced *La Vestale* ("The Vestal"). The libretto was offered to Spontini by Étienne Jouy, one of the two main literary creators of French grand opera, the other being Eugène Scribe. Now this vestal is an officially virgin priestess who, having received a lover into the temple and allowed the sacred flame to go out, is only rescued from being buried alive in punishment by the miraculous intervention of Jupiter himself, the god of the temple. He proclaims her innocence and sanctions her union by rekindling his own fire with a stroke of his own lightning, thus indicating beyond a doubt that he does not consider the sacred flame of the spirit and the secular flame of love to be necessarily incompatible. Spontini's music takes up every melodramatic opportunity with excellent choruses, ensembles, and solo melodies, supported by stirring diminished sevenths in the harmony, by colorful woodwind in the orchestra, and on the visual side, by richly varied and imposing scenery. Yet beneath the melodrama, there remains something of the chaste and classical restraint of Gluck in this last of his true descendants. We are on the threshold of romantic opera, but we are not yet across it.

The next move came a longer way around. The German composer Johann Simon Mayr (1763-1845), having become a fully acclimatized Italian resident, brought to his many Italian operas an extraordinary energy and tunefulness. He used some French scenarios requiring choruses and ensembles; he added a German richness and excitement to the orchestra. Where Mayr sowed the wind, Gioacchino Rossini (1792-1868) reaped the whirlwind. By the age of twenty, Rossini was taking operatic success and failure in his stride; and by the age of twenty-three, besides other triumphs both serious and comic, he had achieved his masterpiece, the comic opera *Il Barbiere di Siviglia* ("The Barber of Seville"), of which the leading role, Rosina, is unusual in being not for a soprano but for a mezzo-soprano. The first performance in Rome in 1816 was a social failure, because it was thought to presume upon Paisiello's beloved opera on the same famous play by Beaumarchais. But in two more nights Rossini's opera had established itself for the popular favorite it has ever since remained. The overture is typically energetic. Now Count Almaviva serenades young Rosina, the closely guarded ward of old Dr. Bartolo, who means to marry her after the unsuitable but familiar fashion of conventional comedy. Figaro, however, will take it all in hand: Figaro, the barber of Seville, the heir to many a trickster servant in folk tale, and in the remoter background, to trickster gods of ancient myth like Thoth, Hermes, or Loge. Figaro has the Count get into the house as a drunken soldier, and then more subtly as a music master, who bows and scrapes himself in with so interminable a mock politeness that Bartolo, determined not to be outdone, is put out of all patience. The joke is caught to a turn by the music (and was remembered by Verdi in *Falstaff*). The pace is breathless; the recitative speeds along; the arioso sparkles; the arias soar; the ensembles dazzle; the orchestra glitters; and the whole intoxicating affair winds up, needless to say, in the young lovers' favor. And if, compared with Mozart, it is all a little smooth and calculated, capable of sentiment but hardly of those sudden catches at the heart, through all the laughter, at which Mozart excelled, there is no time to think of that in the excitement of the moment.

Rossini was brought to Paris in 1824, with the well-justified expectation that he would raise the standards of performance and repertory alike from the decline into which Parisian opera had fallen since Spontini's *Vestale* in 1807. For that sensational success had been little followed up, by the time that, in 1819, Spontini turned against Paris and left to continue his uneven career in Berlin. Besides several existing or adapted operas of his own, Rossini introduced in Paris, to his own disadvantage, *Crociato in Egitto*, the first opera by Meyerbeer to be performed there. He also brought some fresh singers, and encouraged a more Italianate vocal idiom. *Le Siège de Corinthe* in 1826, and still more, *Moïse* in 1827 and *Le Comte Ory* in 1828, entrenched Rossini at the *Opéra*. But he had a rival in the French composer Daniel François Esprit Auber (1782-1871), working with that most successful of Parisian librettists, Scribe, mostly in *opéra-comique;* but early in 1828 (some five months before Rossini's *Le Comte Ory*) the *Opéra* produced their grand opera *La Muette de Portici* ("The Dumb Girl of Portici"), the most lavishly staged so far, with music appropriately massive. This in turn was surpassed in both musical and historical importance at the *Opéra* in 1829 by Rossini's *Guillaume Tell* ("William Tell"), on a libretto offered to Rossini by that same Jouy who had worked so closely with Spontini.

Both the plot and the score of *William Tell* satisfied the Parisian audiences with every fashionable effect of suspense and sentiment. The long overture opens with quite wonderful serenity, and ends with noisy brilliance. Patriotic Swiss peasants are opposed to an oppressive Austrian governor, named Gesler. Now Gesler has a young sister, Matilde, whose life was saved from an avalanche by wise old Melchtal; he in turn has a son, Arnoldo; and the two young people are now in love across all barriers of political interest. William Tell, the leader of the peasants' resistance, rebukes Arnoldo without avail until further atrocities culminate in the brutal murder of old Melchtal, whereupon Arnoldo repudiates Matilde with her regretful consent, and joins in the leadership of the outraged peasantry. For an open insult to the governor, William Tell is condemned to stand an apple on the head of his own son, Jemmy, and to shoot an arrow through the apple if he can. Tell's trepidation at this hazardous endeavor is interspersed with Jemmy's pride and confidence, the suspense being protracted to the uttermost. The shot is successful, but Tell is nevertheless condemned to a lingering death. But now Matilde changes sides. She releases Tell, who is next nearly drowned in a storm across the lake, but escapes by heaven's grace. He raises the peasantry, kills the governor with another splendid shot from the same bow, and goes on to free his country from the Austrian rule, all in one swift and eventful finale. An exultant closing chorus with solo interjections includes Arnoldo and

Matilde, now happily reunited, and, with the clearing storm and the soft evening light, peace and reconciliation prevail.

*William Tell* is emphatically grand opera, and only subsequent developments show it not to have been opera of the very grandest. There is energetic and resourceful orchestration; there are massive choruses taking an active part dramatically as well as musically; there are ballets to match the spectacular Parisian scenery, then approaching its greatest magnificence; there is stirring accompanied recitative and arioso, aria and ensemble to heighten each agitated emotion. Much of this music is extraordinarily beautiful, though the pace is leisurely and the concessions to divertissement are far too great. Spontini was out-distanced; Auber was improved upon; yet a certain balance and proportion still keeps us in touch with classical opera even in this fine romantic heavyweight. For almost forty years longer, Rossini lived on his vast reputation; but as if afraid of not being able to compete with his chief successor in Paris, Meyerbeer (or perhaps with his own earlier self), he composed no further opera and very little other music.

Vincenzo Bellini (1801-1835) was another composer of romantic opera whose native elegance kept him still within the classical tradition. Bellini, like Rossini, showed precocious talent; and by 1827 he achieved with *Il Pirata* an enduring reputation for pure and expressive melody. There is almost always in Bellini an undertone of sadness. His vocal figuration is affecting and delicate, rather than impressive or powerful; it may have influenced Chopin's sensitive figuration for the piano. At twenty-nine, in Milan in 1831, Bellini achieved the first of his two lasting masterpieces, *La Sonnambula* ("The Sleepwalker"), on a libretto drawn by Felice Romani from a typically French scenario by Scribe. The heroine is discovered in the bedroom of the aristocrat villain (but he is quite good at heart); she has walked there in her sleep, but only convinces her affronted hero of it at the end of the opera by again sleepwalking in public, above the raging mill race. The choruses are quietly beautiful, the arias are melting, the orchestra takes an unsophisticated but eloquent share, the creamy harmonies are sometimes nearly but never quite banal. There are hidden depths; and this is still more evident in Bellini's second and only other unqualified success: *Norma*, performed in Milan later in 1831. This is also on a libretto based on a French play and written by Romani. In its own translucent idiom, it is a very beautiful opera indeed.

Pollione, the Roman governor of Gaul, has secretly fathered two fine children to Norma, the officially virgin priestess, daughter of the High Druid. Pollione now deceives Norma by persuading a younger priestess, Adalgisa, to flee to Rome with him; but in all innocence she first confides in Norma, whose rage almost leads her to murder her children before our eyes. Adalgisa magnanimously offers to restore Pollione to Norma; however, he is taken captive in the virgin's quarters. Norma now confesses very movingly, orders a funeral pyre, and mounts it while recommending her children to their startled father's care. This so affects him that he joins her just before the curtain comes down on the impending blaze. As outer drama, it could hardly be more implausible. Yet in the haunting ritual where Norma cuts the sacred mistletoe, and the moon breaks through in full splendor to receive her prayer (*Casta Diva*, "Chaste Goddess"), there is something which recalls the Queen of the Night in *The Magic Flute;* and in the funeral pyre, there is something which recalls the ordeal by transforming fire. Bellini went in 1833 to Paris, where he was encouraged and advised by Rossini, and where his unevenly achieved *I Puritani* ("The Puritans") was well received in 1835, in which year he died.

Gaetano Donizetti (1797-1848) was a pupil of Mayr whose output was compendious and whose contemporary standing was high. His reputation today rests chiefly upon his tragic *Lucia di Lammermoor*, an Italianate grand opera, produced in Naples in 1835, of which the celebrated mad scene is rather heartlessly impressive, but other arias, ensembles, and choruses have considerable eloquence; and his brilliantly comic *Don Pasquale*, a fine favorite in Rossini's lighter vein, produced in 1843 in Paris. There Donizetti settled in 1838 long enough to contribute several further operas, including an *opéra comique* in 1840, *La Fille du Régiment.*

## Early Romantic Opera in Germany

The style of early romantic opera in Germany was established by Carl Maria von Weber (1786-1826), a young composer of wayward temperament but undoubted talent, who after some considerable wanderings settled in Dresden. There he became the leader of the German school, while Spontini in Berlin stood for imported Italian opera. Weber[2] described his aim in opera as "a work of art complete in itself, of which the several artistic ingredients blend and vanish, and in vanishing, combine to form a new world." His colleague, the romantic poet Friedrich Kind,[3] likewise wanted "the union of all the arts of poetry, music, acting, painting, and dancing." This idea of opera as not just a conjunction but a fusion of the arts was a characteristic aspiration of the German romantic movement,[4] and was subsequently taken up by Wagner, who (forgetting for the moment *The Magic Flute*) called Weber's *Der Freischütz* ("The Free-Shooter") "the first German opera."

*Der Freischütz* is a *Singspiel*, having mainly spoken dialogue (with a little accompanied recitative) and a large number of formal arias, some duets and other ensembles, some fine choruses and considerable opportunities for spectacle and dancing. The libretto was written by Kind, at Weber's request, in 1817, on a spooky ghost story from Apel's famous collection of 1810; but Weber, unusually for him, took so long over the music that it was not finished till 1820. Much of this music is fairly ordinary; but it is magnificent in the great scenes—especially the last. The first performance in Berlin in 1821 exceeded Spontini's fine success there, a year before, with his Italian *Olympia;* and the occasion was regarded as a signal triumph for German opera. The overture is long and approximates to sonata form. It introduces some of the main tunes of the opera, and also anticipates the closing chorus. Max, the hero, has mysteriously lost his skill on the eve of a test of marksmanship which he has to pass in order to qualify for the hand of

Agatha, daughter of the hereditary chief forester Cuno, and with her the succession to this coveted position. In a stage aside, the villain, Caspar, thanks the devil's representative, Samiel, for thus inhibiting Max; for Caspar has sold his soul for the power of moulding magic bullets, and is now a dead man and a damned one unless he can corrupt another soul in his place. He exploits Max's desperation by letting him bring down a distant and almost invisible eagle with a last magic bullet. They arrange a midnight assignment in the notorious Wolf's Glen to mould another batch.

In Act II, a portrait of Cuno's paternal ancestor (whom gossip suspects of having himself used a magic bullet) has just disgraced itself by falling down on Agatha's head. She and her confidante, Annie, also tell us about a wise old hermit who brought her some consecrated roses as protection against an unknown danger. At a sound of distant horns, Agatha waves to her approaching lover (Wagner recalled this in Act II of *Tristan*); but when he puts his hat down, the light goes out and magically relights itself, because of the illicitly gained eagle's feathers stuck in the brim. We learn from the ensuing conversation that the picture of the old ancestor fell at the very moment at which the eagle was shot, and this connection seems to hint at something as negative in the father's authority as the old hermit is positive. At the Wolf's Glen, under the fitful light of the moon, there are corresponding hints of mother-symbolism, mainly negative. There is a cave and a waterfall. There is a blasted tree shining with putrid

*Der Freischütz*, Act III. Metropolitan Opera Company.

phosphorescence, there are owls with eyes of fire, and there are invisible spirits howling horribly of "moon's milk" and "spider's web wet with blood." The orchestra responds with tremolando strings, low notes on the clarinets and horns, trombones with their underworld associations, and sinister rolls and sudden taps of the drums. On the stroke of midnight, Caspar sticks a gleaming skull onto his dagger, and gives it three twists, whereupon Samiel, speaking across the orchestra, allows him three years' respite for ensnaring Max, who is at once seen looking down "as into the pit of hell." His mother's ghost now actually opposes him with a gesture of prohibition; but she is countered by a vision of Agatha about to plunge herself into the waterfall. "My fate calls," he rightly decides; for what with the reiterated threes, the waterfall, the fire for melting the bullets, presently the answering lightning from the sky and flames from the earth and a direct reference by the chorus to the four elements of initiation, it is probable that we are being reminded deliberately of *The Magic Flute*, so admired by Weber and other German romantics. If Max drew back now because of his mother's prohibition, he would miss his moment of initiation, and lose his Agatha both as his bride and as his feminine inspiration. But down he goes, and the moon shrinks "to a narrow strip." Three substances are dropped into the transforming cauldron: lead (the base metal of alchemy); glass from broken church windows (presumably in defiance of Mother Church); and mercury (in alchemy the transforming principle). Three spent bullets go in next, and three times Caspar prostrates himself at three pauses in the music. The moon vanishes; spectral huntsmen gallop by; the invisible spirits (holding A flat uncannily against D natural in the orchestra) invoke the four elements—fire, earth, water, and air (Ex. 15). One by one, seven bullets (making three plus four) are molded. At the sixth, the sky flashes with lightning and the earth belches flames; at the seventh, Max, to steady himself, grasps a withered branch which becomes the hand of the Black Huntsman (in German folklore, Odin, now sadly declined to stand for the devil or—like Samiel—the devil's representative); and as with Don Giovanni, he cannot let go. He falls as one dead, but struggles up with difficulty as the curtain comes down.

After an agitated orchestral introduction in D major, and a brief spoken dialogue in which we learn that the last bullet of the seven is at the devil's command, we cross that same ambiguous tritone interval to A flat major for a charming cavatina in which Agatha greets the sunshine on her wedding day. The melody is like Gluck at his simplest and most expressive; the harmony glows with romantic dominant ninths; the solo cello has an exquisite obbligato; yet the omens become more ambivalent than ever. Agatha relates a prophetic dream about a white dove turning into a black bird of prey when shot by Max; Annie caps this with a monster having eyes of fire and clanking chains, turning into the faithful watchdog Nero. At this moment, that persistent ancestral picture comes crashing down again. The dreams may partly relate to Agatha's need to accept her own animal nature now that she is on the point of getting married; the picture hints at something potentially harmful from the negative aspect of the father's authority in her fantasies; and next a black funeral wreath has somehow got into the box which is supposed to be bringing her a white bridal wreath. But the old hermit, she remembers, has already brought her a bunch of consecrated white roses; and in deciding to wear these as her bridal wreath, she puts herself under his positive protection. She sings rather uneasily that a girl wears roses before the altar—and in the coffin. But if there is this thought of death in her mind, it may be symbolic of the transformation already hinted at in the second act when Max fell as one dead. Now, at the test of marksmanship, Max is ordered to shoot a white dove. Agatha runs in screaming: "Do not shoot, Max—I am the dove!" But Max has shot. Agatha in her turn falls as one dead; the devil's bullet has found its mark. Or has it? She wakes, singing: "Was it a dream, that I fell?" It is Caspar who calls out in the agony of death: "Heaven has conquered; it is all over with me." The dove is a Christian symbol for grace descending; and though the Prince sternly banishes Max when the truth comes out about the magic bullets, the old Hermit enters on a heart-warming modulation to E flat major (Ex. 15), and prescribes instead a year's probation for Max, with Agatha's hand and the succession in reward, provided there have been no more self-deceiving dealings with the devil in the meantime. A fine chorus of rejoicing concludes the opera.

EXAMPLE 15    Weber, *Der Freischütz*, (a) II, 4 (Finale), tritone interval for the sinister chorus of Spirits; (b) III, 6 (Finale), modulation for the entry of the wise old Hermit.

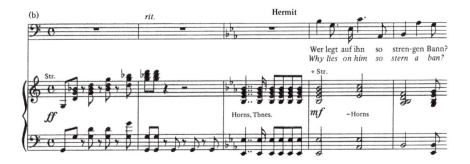

Weber's last two operas were serious but not wholly successful attempts at a close and equal blend of music and drama. They are *Euryanthe,* performed in Vienna in 1823; and the much more uneven *Oberon,* performed in London in 1826, shortly before Weber died there. The next composer of account in German romantic opera was Heinrich Marschner (1795-1861), whose spooky *Der Vampyr* was performed in Leipzig in 1828, and whose *Hans Heiling,* a fairy-tale opera of considerable force and charm, was produced in Berlin in 1833. Gustav Albert Lortzing (1801-1851) achieved a most genial and amusing comedy in *Zar und Zimmermann* ("Tsar and Carpenter"), produced in Leipzig in 1837; and a characteristically romantic fairy-tale opera in his *Undine* (produced in Magdeburg in 1845) on a libretto written (and already set) by the celebrated E.T.A. Hoffmann (1776-1822). From there the succession runs straight to early Wagner.

## The Height of Grand Opera in France

While German romantic opera was thus developing, its influence reached Paris in the powerful person of Weber's friend and admirer, the German-born composer Giacomo Meyerbeer (1791-1864). After failing with some youthful operas of too studied a texture, Meyerbeer went on Salieri's advice to Italy. Here he fell under the fascination of Rossini, imitating his style with much facile success. But wanting to do something more worthy, as he felt, of his own solid talents, he became involved in Paris in a remarkable partnership. The *Opéra* was being successfully reorganized by an able administrator, Véron, who had taken it over as a business speculation. He succeeded because he indulged the Parisian taste for prodigious stage spectacles. Scribe was his cunning librettist; Meyerbeer produced music of just the broad structure and massive appeal required. Their first astonishing triumph was *Robert le Diable* ("Robert the Devil"), first performed at the *Opéra* in 1831. It was the year of Bellini's *La Sonnambula* and *Norma*—a strange contrast of the most elegant of the classics with the least inhibited of the romantics. But *Robert le Diable* is quite the finest specimen of its kind, and we should take a good look at its remarkable exuberance. Nothing could show us better what "grand opera" implies.

Robert is called the Devil because his mother, having been too proud to accept any ordinary suitor, fell at last to a very specious one who proved to be the foul fiend in person. Rather oddly, she is represented as having been a wronged saint on earth, but as having just left it, with pious prayers for her delinquent offspring, who has rebelled against her piety and taken after his father so energetically that he has just been exiled from his own kingdom. Now any man who thinks his mother was a saint and his father the devil has a psychological problem, one symptom of which may be a contrary fantasy of his mother as lascivious and his father as a hero. This fantasy presents itself here as a chorus and ballet of fallen (but now spectral) nuns, and as the attractive Bertram who proves to be Robert's actual father, the devil in disguise. There is also the virtuous princess Isabella, loved by Robert in his better moments, and by the virtuous Prince of Granada at all times. The vacillating Rimbaud is betrothed to Alice, who is foster-sister to Robert, and would like to reform him. Robert is not very happy in his life of evil-doing; and when Alice brings him to meet Isabella again, they are readily reconciled. But Bertram counters by tempting Robert to gamble away not only his wealth but his weapons and his horse, thus excluding himself from a tournament with the Prince of Granada as chief antagonist and Isabella as the prize of victory. She forgives Robert again and provides the necessary equipment. Unfortunately Bertram snares Robert into a dark wood after a spectral counterfeit of the Prince of Granada. The wood recalls Dante's "dark wood" of inner confusion once again—but not Dante's genius.

In Act III, an image is distortedly borrowed from Virgil, whose Aeneas had to take a sacred branch down into hell as a present to propitiate Proserpina. We see a ruined monastery abandoned through the unchastity of all its nuns except for its pious but now defunct abbess. Her statue holds a sacred branch which if stolen will give magical power, wealth, and immortality. But when Bertram mentions that her name was Bertha, Robert recoils in horror from the deed; for this was his mother's name. Bertram invokes the indispensable ballet of fallen nuns out of their graves to encourage Robert—but he merely thinks that the statue is looking accusingly at him in his mother's likeness, until a nun called Helen seduces him into the dark deed, and the nuns all reveal themselves as specters. Demons join them to complete a full SATB chorus, who inform him (rather like Lully's Amadis) that he is now in their evil power.

In Act IV the chorus has changed costumes to congratulate Isabella on her imminent marriage to the Prince of Granada. Robert puts a magic spell as of sleep on them, but wakes Isabella to tell her that nothing can now hinder him from raping her. By dint of very extensive singing she does hinder him, and works on his bad conscience so that he breaks his magic branch, and is at once made prisoner. Bertram enchants him out of prison again, and proposes the usual contract with the devil; but a chorus of monks unsettles him; and on hearing that Isabella is to marry the Prince of Granada, Robert in his anger at last picks up courage to quarrel with Bertram. And at last, Bertram tells him that he is his father. Robert's conflict is now brought to a head by a long-delayed letter from his mother, warning him against his father. He prays to heaven. Clouds fill the stage, and the scene changes to the interior of a cathedral thronged with a chorus of townspeople, to whom another, invisible chorus of spirits answers. Robert is to be united with Isabella after all, having earned this reward, we might suppose, by standing up to the undue influence of both the parents. There is in this ending a certain glittering magnificence; but it cannot compare with what Verdi so finely achieved by modifying grand opera, and Wagner by departing from grand opera, during the second half of the nineteenth century.

The next Parisian grand opera by Scribe and Meyerbeer was *Les Huguenots*, on a political rather than a chivalric theme, and in some ways a more solid (and less immediately popular) affair. *Le Prophète* followed in 1849; then two untypical productions at the *Opéra-Comique* in 1854 and 1859 (the text of the second is not by Scribe); and finally the ambitious but problematical *L'Africaine*, performed posthumously at the *Opéra* in 1865. In grand opera, Meyerbeer's only serious competition was from Fromental Halévy (1799-1862), whose *La Juive* ("The Jewess"), on another typical libretto by Scribe, was performed in 1835 with immense success. But the sentimental or comic alternatives to grand opera continued, as in the somewhat facile charm of the German Friedrich von Flotow (1812-1883), who was in Paris from 1827, though his still mildly popular *Martha* was first performed in Vienna in 1847. There was some exchange of influence with Marschner, Lortzing, and others in Germany; while such secondary English composers as Michael William Balfe (1808-1870), whose *Bohemian Girl* appeared in 1843, also took their style of light opera from Paris. Both in light and in heavy idioms, Paris was the leading nineteenth-century center of opera.

## Notes

1. In a famous letter to his brothers Carl (Caspar) and Johann, left to be read after his death, and known as the Heiligenstadt Testament; an English translation is included in the article on Beethoven in *Grove's Dictionary*, 5th ed., London, 1954, Vol. I, p. 539.
2. *Allgemeine Musikalische Zeitung*, XIX (1817), 201-08.
3. Friedrich Kind, *Das Freischützbuch*, Leipzig, 1843.
4. Christoph Martin Wieland, Franz Grillparzer, E.T.A. Hoffmann, etc.

# PART FOUR

## Act Opera

⌘

## The Fourth Great Period

The second half of the nineteenth century completed the return, in different idioms, to the original Florentine ideal of opera as drama continuously and flexibly unfolding in words and music. As numbers had dissolved into longer scenes or sequences, so these in their turn dissolved into entire acts, or in certain cases (for example, *Rhinegold*), into entire operas. The main musical substance lies neither in recitative nor in aria, but in arioso. Such recitative as remains is orchestrally accompanied, often elaborately, and has a constant disposition to merge into arioso. Arias have a similar disposition to emerge from arioso, and to merge back into it. When arias of clearly defined construction occur, this construction may yet retain some of the fluidity of arioso; and in so far as the construction does conform to pattern, this pattern may range from simple song forms in one or two sections, to full da capo arias of conventional design or some modified equivalent to it. When big "numbers" are found, or big scenes or sequences incorporating several numbers linked or dissolved together, for example in a long finale, there is likely to be good dramatic reason for them. The libretto may be expected (as by Verdi) to serve the drama with the utmost economy of words; or it may be caused (as by Wagner) to enlarge upon the drama

**121**

with the most searching of philosophical comment; but on either method, it is the drama which once more, as in that distant Florentine ideal, conditions both words and music. We are back with music drama in the fullest sense.

The romantic orchestra developed to its greatest extent during the second half of the nineteenth century. Four-part writing was standard for the core of bowed strings, though there was a somewhat greater tendency to give the double basses an independent part instead of merely putting them to play an octave below the cellos, which in turn were left free to play a tenor part or a solo part (or parts) when so desired. Subdividing any or all of the string sections became a familiar although never a standard recourse. The number of players in each string section grew larger than with the classical orchestra and much larger than with the baroque orchestra. The woodwind sections were enlarged correspondingly to preserve a satisfactory proportion, until triple woodwind became virtually a standard provision, and quadruple woodwind a not uncommon requirement. Additional members were added to some families, both in the highest and in the lowest registers. The keywork of woodwind instruments was very much elaborated, which made it possible, or less difficult, to play them with good intonation in the remoter tonalities. Valves added to both the trumpets and the horns increased their availability in different keys, and also allowed them to play both diatonically and chromatically on any notes within their practical compass, so that the brass sections (including three regular trombones and that splendid bass bugle, the orchestral tuba) were completed, to the great increase of orchestral sonority and variety. The kettle-drums were increased to three at the least, and commonly more. The harp advanced from intermittent appearances to regular status; the continuo harpsichord or piano had finally disappeared. The art of orchestration departed still farther from the baroque ideal of differently colored lines, or even from the classical ideal of balanced gradations, and sought a constantly fluctuating mosaic of sonorities which at some times blend imperceptibly one into another, and at other times produce extreme and sudden contrasts.

In using these extended orchestral resources to the full, some composers of opera, above all Wagner, made demands on the singers which only the finest of Italian *bel canto* voice production can meet. The new dimensions of expression thus opened up were quite in the original spirit of music drama. But now Verdi and Wagner brought Italian and German opera to another parting of the ways. Both were born in 1813; both achieved early fame with grand opera in the international Parisian style in the year 1842, Verdi with *Nabucco* under the influence of Rossini (whose *Mosé* he heard at Milan in 1840), and Wagner with *Rienzi* under the influence of Meyerbeer (whose *Robert le Diable* he conducted in Würzburg in 1833); both went beyond grand opera, Wagner after his *Lohengrin* of 1850, and Verdi, with some subsequent regressions, from his *Rigoletto* of 1851. But where Verdi still put vocal expressiveness in the forefront of his advancing style, Wagner put dramatic symbolism, very largely through the independent commentary of the orchestra. Meanwhile, other important national styles evolved in France and in Russia; but with the twentieth century, our modern multiplicity of styles began to reflect personal rather than national differences of aim and temperament.

Other centers of opera overtook the prestige and leadership of Paris. *La Scala* at Milan, with Rome, Naples, and other centers, stood high for Italian opera; London and New York were internationally prominent; Bayreuth was Wagner's personal creation, and remained until recently the authentic guardian of his artistic intentions; Dresden and Munich have the strongest associations with Wagner's heir apparent, Richard Strauss. Not all the operas mounted at these and other centers were romantic operas, nor were they all in one form or another music dramas having entire acts as the effective units of construction. But on a broad view, the century which lay between the middle of the nineteenth and the middle of the twentieth centuries may be called the fourth great period of opera, and its most characteristic species of opera may be called *act opera*.

# 9

# The Italian Verdi

Giuseppe Verdi (1813–1901), though he had no outstanding teachers, was thoroughly steeped in the Italian opera of his youth. In his *Nabucco* of 1842, Verdi combined the influence of Rossini's excellent construction with splendid choruses, effective if noisy orchestration, and a vocal intensity which later developed into Verdi's own most characteristic quality. Where Rossini was brilliant and Bellini was elegant, Verdi became dark and powerful. He showed this already in *Macbeth*, performed in Florence in 1847, and revived, with extensive revisions, in Paris in 1865. The librettists, Piave and Maffei, attempted a fidelity to Shakespeare which, while only relative, was new at the time; and Verdi was equally determined to put dramatic truth before all purely musical considerations. The rousing choruses and the virtuoso arias are of conventional pattern; but much of the opera (such as Lady Macbeth's sleepwalking scene in the last act) consists of free and even fragmentary arioso supported by concentrated melody in the orchestra—a technique not altogether new, but increasingly developed by Verdi in his most individual operas, above all his last three.

For Paris in 1847, Verdi worked over his *I Lombardi* of 1843, as *Jérusalem*, adding a full ballet. He was in Paris until 1849, in which year Naples produced his *Luisa Miller*, a blend of convention and experiment rising to an extraordinarily free and expressive last act. In Venice in 1851, *Rigoletto*, on a libretto by Piave after a play by Victor Hugo, further decreased the number and the virtuosity of the arias, and increased the continuity and the flexibility of long passages of orchestral melody with the voices often inserting no more than declamatory phrases. Only where some relaxation of the drama suggests it do the vocal lines flower into lyrical arioso or full aria. The Duke of Mantua pursues the wife of Count Ceprano, with the cynical encouragement of his hunchback jester, Rigoletto. Ceprano conspires to steal Rigoletto's supposed secret mistress, actually his rigidly guarded daughter Gilda. Old Monterone insults the Duke for having previously dishonored *his* daughter; when Rigoletto mocks him, he curses them both and is arrested. A professional murderer, Sparafucile, offers Rigoletto his services, not "at the moment required"; but Rigoletto seems worried by the old man's curse. He warns his daughter to let no one in, but the Duke, in disguise as a poor student, contrives to court her very agreeably for both of them until a disturbance in the street sends him off; it is the conspirators, who are tricking Rigoletto so that he holds their ladder while they steal, not Ceprano's wife as they are pretending, but Gilda. When Rigoletto finds her gone, he cries out: "Ah, the curse!" and faints.

In Act II, Rigoletto is prevented by the courtiers from pursuing Gilda into the Duke's apartment, but astonishes them by protesting that she is his daughter and not his mistress. To his joy, she runs out, but agonizes him by telling him of her shame (it never occurs to him that it may have been also her desire). Old Monterone is led by, remarking that the Duke seems so far to have escaped his curse; Rigoletto, speaking now as one outraged father to another, swears to take vengeance for them both. In Act III, Sparafucile is hired to attend to this in his professional capacity. His sister Maddalena lures the Duke to a lonely tavern. He sings an outstandingly ear-catching aria, *La donna è mobile* ("Woman is fickle") and makes love to Maddalena, seen and heard through a crack in the wall by Gilda, whom her father has brought there for the purpose of disillusioning her. A celebrated quartet builds up, which keeps each of the four perfectly in character, but combines them with a skill and inspiration deriving substantially from Mozart. Maddalena so likes the Duke that she persuades her brother to spare him, provided someone else arrives who can be murdered instead, in order not to lose the fee. Gilda goes in deliberately to save her faithless lover's life, and is stabbed and handed to Rigoletto in a sack. He gloats over what he supposes to be the murdered Duke, and is about to drop the sack in the river, when that same cynical *La donna è mobile* is sung, by the Duke, unseen but in perfectly good voice; and on opening his sack, Rigoletto finds Gilda dying but still able to give him the explanation in moving melody and to promise him her prayers in heaven. For the second time, and to the same music, he cries out: "Ah, the curse!" and falls senseless across the dead body of his daughter.

By thus piling sensation on sensation, the libretto gave scope to Verdi's immense talent for dramatizing in music a good theatrical situation. There is plenty of confused archetypal potency in the surge of images. Rigoletto's possessiveness as a father, for example, which leads the courtiers to think that his virtually imprisoned daughter must be his mistress, touches obscurely on that theme of unconsciously incestuous desire which Freud called Oedipal, and makes the stabbing feel on one level like some vicarious but horrible consummation. Of course we do not think of that; but the whole mood is grisly beyond all rational credibility, and it is the mood—distasteful as it is to quite a few listeners—which Verdi has caught musically with masterly conviction. The images, separately powerful as they are, do not add up to a coherent inner drama like Mozart's *Magic Flute* or Wagner's *Ring*. We are not purged and renewed as Aristotle said that tragedy should purge us through fear and pity. But we are magnificently gripped.

There is no less archetypal potency but there is much worse confusion in *Il Trovatore* ("The Troubador"), on a libretto mainly by Cammarano after a Spanish play, and produced in Rome in 1853. The musical construction of the opera is less advanced. Recitatives and arias are kept more conventionally distinct, though skillfully disposed. We learn retrospectively (and therefore undramatically) that the old Count di Luna burned at the stake the mother of the gypsy Azucena, for having cast a spell on his baby son, brother to the present Count. Azucena revenged herself by stealing this baby, and reportedly burning it; but by some unexplained aberration it was her own baby son that she burned. She then brought up, as her son, the stolen baby, now grown to manhood under the name of Manrico. He comes disguised as a troubador to serenade the Lady Leonora at the palace of his (unknown) brother, who also loves her. The curtain comes down on their threatened duel. But in Act II, at the gypsy encampment, Azucena unfolds her great mezzo-soprano role by telling Manrico that she burned her own son, yet that her own son is Manrico, which increases his bewilderment without appreciably diminishing ours. Later the Count and Manrico are each trying to abduct Leonora before she, on a false report of Manrico's death, can take the veil at a neighboring convent. With their followers they fight it out to Manrico's advantage. In Act III, Azucena is captured by the Count, with a view to burning her; and the news reaches Manrico just as he is about to marry Leonora. So he rushes off again, only to be captured himself when his castle falls (but all these stirring misadventures occur off stage). Act IV brings to our ears the voices of unseen monks praying for Manrico; while in the foreground, Leonora hears them, and hears Manrico too as he sings briefly from his prison tower. The Count enters, telling his guards to behead the son and burn the mother at break of day; and on being asked by Leonora for mercy, refuses until she promises him her own person in return. But even as the Count rescinds the order of execution, Leonora swallows poison from her ring, which she seems to think restores her honor in the matter.

The closing scene is inside the prison, where Manrico tries with small success to comfort Azucena, already seeing the flames rising in a half-crazed vision of her burning mother. She sleeps at last, and Leonora comes in to urge her beloved to fly while flight is possible; he at once guesses the price of his release, and condemns her ungratefully until the poison fells her and he sees the measure of her fidelity—too late. For the Count, taking in the situation at a glance, sends Manrico to his death, and reports it as he drags Azucena to the window; whereupon she tells him that he has killed his brother, and that her mother is avenged. As she falls fainting, the curtain comes down on his horror at still being alive. There are remote hints here of the familiar mythological brothers (such as Castor and Pollux) each standing for the other's unconscious shadow; of the woman who (as in Wagner) redeems by self-sacrifice; and of the potentially transforming fire. But it is only Verdi's superb vocal eloquence which really gives any semblance of coherence to this remarkably inconclusive and disorderly libretto. Once more, the opera is musically, although not dramatically, magnificent.

*La Traviata* ("The Strayed Woman"), produced in Venice later in 1853, has a very much better libretto by Piave after a play (at first a novel, *La Dame aux Camélias*) by the younger Dumas. The proportion of arias is a little smaller, and the scenes are connected with rather more orchestral continuity; but it remains fairly conventionally a singer's opera, and Violetta, the soprano heroine, has some of Verdi's most ornate and exacting melody. She is hardly shocking to us now, but was so at the time, since although she entertains only the most exclusive clients, she nevertheless makes her living by entertaining them. At one of her brilliant parties, for which Verdi's music is still more brilliantly sustained and organized, the hero Alfredo Gaston, who has loved her at a distance throughout her recent illness, asks: "Have you a heart?" She answers: "A heart . . . yes . . . perhaps"; but having dismissed him, she sings one of Verdi's most splendid arias, of which the slow first section (*cavatina*) dwells radiantly on her dawning hope and wonder, but the fast second section (*cabaletta*) dismisses it all for wishful thinking, from which she had better return to perish in her accustomed whirl of pleasure. But she does not sound as if it would please her in the least; and as Alfredo's voice is heard outside, she seems in mingled doubt and hope again until the curtain falls.

By Act II, Alfredo has been living happily for some time with Violetta in a country house, until he suddenly discovers that she has been selling her possessions to pay for it. No sooner has he departed for Paris to ask his father for some money than the father arrives to ask Violetta to give up Alfredo, so that the scandal shall not prevent the suitor of Alfredo's sister from marrying her. It is a grossly unfair abuse of parental authority, but he beats down her resistance by arguing that there can be no future in her illicit union once her beauty fades. She returns in fact though not in feeling to her old life, which so confounds Alfredo that he wounds her reestablished protector in a duel and has to flee the country. Act III finds Violetta abandoned, impoverished, and very ill; but father Germont, in remorse at his disastrous intervention, has explained everything to Alfredo, who is hurrying back. And as the joyful sound of masquers is heard outside, in dramatic contrast to the hushed sickroom on the stage, Alfredo comes. The lovers sing ecstatically of their reunion forever; but as Germont arrives to ask for her forgiveness, she gives Alfredo a miniature portrait of her own young self; tells him to marry and give the portrait to his bride; feels a sudden access of illusory strength; and dies. Verdi's music makes sure of our compassion; but there may also be some mythological intuition of the hero's inner femininity transformed. The scene as Verdi has composed it rises far above mere sentimentality, and is genuinely affecting.

In 1853, Verdi went to Paris in order to produce a grand opera on a libretto by the famous Scribe. The result in 1855 was *Les Vêpres Siciliennes* ("The Sicilian

Vespers"), a not very successful imitation of Meyerbeer, and hardly better in an Italian version in Milan in 1856. *Simon Boccanegra* was a failure in Venice in 1857, being too dramatically inept for its intermittently splendid music. But *Un Ballo in Maschera* ("A Masked Ball"), on a libretto adapted from Scribe, was very well received in Rome in 1859, partly for patriotic reasons connected with the liberation of Italy from Austrian rule, but partly because the influence of Meyerbeer is better assimilated. There are dark scenes of massive grandeur, and light scenes of brilliant energy; but the drama, based as it is on the historical assassination of Gustavus III, is not as interesting as the music. *La Forza del Destino* ("The Force of Destiny"), on a libretto by Piave after a Spanish play, was produced in St. Petersburg in 1862, and had some influence on the Russian school. The grand scenes are of a deep and gloomy tragedy, but they are mixed with comic scenes so incongruously that the whole does not altogether carry conviction. *Don Carlos*, on a libretto by Méry and Du Locle after Schiller's intensely poetic drama, and produced in Paris in 1867, contains characters of great tragic power, which Verdi presented in music of extraordinary emotional range and subtlety; but the wish to please in Paris led to too many distracting episodes and showy choruses, and this is also an opera better in its parts than as a whole. It was performed in St. Petersburg in 1869, while Mussorgsky was actually at work there on his *Boris Godunov*.

## Verdi's Maturity

Verdi's full maturity came when he was not far short of sixty, with *Aïda*, produced in Cairo for the new opera house there in 1871, and in Milan in 1872, to great acclaim. Verdi himself tightened up the libretto by Ghislanzoni, on a French scenario. The score breathes a strange and haunting nostalgia, not so much for ancient Egypt as for some equivalent in Verdi's imagination to pastoral Arcadia. The orchestra maintains an almost unbroken flow of free symphonic development, into which the voices bring short phrases, or reiterated notes; or they may fall into passing unison or counterpoint with an instrumental melody more continuously sustained; or they may expand into lyrical arioso or formal aria; or they may join in duets or ensembles, or interweave with choruses, or give way to marches, ballets, or interludes. The orchestra is the ground; the vocal drama appears to grow out of it, though really conditioning it in every way. This is the idiom perfected by Verdi in his full maturity, to produce in *Aïda*, and still more in his last two operas, a form of music drama as continuous and flexible as Wagner's by another method.

The overture starts soft and high with muted violins which soon draw the orchestra into a short but free fantasia, mounting to full strength before diminishing again to yet softer heights for a swift rise of the curtain. Young Radames hopes to be chosen by Isis as Egypt's general against an Ethiopian invasion, and to return victorious so that he can seek the hand of Aïda, an Ethiopian captive. She

Triumphal scene from *Aïda*, Act II, performed in the outdoor arena of Verona, Italy.

has kept it secret that she is a princess, daughter to the invading king Amonasro. Yet Radames, who wants to place her "on a throne near to the sun," seems to sense her hidden worth; and this is noticed jealously by Aïda's mistress Amneris, daughter to the king of Egypt, who desires Radames herself. The court sweeps in with pomp and circumstance, and Radames is named general, to the distress of Aïda since she already loves him, and he will be fighting against her own father and her own people. Left alone, she sings an eloquent arioso above one of those ongoing orchestral passages which now largely serve Verdi in place of recitative. This leads her to a *cantabile*, suggesting the start of a formal aria, as she compares Radames to "a ray of the sun" (for Egypt seems to stand here for bright conscious-ness against the dark upsurge from Ethiopia). But her incipient aria dissolves quietly into a "grand scene of the consecration" of Radames, which the high priestess opens mysteriously to an accompaniment by two harps, with priests and priestesses answering in chorus. A ballet of priestesses is still quite lightly scored, with some colorful (but not literally Egyptian) chromatic intervals to convey Verdi's imaginative fantasy. But as the long scene builds up, with another ballet for little Moorish slaves, followed by a crescendo of choral and orchestral rejoicing, we are given spectacle and brilliance on the scale of Meyerbeer, but with far finer musicianship and far more genuine characterization.

Act II confronts the two princesses, as Amneris easily tricks Aïda into confes-sing her love for Radames. When he returns triumphantly, Aïda recognizes her father, King Amonasro, disguised among the captured Ethiopians, who are all magnanimously spared at Radames' pressing request. Act III opens yet more evocatively in moonlight on the banks of the Nile, as Aïda sings regretfully of her own lost country. She is expecting Radames; but instead her father comes and persuades her (but again it is an illegitimate abuse of the father's authority) to trick Radames into betraying to her the route which his army is to follow next day, so that the Ethiopians can ambush it. No sooner has Radames arrived than she does trick him, with a womanly guile on which Delilah herself could not have improved. Amonasro comes rushing out of hiding; so do Amneris and the High Priest, who have been listening too. Amonasro runs off with Aïda, after Radames has quixotically prevented the High Priest from killing him. Still more quixotically, Radames surrenders himself in an agony of shame.

This clash of two worlds is somewhat unexpectedly resolved in Act IV. Amneris will save Radames on condition of never seeing Aïda again. When he refuses, he is condemned to be buried alive. We see the bright temple above ground, with Amneris praying and the priests chanting; we also see the dark vault below, where Radames is shut in with a great stone, only to find Aïda already hiding there so that she can die with him. They sing quietly of their shared destiny, to a melancholy counterpoint from the princess and the chorus of priests above. For all the resigned beauty of Verdi's ensemble and antiphony, the situation would be false and unendurable if there were not some aura of mythological association with the traditional descent into the underworld, for rebirth into greater consciousness and maturity. The stone which closed Christ's sepulcher did not prevent him from descending into hell in order to ascend again. "Heaven opens to us," our imprisoned lovers sing; and Amneris adds the last word, "peace," thus bringing down the curtain not on the expected hate and vengeance, but on reconciliation. It was surely this sense of reconciliation which inspired Verdi's serenely beautiful closing music, and which finds an answering echo in our hearts.

EXAMPLE 16   Verdi, *Aïda*, III, 1, the poignant nostalgia by the moonlit Nile.

(etc.)

o
oh

pro - fu - ma - te
sweet - ly  smell - ing

ri
banks

ve

# Verdi's Old Age

In 1874, Verdi produced his magnificently dramatic *Requiem Mass,* and in 1881 and 1884, revisions of *Simon Boccanegra* and *Don Carlo;* but he was only persuaded to undertake another opera with great difficulty by Arrigo Boito, who derived from Shakespeare's *Othello* a libretto so masterly that it won Verdi over. The delays were protracted, the composing was slow, but early in 1887 *Otello* was produced in Milan to immense enthusiasm. Boito (himself a composer of opera) sensibly omitted Shakespeare's first act in Venice. After a mere three bars of orchestra, the curtain rises upon a violent storm as Othello's ship is sighted by the garrison at Cyprus. He lands, announces briefly the destruction of the enemy fleet, and goes into the castle. Iago is already playing upon his dupe Roderigo to work fraudulently on Othello's weakest point, his jealousy. As the storm and the orchestra subside into welcome tranquillity, Iago entices the honest but not especially perceptive soldier, Cassio, into drinking too much, and Roderigo into insulting him. They fight, and the disturbance brings out Othello and also Desdemona, which so enrages him that he impulsively demotes Cassio. Left alone, Othello and Desdemona sing of their love through a long and lyrical passage of symphonic development in the orchestra, their voices floating freely over it. The night has cleared, and their hearts with it. They recall with joy their courtship in Venice, when his dark Moor's face lit up with beauty for her, the fairest of Italians; yet even in this radiant scene, which melts our hearts too, Othello has the strangest premonition. "Let death come!" he sings; "let it take me in the bliss of this embrace"—for "such is the joy of my soul [*anima*] that I am afraid." And as he asks her for a kiss, and a kiss again, and yet another kiss, Boito and Verdi prepare for us a stroke of theatrical genius which is not in Shakespeare. It is wonderful here, but still more wonderful when the full irony of it is accomplished at the end of the opera.

EXAMPLE 17    Verdi, *Otello,* the intense music for the kiss at the end of Act I; recapitulated twice in the finale of Act IV.

In Act II, Iago insidiously recommends Cassio to ask Desdemona, "the captain of our captain," to intercede for him with Othello, knowing that this will do all three of them the greatest possible disservice. And then, as Cassio goes off, Iago launches into his finest passage, in which Boito and Verdi made explcit what Shakespeare did not: Iago's motivation. "Your demon drives you," he sings after the departing Cassio; "and I am your demon; mine draws me, in which I believe, an inexorable deity." Then, with no more thought of Cassio, "I believe in a cruel God who created me in his own image." For that indeed is what Iago is: an image of archetypal evil. Iago is not just an evil man—no actual man could be so consistently and exclusively evil. Iago is a personification of evil itself. Since every man has some share of archetypal evil, Iago can conclude: "I am evil because I am a man." Othello is only vulnerable to Iago because Iago corresponds to his own dark shadow, and is therefore really getting at him from the inside.

Thus when Iago, without actually saying so, insinuates that Cassio and Desdemona not only share but have already consummated a guilty passion, it is

Othello who puts it into words, which Iago repeats, so that they appear to Othello (more truly than he realizes) to originate from himself. When Desdemona pleads for Cassio, it is Othello who now suspects the worst. When through a chain of circumstances more neatly contrived by Boito than by Shakespeare, Iago gets possession of the handkerchief given by Othello's father to his mother, and by Othello to Desdemona as his first love gift, it is Othello who never thinks to inquire whether there might not be some perfectly innocent explanation; and in the course of Act III fearful play is made with this handkerchief, as if it were proof positive of Desdemona's iniquity. No wonder she confides to Emilia that "a great cloud disturbs Othello's wisdom and my destiny." A hateful climax follows when Othello throws Desdemona to the ground, in the presence of a party of ambassadors come to summon him to Venice in still more honorable employment (leaving Cassio as governor of Cyprus in his place). She grieves that "the bright Sun" is lost to her, and the bystanders call him "that black man" in whom there is "a blind shadow of death and of terror"; but remarkably enough he cries out to her "my soul [*anima mia*], I curse you!" Outside, the chorus sings "Long live Othello! Glory to the Lion of Venice!" But on the now-deserted stage, Othello has fallen in a frenzy to the ground, while Iago stays behind to sneer at him in fearful triumph: "See the Lion!"

Act IV, again more tautly than in Shakespeare, is all in Desdemona's bedroom. As she waits for Othello, she sings that sad song "Willow, Willow," which in Shakespeare's poetry conveys so heart-rending a pathos and so sinister a foreboding. Boïto did not quite catch the very English reticence of that, nor its haunting poetic resonance, but it is nonetheless very moving in Verdi's music; and Desdemona's *Ave Maria*, her famous prayer to the Virgin Mary, which follows in place of Shakespeare's change of scene, is a set piece both justified by the situation and beautiful in its effect. As the high violins and violas die away with their 6-4 chord of A flat on its E flat bass, and the double basses enter on their bottom E natural almost three octaves below, Othello comes in by a secret door. She sleeps; he watches her with intense but troubled feelings, then kisses her awake with three kisses to the same music as at the end of Act I; and very poignantly we remember it (Ex. 17, p. 133). She denies with the most evident sincerity his reiterated accusations of infidelity, soon mounting to stark hysteria; but not believing her, he smothers her. As the alarm is raised by Emilia, and all the main characters are brought on stage, the truth about Iago is relentlessly pieced together, and Othello in his agony of belated realization stabs himself at Desdemona's bedside. "Before I killed you, wife, I kissed you. Now dying, in the shadow in which I lie, a kiss, a kiss again, ah! Another kiss. . . ." And these three kisses are given once more to that heartfelt music and tight-stretched scoring of their lovers' kisses, three long acts and a world of passion ago. On the last of them, Othello dies.

All operatic deaths hold at a deep enough level some hint of transformation; and the overall human character suggested by the various characters in *Otello* certainly stands in need of being pulled together by some transforming inner reconciliation. But it is not as it was at the end of *Aïda*, a situation only making much sense when regarded as the naive surface of a deeper symbolism. The end of *Otello* is not naive on any level: that is the difference between a merely competent playwright and the genius of Shakespeare; the difference between good melodrama and great tragedy.

Having shown themselves equal to that Shakespearean greatness in tragedy, Boito and Verdi showed it six years later in comedy, where Verdi had never previously succeeded. The comedy is *Falstaff*, on another superb libretto by Boito, most skillfully culled from Shakespeare's *Merry Wives of Windsor* and those of his chronicle plays in which Falstaff appears. It was not so hard this time to persuade the old maestro to get to work; and by 1892 he had *Falstaff* ready for performance, in Milan in 1893, his eightieth year. There is again no overture; and in a swift scene of the sharpest dialogue, threaded through the wittiest orchestration, Falstaff and his shocking comic followers, Bardolph and Pistol, first wrangle with the pompous Dr. Caius, and then fall out when those two dishonorable figures of fun bethink them of their honor; for Falstaff has asked them to carry his love letter to Mistress Ford and Mistress Page, the Merry Wives of Windsor. On this excuse, Boito has Falstaff deliver himself of that notable speech in dispraise of honor which Shakespeare gave him on the battlefield in quite another context; and a very mock-eloquent passage of mingled recitative and arioso Verdi makes of it. In the following scene, the Merry Wives find themselves the astonished recipients of identical love letters from Falstaff, who is evidently indifferent as to which of the fair temptresses falls to his lot, provided that one of them does. They plan a teasing revenge; but into their planning there interweaves the courtship of young Fenton and Nannetta, Ford's daughter, who take every brief opportunity of snatching a word and a kiss. Their charming endeavors and their lyrical melody run all through like a counterpoint of another color, giving to the witty comedy a warmth of sentiment it would not otherwise possess.

In Act II, Mistress Quickly, a friend of the other two wives but a little more staid in years, visits Falstaff with that prolonged curtseying and exaggerated reverence (*reverenza*) which Verdi made quite as funny in his music as Rossini made the same joke in his *Barber of Seville;* and perhaps the tribute was deliberate. She assures Falstaff that each of her friends ("the poor woman") is burning for him; and an assignation with Mistress Ford (Alice) is arranged. But Ford has been warned by Bardolph and Pistol. He arrives at Falstaff's inn disguised under the name of Brook, and by pretending to want an illicit affair with his own wife, which he suggests would be made easier if Falstaff made the first breach in her chastity, he gets it out of Falstaff not only that this is just what he is expecting to do, but the actual time of the assignation. The dramatic irony of all this is a little crude, but it is very amusing. The music is as flexible as it is lively and inspired.

The big second scene of Act II opens quietly with Mistress Ford (Alice) and Mistress Page (Meg) preparing their trap for Falstaff, and enjoying it; but Nannetta is in tears. Her father Ford wants to marry her to dry old Dr. Caius. The women, we are given to suspect, are not going to let him do any such thing. All but Alice now hide as Falstaff approaches, and rather touches us by singing to her of his own youthful slenderness, the loss of which does not lessen his love for her now. She leads him on with honeyed words and music until, by prearrangement, Mistress Quickly rushes on to announce Meg, and Meg rushes on to announce Ford in a fury. No sooner has Falstaff been hurried behind a screen than, not at all by prearrangement, Ford does rush on in a fury, followed by Dr. Caius, Bardolph, and Pistol. There is a great laundry basket, into which Ford looks with immediate suspicion, but from which he pulls out only the dirty linen. The pursuers now rush upstairs, and Falstaff gets with difficulty into the same basket, where the dirty linen is stuffed back on top of him. The orchestra keeps up the excitement; the voices interject and combine; Falstaff groans and grumbles from his smelly basket; and now from behind that useful screen, visible to us but not to the other characters, Fenton and Nannetta join their fresh voices and lilting melody to the medley with indescribable charm, until they climax with a noisy kiss. So Ford and his followers, sure now, as they think, of their man, tiptoe elaborately up, throw down the screen, and find—the young couple, with whom Ford, of course, is more furious than ever. The hunt resumes; but the women contrive with enormous exertions to heave the basket onto the window ledge. Just as "the basket, Falstaff, and the linen tumble headlong" into the river below, Alice draws Ford to the window to witness his supposed rival's discomfiture, and one and all join in delighted laughter.

A much dampened Falstaff opens Act III by at first rejecting furiously, but soon falling into the snare of a renewed assignation, this time for midnight in the Royal Park of Windsor, at Herne's Oak, in disguise as that Black Huntsman whose sinister implications and nocturnal habits we have already encountered in the Wolf's Glen of Weber's *Freischütz*. There Alice renews her seeming blandishments; and this time the interruption comes from a ballet of children led by Nannetta and disguised as fairies. Falstaff throws himself to earth face down in terror; for "who looks upon them, dies." They dance "under the brightness of the moon, toward the dark oak of the black Huntsman"; and through the beauty of the music, the spell of the ancient forest falls hauntingly upon us, even though we know that this is only a pantomime set up for teasing Falstaff, who is completely taken in. The jest and the beauty go hand in hand: that is the secret of Verdi's enchantment. The jest grows rougher when the other characters come on variously disguised, followed by small boys as goblins, sprites, and devils; for now Falstaff is pushed, pinched, and beaten with sticks and words, until Bardolph's hood slips off in the turmoil, and Falstaff recognizes that bright red nose. His disillusioned outburst of indignation is so powerful in words and music that it wins an unstinted "bravo" from all his persecutors; and that jest is over.

But there is more to come. Ford is about to bestow the veiled Nannetta on the masked Dr. Caius in marriage; but the women are too much for him. He does indeed bestow on Dr. Caius a figure all veiled in white; but there is, it seems, another masked and veiled couple seeking his sanction in marriage, which he gives without the least inquiry: "So be it . . . a double ceremony." But when the masks and the veils are taken off, there is Dr. Caius coupled with that preposterous Bardolph, and here is Fenton coupled with his beloved Nannetta. Ford, after his initial shock, has the good grace to admit that the joke is on him now, and the hard facts as well. As Nannetta asks his pardon, he grants it gladly, and calls down heaven's blessing on the happy pair. But as is proper, Falstaff, he whose "wit creates the wit of the others," has the last word. He calls for a chorus to conclude the scene; while Ford invites them, when it is done, all to join with Sir Falstaff at dinner. And then Falstaff starts off that lightest and most dazzling of fugues: "All in the world's for laughter (*tutto nel mondo è burla*)." And so Verdi, too, ended his long career in lightness and in laughter. What can any man do better than that?

EXAMPLE 18    Verdi, *Falstaff*, III, 2, the final fugue.

# 10

# The German Wagner

Richard Wagner (1813–1883) lost his father in the year of his birth, and his very sympathetic and affectionate stepfather Ludwig Geyer (possibly though not probably his actual father) in his eighth year: a double deprivation which left him with some psychological problems not of his own making. Wagner's family background was favorable to the arts, but he had no formal training in music, and not much advanced education in any direction. He took his own musical education in hand at an early age, not only studying but in some cases copying scores, just as J. S. Bach did, in order to reach a better understanding of them. He was particularly impressed and influenced by Mozart's *Don Giovanni*, by Weber's *Freischütz*, and by Beethoven's *Fidelio*. In his early twenties, Wagner was already conducting operas by Bellini, Marschner, Meyerbeer, and others. Spontini and Meyerbeer were his chief models for *Rienzi*, a grand opera (completed in Paris in 1840 and performed in Dresden to great applause in 1842) of which the last three acts show some unconventional arioso. But Wagner's true individuality first appears with *Der Fliegende Holländer* ("The Flying Dutchman") performed in Dresden in 1843. This is an early German romantic opera, normal in all respects except in being in music throughout, without spoken dialogue. Instead it used (very much as Bellini might have used it) orchestrally accompanied recitative, worked effectively into the excitement and impetus of this extremely consistent score—a score which carries to its highest expression the romantic freshness and naive confidence of Weber's *Freischütz*.

The libretto of *The Flying Dutchman*, like those of all Wagner's operas, is by the composer. The score, with its chromatic harmony and surging melody, recalls the restless voices of the sea and the wind in almost every scene. A stormy sea in opera is always liable to touch upon our uneasy intuitions of hidden depths from which may rise up trouble or treasure, but neither of them within our rational control. Here is this ghostly wanderer from the sea, this Dutchman doomed to sail forevermore unless he can find a woman to redeem him by her willing sacrifice. Once every seven years he can come on land to search for her. He brings treasure, by which he pays for his welcome in Daland's home. And there is Senta, Daland's daughter, who has already felt a mysterious sympathy with the Dutchman's portrait hanging on the wall, and with his legend. She pointedly refrains in Act II from the brilliant Spinning Chorus of the other women with their normally domestic aspirations, and sings that pure and haunting aria known as Senta's Ballad, about her own compassion for the legendary wanderer. Its diatonic stability well conveys the peace which her compassion holds in promise for him. She has, however, also a normal suitor, Eric, who also has been troubled by a prophetic dream of his ghostly rival. Now when Daland brings the Dutchman in, an almost hypnotic sense of recognition takes hold of this couple so strangely destined for one another. The recognition implies that they are reenacting for us an archetypal situation: some familiar scenario of wandering masculinity and quieting femininity repeated down the generations of our troubled species. Ghost that he is, the Dutchman stands for something stronger than any human suitor, and more uncanny. In fey tones, the man and woman give each other greeting. So direct an encounter with archetypal imagery is inevitably disquieting, and in the last act, a chorus of townspeople are seen entertaining with understandable uneasiness that other chorus who are the ghostly crew. Eric appeals to Senta in urgent arioso; the Dutchman, incompletely overhearing, gives himself up prematurely for lost and puts impulsively out to sea, announcing his true name and nature as he goes. But faithful Senta plunges into the waves to redeem him, as the legend requires. Some sort of united transfiguration is depicted in a lingering plagal cadence anticipating (and later remodeled like) the end of *Tristan,* where the implications are more clearly drawn. Here the representation is so naive that we can appreciate it best as pure fairy tale, set to music of a romantic freshness and confidence of which Weber, Lortzing, and Marschner set the character, and which was only possible for a brief phase in the history of music before growing threadbare and banal. But Wagner caught it here in all its pristine bloom, and made of it a particularly spontaneous, radiant, and consistent opera.

*Tannhäuser,* performed in Dresden in 1845, is a modified grand opera with a yet more continuous and flexible construction than *The Flying Dutchman,* but a less consistent dramatic and musical inspiration. The overture depicts moral purity in a stately pilgrim's march, against which an agitated theme of lust is brilliantly counterpointed until it predominates; these same events are then reversed, to give us in a concentrated orchestral form the basic conflict of the opera. Tannhäuser has been experiencing his sensual side in the mountain cavern of Venus, but returns to be pardoned just in time for a contest of song, with his old love, Elizabeth the Landgrave's daughter, as the prize of victory; and she (like Plato's heavenly Venus) evidently stands for his aspiring side. Wolfram, who is also in love with Elizabeth, sings of his love in chaste words and noble melody; but Tannhäuser, carried away by his own still unresolved ambivalence, sings unchaste words to a melody of unashamed impulsiveness. This is his famous song in seemingly compulsive praise of Venus, very obviously in her sensuous and not her spiritual role. He is with difficulty rescued from the righteous indignation (perhaps not unmixed with envy) of the respectable knights, and sent off to seek absolution from the Pope, who tells him puritanically that sooner shall his papal staff put forth flowers than Tannhäuser shall be absolved. He struggles home to seek such solace as he can with Venus again, and narrates his story in a long and elaborately accompanied arioso which is one of the best passages of the opera. But he is met by the funeral procession of Elizabeth, who has died of a broken heart for him; this sacrifice, like Senta's for the Dutchman, redeems him, and he dies with a kiss across her body. The pilgrims bring on the papal staff, flowering in a beautiful symbol of new growth. What is not so beautiful is the moralistic censoriousness and the abject, almost masochistic, guilt to which Tannhäuser is subjected on the way to his redemption. The hero of *Tristan* later undergoes a comparable experience, but with a warmth of sympathy and understanding incomparably more mature, not only in the drama but also in the music.

*Lohengrin,* composed from 1846 to 1848, and performed in Weimar under Liszt in 1850, was Wagner's magnificent last contribution to grand opera. The overture again presents the essence of the coming drama in orchestral form. We hear divided violins in a very high register: it is the heavenly music of that potent Christian symbol, the Holy Grail. The hero, Lohengrin, turns out to be a Knight of the Grail, though this is not revealed until the last scene of the opera. Little by little the music comes down to more earthly levels, gaining warmth and substance, but presently returning to the heights, as Lohengrin is going to return home when the opera concludes. The curtain rises on a chivalric scene as the heralds with their trumpets announce the arrival of the overlord of this province of Brabant: King Henry I of Germany. The regent, Count Telramund, reports that the young ruler, Gottfried, has been murdered by his sister Elsa with a view to usurping the throne, which Telramund now claims. He believes this story, because his wife Ortrud has told him that she saw the murder. The King sends for Elsa and asks her with great kindness if she will accept the results of a "judicial combat" between Telramund and whichever knight will fight in her cause; for it is believed that God will grant the victory to whichever knight is fighting for the just cause. She accepts, but no knight comes forward. Then Elsa sings an aria reminiscent of Senta's ballad in its hauntingly beautiful and sustained serenity, in which she narrates a dream, very movingly, and almost as if she and we were still taking part in it. At the last possible moment, this dream comes true. Lohengrin appears in a boat drawn magically by a swan, not only to be her knightly champion but to marry her, on one condition: she must never question him about his name and origin. Telramund is defeated; but in the second act, his wife Ortrud urges him to a treacherous revenge, persuading him that it was only by sorcery that Lohengrin prevailed. She throws herself falsely on Elsa's compassion, in order to insinuate doubts as to what disreputable secrets Lohengrin must surely be concealing. In a scene worthy of the most brilliant traditions of grand opera, Ortrud arrogantly tries to press in front as the bridal procession approaches the cathedral; Telramund weakly accuses Lohengrin of sorcery; but Lohengrin quietly maintains his dignity, without betraying his identity, and the procession passes on. There is a long, heroic orchestral introduction to the third act, and a bridal chorus full of tender feeling, which moves away to leave the happy couple at last alone. They sing very lyrically of their mutual love and confidence; yet Elsa cannot forget Ortrud's cunning words, and gradually she brings the subject round to that fascinating but forbidden question of who and what Lohengrin is. He tries to divert her, but in the end she comes right out with it. At this moment, they are interrupted by an armed attack from Telramund, who has been promised by Ortrud that the slightest scratch will destroy Lohengrin's magic power; but instead, Lohengrin quickly kills him. Next day, Lohengrin gives, before the King and all the people, that answer which, once asked, he is compelled to make by the sacred conditions of his calling. In an eloquent but quiet arioso, supported by the high violins as in the overture, he sings of the distant castle of the Holy Grail whose ruler is his father, Parsifal, and to which he must return once he is known. Even as he finishes, the swan brings up his magic boat. Ortrud breaks out, in terrible exultation, that the swan is Gottfried bewitched by herself, in vengeance on the people for leaving the old pagan gods: a powerful motivation which we had not previously suspected in her. But now to the same heavenly music the white dove of the Holy Grail itself flies down; Gottfried is restored to human form and named ruler of Brabant by Lohengrin, to the delight of the people and above all of Elsa; Ortrud falls to the ground with a shriek; the dove draws Lohengrin away.

We are left with a strangely open-ended impression, as if there might be more to come. There was more to come, for Wagner's last opera, *Parsifal*, though it steps a generation back, takes the issues of *Lohengrin* on to a much completer resolution. Parsifal has to learn there the hard lesson that the crucial questions must be not avoided but, on the contrary, asked. Elsa here was forbidden to ask; but in fairy tales, the forbidden deed is the necessary deed, put in that form as a test of character. It feels wrong, and it feels dangerous, but if it is dared, it brings an increase of consciousness. Elsa lost a dream lover but gained a real brother, and became herself more real by doing so; for if she had not asked the crucial question about what Lohengrin stood for, she would have remained a child content with her fantasies of the all-protective knight in shining armor. What Elsa needed was to grow up. She did grow up; but there is sadness, too, in letting go our youthful fantasies, and we hear it in the music as the parting comes.

*Lohengrin* was the culmination of Wagner's early prime. Recitative, arioso, and aria are recognizably present, but they merge and they gather momentum irresistibly, together with choruses which enter powerfully into the dramatic action. It is a wonderful score; and we might have regretted that Wagner never returned to grand opera, if it were not that in his later manner he matured to still greater masterpieces.

# Theory and Practice

So far-reaching were the changes in Wagner's maturer manner of opera that for five years after *Lohengrin* he composed no music, though like a fallow field he was preparing inwardly for the coming harvest. His career was also in transition, since his confused but serious involvement in the unsuccessful revolution in Dresden in 1849 had ended his prosperous employment there, and driven him into a long exile in Zurich. Here he produced the poetry for his next librettos, and a number of theoretical prose writings. Wagner's prose writings are voluminous, inconsistent, historically inaccurate, and sometimes shamefully abusive; but they abound in passing insights, and helped in clearing his own mind for his continually evolving practice. *Art and Revolution* in 1849 and *The Art Work of the Future* in 1850 led up to the important *Opera and Drama* of 1851, which deliberately restates the original Florentine ideal of opera as a drama for which the words are the end and the music is the means, the music being therefore subordinated to the poetry. On the theory elaborated in *Opera and Drama*, the poetry is to be condensed and allusive, so far as possible without emotionally neutral words such as articles and conjunctions, but emphasized by alliteration with or without the more regular resources of rhyme and meter. The vocal melody should then follow in close detail the sonorous qualities of this poetry; the harmony should reflect its fluctuations of emotional intensity; there should only be modulations for changes in the dramatic situation. The result was to be a total art work (*Gesamtkunstwerk*), which was even seen as rendering obsolete the separate arts (but this last was a preposterous suggestion not long maintained). *Rhinegold* comes nearest to this stage in Wagner's theory; but *Die Walküre* still follows it quite closely, especially in Act I.

Three years after this first important statement of his theory, Wagner came under the strong influence of Schopenhauer, who put music at the head of all the arts.[1] Since that view suited the way in which Wagner's own practice was by then developing, he little by little came around to it. By *Music of the Future* in 1861, poetry and music were allowed separate and equal value, and were to be matched to one another not so much in detail as in the broad sweep. By *Beethoven* in 1870 and *On the Destiny of Opera* in 1871, the poetry was to be subordinated to the music, though the music could be all the bolder because the unfolding of the drama would itself provide coherent form enough. And in 1872, Wagner rather beautifully described his music dramas as "deeds of music made visible" (*ersichtlich gewordene Taten der Musik*), which exactly fits the style of *Parsifal* shortly afterward ("Essay of the Term 'Music-drama' ").

In his operas after *Lohengrin*, Wagner discarded almost entirely any such set numbers as recitatives and arias, duets or choruses. Instead, he spun out an indefinitely prolonged and seamless arioso in which full cadences are postponed with great formal and harmonic resourcefulness to the ends of the acts, where the drama arrives at a natural break. Wagner very seldom allowed an actual tune to round itself out for long enough to impose a regular pattern of its own on this unending melody. The subjects of his music are most often (especially in *The*

*Ring*) short themes for symphonic development and contrapuntal combination. These themes may be attached, by natural affinity and frequent association, to specific characters or situations, objects or ideas, which they bring consciously or unconsciously to mind whenever they are introduced. In this form, we call them leading motives—a system which Wagner did not invent, but did most to establish. Sometimes (especially in *The Mastersingers*) a leading motive is allowed to grow into a longer melody, while still remaining associated with some specific element in the drama. And sometimes (particularly in *Tristan* and still more in *Parsifal*) the association may not be specific, but suggestive in a more elusive manner; in that form, we may not quite think of the material as a leading motive, yet it may nevertheless function similarly as a link between the musical situation and the dramatic (Leitmotif, from the German *Leitmotiv*, is also used).

By symphonic development we mean breaking down musical material and reassembling it in various transformations; and since in Wagner the musical material is also the dramatic material, the development of the leading motives is also the development of the characters and situations. By contrapuntal combination we do not here mean the fugal interweaving of the same musical subjects, but the dramatic interweaving of different musical subjects; and since these musical subjects are in effect the characters and situations, we not only hear different personalities in the music, but hear them in relation to one another and to other elements of the drama—a counterpoint of characters as well as of leading motives. It is a wonderful method for unfolding drama as much in the music as in the words; and in evolving it, Wagner opened up a new technique for opera.

## The Ring Cycle

The poem of *Der Ring des Nibelungen* ("The Ring of the Nibelung")[2] was first sketched, as one opera, in Dresden in 1848, and completed in exile, as four operas (*Das Rheingold, Die Walküre, Siegfried, Die Götterdämmerung*), in 1852. By 1857, the music was composed in an orchestral sketch up to the end of *Siegfried*, Act II, then set aside as impracticable for twelve years, but resumed and performed entire at Bayreuth in 1876, more than a quarter of a century after the vast undertaking was first begun. In his autobiography for September of 1853, Wagner tells us of a strange waking vision in which he seemed to be flooded along by waves of water which were the E flat major arpeggios of "the orchestral introduction to *Rhinegold*, as I had been carrying it about, without being able to find it," and which somehow impressed upon him that "the flow of life would never pour into me from the outside, but only from inside." As *Rhinegold* opens (Ex. 19, i, p. 153), we find ourselves in the waters of the Rhine; it is like the waste of waters engendering the first creatures in a creation myth, which is an intuitive image, not literally for the origins of species, but symbolically for the origins of consciousness. "The world's beginning," Wagner called it in a letter to Liszt on February 11, 1853: "the depicting of reality," as he wrote of *The Ring* in a famous letter to Röckel on January 25, 1854. But we can see at once that he means inner reality. The creatures first seen here are three Rhine maidens with the traditional mermaid's way of luring men down to their destruction, as Fricka presently informs us. We are back symbolically in the state of nature from which our species at length emerged into that measure of conscious awareness which is our human state. But with consciousness, we have brought on ourselves choice and conflict and responsibility, just as we found Circe fabling in the *Ballet Comique de la Royne* when she spoke of nature ruling men contentedly by their instincts until Jupiter gave us at the same time care and understanding, change and desire. Because our human state is a mixed blessing, we can be tempted by debilitating fantasies of being carried along again by mother, like infants, or by mother nature, like animals; and it is perhaps for this reason that mermaids are fabled as dangerous. For 157 bars of tonic E flat major (Ex. 19, i–ii), the mermaids swim around, while nothing changes; then, with the first change of chord, there arrives a dark and sinister dwarf, Alberich, who is the main villain of the piece. But in a fairy tale, the villain is the instigator who gets something happening; and if it were not for Alberich, we should still be stuck fast with E flat major, and nothing human and conscious would have come out of it at all. The Rhine maidens cruelly mock his clumsy longings; but suddenly the rising sun strikes down through the water onto a great lump of gold (Ex. 19, xviii), very much as the light of conscious spirit penetrates the waters in creation myths. The Norse sagas make many references to gold lighting up like fire beneath the water, in token of the illuminating spirit and burning energy of life. Those who are enough in touch with their own true value to let life burn through them have no need of mermaid fantasies. The crude gold stands here for that potential value in ourselves; but the Rhine maidens have not done anything but enjoy like children the mere glitter of it (Ex. 19, xiii). Accidentally on purpose they now let it out to Alberich that he who forges the gold into a ring (Ex. 19, xv) will be master of the world—but that only by renouncing love can he forge the gold (Ex. 19, vi–a). Having just frustrated the ugly little fellow of their own love, they should not be so surprised when he does renounce love with a fearful curse (Ex. 19, vi–b). But what kind of love was this of which they have frustrated him? Mermaid's love, fantasy love. And the fantasy is that insidious one of slipping back to childhood bliss and mother's protection which we saw unmanning Don Giovanni, and which might have unmanned Wagner too if it had not been for his power of working out his inner problems in his art. On one level, it may be part of the symbolism here that Alberich was renouncing on behalf of Wagner (but tentatively as yet) not so much love's person-to-person reality as love's compulsive counterfeit. For the music of Alberich's renunciation is not harsh nor cynical, but of a resigned and courageous dignity (Ex. 19, vi–a and b). Wagner himself told us that in this scene, he felt inexplicably on the side of Alberich. Nevertheless, Alberich is the villain of the piece, and we need to experience the full horror of his evil aspect. Like all our archetypal personifications, he is ambivalent. But he is unquestionably dark.

Opposite to Alberich comes Wotan, a sky god who stands traditionally for light and consciousness; but he too has his ambiguities like the rest of us. He is at present an impetuous redhead of a Nordic god in his early prime, in trouble because he has contracted with the giants to build him a fortress, Valhalla, in return—of all bad bargains—for the goddess Freia, who stands not only for youthful love but for every form of spontaneous joy in life. Wotan is evidently trying to live too much by willful planning and not enough by his own spontaneous values. His obstinacy and the spear which betokens it have almost the same music (Ex. 19, ix–b and x–a). But Loge, the trickster god of flickering fire and cunning deception—we all have a bit of him—persuades the giants to accept in Freia's place the lifeless hoard of gold which Alberich has, by the power of the ring, bullied his fellow dwarfs into amassing for him. Down we go past the sound of many anvils to a cavern full of underworld associations. By a trick, Alberich and his gold are brought up, which he tolerates well enough until Wotan robs him of his ring as well. Then with the utmost violence he curses it, so that its future holders shall reap envy, care, and death (Ex. 19, xvi–c).

Yet what are envy, care, and death but aspects of our common human lot? The music of the ring (Ex. 19, xv) is round and cornerless; chromatic where the music of the crude gold (Ex. 19, xviii) was diatonic and leaping; harmonically ambiguous and adaptable to many different contexts. The ring, forged in the underworld as a man may forge his own character by renouncing childish fantasy, is a symbol for that force of life which can be used or misused, but only to a man's ultimate advantage when he really lets it make use of him instead. The music of Alberich's curse is a leaping variant of the same chromatic notes which form the music of the ring. The power of the ring and the power of the curse are both of them the same ambivalent power for which Circe stood: the power of life itself for pain and for joy inseparably.

Wotan, just in time, lets himself be warned by his own deeper intuition, in the person of Erda the Earth Mother (Ex. 19, iii), not to hold onto the ring for his own willful uses, since without it, the giants will not let Freia return. She does return, and the joy of life with her, as the stage lights up and the music glows. But to the grim motive of Alberich's curse, one giant kills the other for possession of the ring. From a sudden orchestral storm, a rainbow bridge arches across the Rhine, and the gods line up to cross to Valhalla, whose solid motive (Ex. 19, xvii) depicts the many years of prosperous achievement still ahead of them, and all the valid side of Wotan's authority. And this motive, too, is a diatonic version of that most central musical image, the motive of the ring. Suddenly there floats up, from the hidden valley below, the creamy harmony and timeless enchantment of the Rhine maidens (Ex. 19, xiii), catching at our hearts once more with nostalgic longing; for we are not only spirit and reason but flesh and instinct too, and while we cannot return to nature we must not lose touch with her. To be human is to be ambivalent, and pulled two ways. But now the gods form up again with a proud gesture, and to the sound of many harps above the warm brass of the Valhalla motive, they pass over into their impressive fortress.

*Die Walküre* ("The Valkyries") opens with a grander storm, in the long tradition through Gluck's *Iphigenia in Tauris*, Verdi's *Otello*, and others. Such storms are apt to hint at an inner rather than an outer turbulence. An exhausted and weaponless hero, Siegmund, takes refuge in a forest dwelling, and the mistress of it, Sieglinda, brings him first water to drink, and then mead, to music in such companionable counterpoint (Ex. 19, xi) that it seems like mutual recognition—as indeed it proves to be—and undoubtedly is mutual love. The master of the house, Hunding, arrives to a motive so pounding and sinister that we know him for an enemy; over supper, he proves to be a kinsman of those very enemies of Siegmund who have already broken his weapons although not his courage. Sieglinda disposes of Hunding with a sleeping potion, and comes back to unravel with Siegmund a complex story of violent separation, and of his homeless wanderings and her forced marriage, until they know each other for twin brother and sister, long parted and now impetuously in love. With a wonderful gesture of inspired stagecraft, the great door swings open to the clear moonlight outside—for both outwardly and inwardly, the spring has come. The music of the entire act has been in astonishingly free and eloquent arioso, within an orchestral sonority never obtrusive but constantly expressive. Now the hero soars virtually into aria as he welcomes the spring within their radiant hearts. We and he have already caught glimpses, though he has not yet seen what they are, of a sword (Ex. 19, xx) thrust into the roof tree (as she tells him now) by Wotan (Ex. 19, xvii) in disguise at her forced wedding, which no hero has yet been strong enough to pull out again. Siegfried pulls it out, and is no longer weaponless. He sings of his "yearning love"—but also, with typically mythological premonition, of "death"; and the music to which he sings is that same nobly resigned (Ex. 19, vi) to which long ago Alberich renounced love—of a sort. The common element seems to be the courageous acceptance of what life is actually bringing, which unavoidably extends to what life is taking away. Siegmund and Sieglinda are going, not into escapist fantasies, but right into life, *accepting* all the possible consequences of their actions: consequences which do in fact include his death almost at once and hers some nine months afterward. At the height of their triumphant love music, the curtain comes down upon their impending union.

But in Act II, Fricka, Wotan's consort and here presented as the guardian of conventional morality, wants Siegmund to die in punishment for his double offense: the adultery and the incest. Now Wotan has fathered Siegmund with the very intention that he should be a free hero, able to cut his way through a whole series of inhibiting compacts and conventions which Wotan dare not dishonor in his own person. And why does he not dare? Because in part of himself he has accepted Fricka's view that to bring law and order and social institutions such as marriage into disrepute would undermine his own willful authority. He has not yet seen that this is the wrong kind of authority anyhow, since it makes him the prisoner of his own inhibitions, and the enemy of his own true self. He is probably both willful and inhibited largely through having internalized a domineering, puritanical, and altogether too Fricka-like mother-image; for when he tells Fricka now that the gods have need of a free hero who does not even know that he is helping them, and whom they have not helped, Fricka deflates him at once with the single dry comment: "Then do not help him now; take back the sword." The sword is a symbol for manhood, and sounds like it (Ex. 19, xx). But manhood is a quality which can only be truly forged by growing independent of one's father. Because Wotan fathered Siegmund to set Wotan free, Siegmund is not the free hero who could set Wotan free. Siegmund's courage is the courage that Wotan breathed into him. Siegmund's sword is the sword that Wotan left for him. Siegmund is Wotan himself at one remove. And so Wotan agrees miserably to let Siegmund die.

We are altogether on the side of the young lovers. In the ordinary world outside, this could hardly happen, because literal incest would imply a pathological situation and not a romantic one. But this is incest in a myth, and at some level of our intuitions we seem to pick up the profoundest sense of its symbolical rightness. The mating of twins is an archetypal image for the reconciliation of our own inner components of masculinity and femininity. Mythology is full of it, from Isis and Osiris onward. We do a sort of double take. When Vaughan Williams[3] first heard the love music (e.g. as in Ex. 19, xii–b) in Act I, he "experienced no surprise, but rather that strange certainty that I had heard it all before," that "recognition as of meeting an old friend which comes to all of us in the face of great artistic experiences." What we recognize is the underlying archetype; and because we recognize the archetype, we can also accept at face value the young lovers who are standing in for it so movingly. But Fricka cannot, because the aspect of archetypal femininity which she represents is negative—as Goethe might have (but did not) put it, the eternal nagging. The part of Wotan which is not subject to Fricka's nagging, on the other hand, and which now to our sorrow must die in Siegmund's person, will be reborn more effectively in Siegfried; and this cycle of death and rebirth is another commonplace of mythological imagery which perhaps helps us to feel that the tragedy, although full of bitter grief, is not hopeless. Above all, it is not meaningless.

Wotan's favorite daughter, the Valkyrie or War Maiden Brynhilda, persuades him to confide in her because, as she says herself, she is a part of him; but having previously instructed her to give Siegmund the victory over Hunding, he now to her dismay reverses this. She appears ominously to the doomed hero, but is so moved by his courageous refusal to accept the consolations of Valhalla, since he may not bring Sieglinda with him, that she changes sides. In the battle which swiftly follows, Brynhilda shields Siegmund; Wotan splinters Siegmund's sword on his spear; Siegmund falls defenseless to Hunding's thrust; Hunding falls to a mere contemptuous glance from Wotan. It is all depicted in the music with shattering violence, and not a measure to spare. Brynhilda collects the pieces of the sword, and persuades Sieglinda to escape by telling her that she now carries a hero's seed—Siegfried, as the music (Ex. 19, xix–b) tells us.

In Act III, the "Ride of the Valkyries" sets a mood of demonic energy, on which Wotan enters in an evil temper, telling Brynhilda that she has passed sentence on herself by cutting herself off from him, thus ceasing to be a war maiden and becoming "merely herself"—as if there were anything she could more valuably become. She has indeed become more of a real woman in her own right, and less of an archetypal father's daughter, by standing up to him; but it is Wotan who is actually cutting himself off, projecting his own bitterness by getting angry with her instead of accepting the consequences for himself of his own painful decision. She tells him quietly that in causing Siegfried to die, it was he who was being false to his own true self; and she recalls that it was he who planted in her the love for his children which she obeyed in disobeying him. He flares out that since she thinks love's desire is so lightly to be gained, she shall lie asleep on the mountain to be lightly possessed by the first man who finds her. Not by a weakling, she beseeches; and she adds pointedly that there are no weaklings in Wotan's race. But he has just destroyed his own race! Not so; Sieglinda is pregnant, and has moreover the pieces of the broken sword. Wotan instantly repudiates his unborn grandson; but when with sudden inspiration Brynhilda asks to be surrounded with flames which no one but a free hero will dare to pass, their thoughts become one thought, to which the music (Ex. 19, xix–b) again puts the name of Siegfried. It is their great moment of reconciliation. He lets go his father's authority over Brynhilda, and together with it his own stubborn willfulness, to that same noble and accepting music (Ex. 19, vi–a) to which Alberich long ago and Siegmund more recently accepted the full consequences of being what they truly are. With a last willful gesture of his spear (Ex. 19, x–a), Wotan calls up the magic fire; and the flicker and the roar of it blend into the slow drift of the magic sleep (Ex. 19, xiv–c). Before the flames are passed through and the sleeper awakes (in the next opera, *Siegfried*), a further growth of character will have been inwardly prepared. That is the meaning of the magic sleep.

*Siegfried* opens with a brooding motive (Ex. 19, xvi–a) which seems new, but is only a condensed version of the ring's motive (Ex. 19, xv), as Alberich's weaker brother Mime (Ex. 19, ix–a) plots to get back the ring—now guarded with the rest of the unused treasure by the dragon into which the giant Fafner has turned himself. Mime has brought up young Siegfried, whose mother Sieglinda died in giving birth to him, and now he is trying to forge a sword strong enough for Siegfried to kill the dragon with; but Siegfried smashes it contemptuously on the anvil, and goes off furiously. An older and wiser Wotan comes in, now known as the Wanderer; and in a very mythological exchange of questions, he refers to his old enemy as "black Alberich" and to *himself* as "light Alberich," thus in so many words treating the two of them as opposite aspects of the same character. He also informs Mime that the sword needed for killing Fafner can only be forged by him "who knows not fear," and that to him, Mime's head shall pay forfeit. It is one of Siegfried's immaturities that he does not yet know fear; but now to our relief he sets about forging the fragments of his father's sword for himself, the radical way, by filing them, melting them, and casting them again. His forging song is crude but powerful; he is forging his own manhood, not merely Wotan's at a second remove. He tests his sword by splitting the anvil sensationally down the middle.

In Act II, Wotan refuses to treat Alberich any longer as his enemy, convinced as he now is that life itself has got the matter well in hand. Siegfried muses about his unknown mother (Ex. 19, xii–b), of whom the very birds of the forest seem to be trying to talk to him. Their motive (Ex. 19, xiv–b) is a variant of the Rhine maidens' motive (Ex. 19, xiv–a), as if there may be some danger of his getting drawn back by these nostalgic longings for the mother he never saw; but suddenly he blows on his horn in the traditional fairy-tale challenge, and out comes Fafner the dragon, representing—as such monsters do—the obstructive aspects of those same regressive fantasies whose seductive aspect Siegfried has just experienced in his tender musings.[4] He kills the dragon manfully, and a drop of its burning blood which he licks from his hand teaches him the speech of the birds. One of them warns him to listen to the murder in Mime's heart and not the flattery which he tries to utter. After disposing of the little scoundrel, Siegfried, with the ring on his finger, follows his forest bird toward Brynhilda's mountain; for having overcome the fantasy, he is ready for the true voice of nature. On his way, in Act III, he encounters Wotan, who does him the service of interposing his spear so that Siegfried can also experience and overcome the forbidding aspect of the father's authority; he cuts it through with his sword, thus confirming in both their best interests the end of Wotan's willfulness. The flames blaze up like the burning energy of life, and there on the other side of them Siegfried finds Brynhilda, and learns at last to know fear. It is his first sight of a woman. There is no force more formidable than the eternal feminine; and it is with true courage, now, that he kisses her awake. To a spacious pair of chords in mediant relationship she greets the sun, the light, the radiant day. His greeting is "Hail to thee, mother, who gave me birth"; she, however, answers: "If I have your holy love, I am your own self; what you do not know, I know for you; yet my knowledge comes only from my loving you," by which she seems to mean that as an archetypal image, she is part of him, but that as a woman, she has the kind of intuitions about him which a loving woman may. The flames are now burning in her blood as well as his, and she too learns what it is to fear. But they are right to let instinct take them over now; and for the second time in the *Ring,* the curtain comes down not one moment too soon on love's imminent consummation.

*Die Götterdämmerung* ("The Twilight of the Gods") opens with the two spacious chords in mediant relationship, not, however, in bright C major as they were for Brynhilda's return to consciousness and light, but in veiled C flat major for three grisly old Norns or fates in the dark wood at the world's end, where they spin their rope of destiny, and as they spin it, sing that which they spin. The light and the dark are polar opposites—the same essence in contrary tonalities—as Goethe so often insisted. But for all their archaic premonitions, the Norns can make little of the approaching crisis, and when in token of their confusion the rope breaks, they descend to their sleeping Earth-Mother. A wonderful orchestral daybreak brings on Siegfried and Brynhilda, radiant with genuine happiness, but convinced that Siegfried should now seek further adventures in the great world outside. He gives her the ring, in token of the value he sets on her; she gives him her horse, which is commonly a symbol for natural instinct. She waves him out of sight to that gloriously extroverted orchestral interlude known as "Siegfried's Journey to the Rhine." He is there received by Hagen, whom Alberich has fathered lovelessly on a mortal woman, and by Hagen's half-brother and half-sister, the chivalric but weak Gunther and the beautiful but vulnerable Gutruna. In a plot to get back the ring, Hagen has Gutruna give Siegfried a magic potion to make him forget Brynhilda and his own true self, and desire the woman he next sees: Gutruna, in fact. The potion seems symbolical of that commonest of male delusions: that each new attractive woman holds irresistible value. She may indeed have value; but she is only irresistible because she carries for the time the man's projections of his own inner femininity. By the power of another symbol of wishful thinking and split personality, Tarnhelm the magic helmet, Siegfried is at once sent off, in the disguise and (what is worse) the personality of Gunther, to carry his own Brynhilda away through her protecting flames for Gunther to marry. Even the power of the ring as she holds it up against him cannot avert the course of the drama, which suggests that it is not meant to be averted but worked through to its own due conclusion. He pulls the ring from her finger, and her strength is overborn.

As if in some dream or waking vision, Hagen is urged on by Alberich to get back the ring, with such dark longing in words and music that once again we feel some shift in our sympathy which intensifies the balance of the drama. Siegfried returns instantly by Tarnhelm; Gunther and Brynhilda a little later by boat, to the noisy acclaim of a full grand-opera chorus of vassals—a welcome enough relief after so much concentrated and baleful music drama. And Siegfried greets Brynhilda politely, as a perfect stranger—with their precious ring now clearly visible again on his own finger. She denounces him in honest fury; he protests his innocence as honestly, so far as he knows, since he is still possessed by the schizoid amnesia for which the magic potion seems to stand. Their opposing oaths on Hagen's spear are still grand opera, and so is the dark conspiracy to plot Siegfried's death in which Hagen soon involves her, and also Gunther (more reluctantly); upon which with sudden brightness there enters the bridal procession of Siegfried and Gutruna. There are only a few measures of sustained orchestral glory before the curtain falls; but when imaginatively produced and tensely conducted, it is one of the most moving strokes of dramatic irony in all opera.

The glad sound of horns tells us in the introduction to Act III that the hunt is up, and the rippling arpeggios bring us to the Rhine as they did so long before at the start of *Rhinegold*—but we see the surface of the great river now, and the three Rhine maidens swimming and singing to a lilting flow of creamy six-three harmonies till once more the world seems as nothing, and our conscious human state but a poor reward for such relinquished ecstasy. Siegfried has lost his party. The Rhine maidens entice and tease and cajole him to give them back their gold, in the shape of the ring, which he is about to toss to them quite casually when one of them warns him that if he does not, he will die this day, upon which he grows as suddenly obstinate. As they plunge out of sight, it occurs to him that but for the thought of Gutruna he might have taken advantage of one of the pretty creatures—but that he thought of Gutruna at all under such tempting circumstances already argues a certain improvement on the unconsciousness which once shut out Brynhilda, and still does.

The hunting party finds him, and Hagen leads him on into telling the story of his life. We hear again in the same words and music all that brought him . . . brought him—he cannot remember where, until Hagen slips into his wine an antidote which brings him back to himself in the last rapt moments of his life; and we may realize with something of a shock that this villain, too, is showing an archetypal ambivalence by acting as the instigator of a symbolical transformation. "Straightway I pressed through the fire," sings Siegfried, "and found her asleep, and woke her with a kiss—ah, then like the fire enfolded me Brynhilda's arms!" We are with him on that distant mountain, and have hardly noticed the growing consternation of the vassals until Gunther cries out "What do I hear?" Hagen spears Siegfried from behind; but as he dies we hear again that spacious C major harmony to which Brynhilda first opened her eyes to his kiss. He sings that he kisses her awake again, and that "those eyes are open now forever." So in a symbolical sense are Siegfried's eyes; for as she told him then, she is himself, and as archetypal images they are due for reconciliation. But as characters, they have met with tragedy, which the great Funeral March now brings home to us so that we experience in full our grief and our shock—the only way in which great grief can be lived through to eventual healing.

When the dead Siegfried is brought back to the hall, Gutruna knows at once that this was no hunting accident. Hagen makes for the ring, and kills Gunther when he claims it for Gutruna's dower. Hagen again stretches out to grasp it, but recoils as the murdered man raises his arm in the legendary miracle of denunciation. And the motive which cuts through the music here is, unexpectedly, not the motive of the ring (Ex. 19, xv) but the motive of the sword (Ex. 19, xx), still the symbol of manhood, which at this moment of seeming defeat triumphs over all that is darkest in our complex natures. As if in answer, Brynhilda comes forward, in her own right mind again, and now in full possession of the facts. Gutruna, herself singing "my eyes are opened," sinks to the ground. Already Brynhilda seems to see light pouring from Siegfried's funeral pyre. She calls to her horse: "Does the fire's light which is Siegfried's light draw you to it too?"—as if to imply that instinct is not to be left behind in all this fine growth of character. And into the flames she rides. As the entire hall takes fire and falls in ruin, the modulations in the harmony range far and wide, but with a profound purposefulness which is certainly no mere collapse. The ring, now on Brynhilda's finger, is purged by the fire and cleansed by the overflowing waters of the Rhine, recalling symbolically the ordeal by fire and water at the end of *The Magic Flute*. Ruin on earth spreads to ruin in the sky as the flames take hold of Valhalla, seen far away with Wotan and his old order waiting acceptingly for whatever new order the transforming fire may bring. The Rhine maidens swim up to take back their ring, and to pull down Hagen when he tries to stop them, though Alberich no doubt survives to represent that force of darkness which is also part of life. The last motive to be heard is a soaring theme which at its rare appearances (for example, in connection with Sieglinda's pregnancy) has to do with rebirth (Ex. 19, xxi). The symbolism of *The Ring* is basically rebirth symbolism; and rebirth in ordinary human terms means growth of character.

EXAMPLE 19    Wagner, *Der Ring des Nibelungen*, leading motives and their connections.

i.      The depths of the Rhine

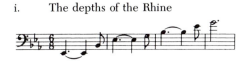

ii.     The first stirrings (version of i)

iii.    Erda as native intuition (version of ii)

iv.     Twilight of the gods as the end of the cycle (inversion of iii)

v.      Acceptance of destiny (version of iv)

vi.    Renunciation, (a) Woglinde; (b) Alberich

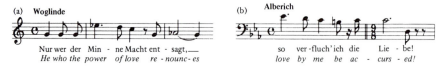

(a) Woglinde

Nur wer der Min - ne Macht ent - sagt,—
*He who the power of love re - nounc-es*

(b) Alberich

so    ver -fluch' ich die    Lie - be!
*love by me be ac - curs - ed!*

vii.    Grief as such (the falling semitone of vi)

Alberich

We - he!    ach we - he!
*Woe's me!    ah, woe's me!*

viii.    Destiny (a) as such; (b) symphonically extended to include the idea of resigned
       relinquishment (developments of vii)

(a)                                    (b)

ix.    (a) Mime's petty will frustrated (version of vii); (b) Wotan's mighty will frustrated
       (extension of vii)

(a)                    (b)

x.    (a) The spear as Wotan's willfulness (variant of ix–a); (b) Siegmund as Wotan's son
       and proxy (variant of x–a)

(a)                                    (b)

xi.     Sieglinda (derivative of end of x–b) in contrapuntal combination with Siegmund's x–b

xii.     Agitation (a) as such; (b) softened to tenderness (extensions of vii)

xiii.     The siren call of the Rhine maidens (major version of vii)

xiv.     (a) The Rhine maidens as the ambivalent call of nature; (b) the first bird as a positive call of nature; (c) return to nature in Brynhilda's magic sleep (extensions of xiii)

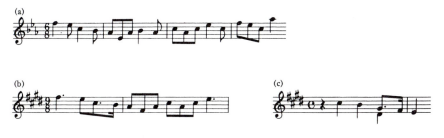

xv.     The Ring as symbol for the ambivalent force of life (a much modified derivative of ii)

xvi.     (a) Mime's brooding; (b) Alberich's hatred; (c) Alberich's curse (elements from xv)

(c)     Alberich

Wie durch Fluch    er    mir    ge - rieth,    ver - flucht    sei    die - ser    Ring!
*As    by    curse    it    came    to    me,    ac - curs    -    ed    be    the    ring!*

xvii.     Valhalla and the positive aspect of Wotan's authority (a diatonic variant of xv)

xviii.     The unforged gold as undeveloped potential (derived from i)

xix.    (a) Siegfried's heroic horn call; (b) the same motive symphonically developed (related to xviii)

xx.    The sword standing for true manhood (derived from i and related to xviii)

xxi.    "Redemption," especially by "rebirth" as a result of accepting "destiny" (a transformed variant of viii–a)

Wagner's symbolism is at its most complicated in this immense four-part work, the longest in the history of opera. So, too, is the tight network of interweaving themes by which he gave the symbolism such detailed musical expression. Both these aspects are examples of the romantic imagination at its fullest development, and both can be traced, if the reader wishes, at much greater length.[5] The complexity is not disturbing to us in the theater, however, since the hidden meanings are carried along by images and situations which are simple in themselves, dramatically convincing, and of the most direct human feeling. It is a heavily loaded masterpiece, as romantic masterpieces were apt to be. But we have always to remember that symbols which take some time to discuss in words may get across to our intuitions with an immediate impact. One of the assets of opera is its ability to do this on so many channels of communication simultaneously: the poetry, the music, and the dramatic staging. On all these channels, Wagner's *Ring* adds up to a great experience for anyone who has the temperament to go along with the abundant flow of his invention.

# Night and Day

*Tristan und Isolde* ("Tristan and Isolda") was composed from 1857 to 1859 (when Wagner had set aside *The Ring* as too problematical) and proved so problematical itself that it was not performed until 1865 in Munich, after the tide in Wagner's affairs had turned through the powerful patronage of Ludwig II of Bavaria. The text is a courageous confrontation of darkness, brought to a creative resolution. The score comes the nearest of Wagner's operas to Schopenhauer's view[6] that "music speaks of the essence" while "the libretto" should remain "subservient." So continuous is the construction and so dissolved is the harmony of *Tristan* that it precipitated that "romantic crisis of tonality" from which derived most of the modern music of the next three-quarters of a century.[7] The prelude begins with a characteristic and for long controversial phrase (Ex. 20a), of which the chromatic ambivalence and uneasy longing are maintained with extraordinary intensity and consistency throughout this protracted opera. The curtain rises on shipboard, as Tristan brings Isolda from Ireland to be the young bride of his old uncle and father by adoption, King Mark of Cornwall. But behind this outwardly honorable situation, a very curious and disquieting background is gradually revealed. Tristan has previously been healed by Isolda of a wound given him by her betrothed, Morold, whom he himself had killed. The reason why Isolda healed Tristan instead of killing him in revenge was that their eyes met, and she could not. But now Tristan has come to fetch her, not for himself, but for his adoptive father. Her fury is bitter and unconcealed. His embarassment is masked by his show of honor; but he feels so guilty underneath, and so oppressed by the sense of having put himself into an utterly false position, that when she invites him to share a drink which they both believe to be poisoned, he accepts. However, her serving maid Brangaena has substituted a love potion, symbolizing not the start of their fatal passion, but simply the moment of truth at which it breaks through uncontrollably into awareness.

We hear the full force of this passion in the orchestral introduction to Act II. Melot, pretending to be Tristan's friend, has arranged a night hunt from which King Mark can unexpectedly return to test the rumors of Isolda's adultery. The horns of the hunt, heard off stage, grow more distant, and are presently muted for the most romantic of fanfares (Ex. 20b, p. 161), their poignant dominant ninths calling up the magical stillness of the warm night, and presently yielding to the mounting ecstasy in the orchestra as Isolda, refusing to be warned by Brangaena's fears, puts out the torch and waves her scarf to signal Tristan to her. He comes, and their yearning glows out at first more plainly from the music than from their almost incoherent words. But soon they are singing of the hateful day and the daylight illusions to which Isolda attributes Tristan's betrayal in claiming her with false honor for King Mark, instead of with true honesty for himself: "the daylight sun of worldly honor," as he at once disparagingly agrees. But this is a rationalization; the truth proves to be much more deeply hidden. They settle into their wonderful love duet. Mark presently surprises them, and in his long and bewildered monologue reveals that he would never have taken Isolda, nor a

*Tristan und Isolde*, Act I. The Salzburg Easter Festival, Austria.

second wife at all, if Tristan as his adopted son had not so strongly urged her upon him. So it was Tristan himself who set up this disastrous situation by which his intrinsically legitimate love for Isolda became not only illegitimate and adulterous, but a sort of token incest. In real shame, now, Tristan asks Isolda if she will follow him to that dark land—and he means the land of death—where his mother went in giving birth to him. We thus learn of a childhood bereavement for which it might well have been tempting for Tristan to compensate unconsciously by putting Isolda into a mother's place. Seeking death, Tristan opens his guard to Melot's sword, and falls grievously wounded.

In Act III, faithful Kurwenal has brought Tristan home to safety and sent for Isolda to heal again his desperate wound. The doleful tune (it is usually given to the English horn) played by the shepherd who is watching the empty sea for Isolda's ship calls up in Tristan two further associations with his childhood. He remembers hearing it when they told him of his father's death in battle, and also when they told him of his mother's death in childbirth. The second bereavement thus brought to our notice, when he lost his father, must have done yet worse damage to his growing personality through following on the first bereavement, when he lost his mother. Distraught and intermittently delirious as he now is, Tristan is showing the greatest courage, as Joseph Kerman first perceptively observed,[8] in letting himself associate these profound childhood hurts with his adult experiences of being wounded by Morold, and healed by Isolda; of repressing his own passion for Isolda, and giving her instead to Mark; of being overwhelmed by that repressed passion, and atoning for it by letting himself be wounded again. It is normal for children to experience jealousy and desire in relation to their parents, and to have to work through guilty fantasies in consequence; but this is harder for children who have been prematurely bereaved, because their guilt seems to be catastrophically confirmed by their obscure fear that their own hostile moods may have been the cause of death. If Tristan has transferred to Mark the guilt toward the father, and to Isolda the forbidden fascination of the mother, then we can understand his feeling compelled to make unconscious reparation. He certainly knows now that he has brought this fearful punishment on himself. "The terrible potion which acquainted me with pain, I myself brewed! From father's suffering and mother's woe"—so he spells it out to himself—"I have prepared the poison of the drink." This is the bitter truth which alone, at this late stage, can be the healing truth. It makes so violent an impact that it pushes him back at first into his delirium. But when the shepherd changes to a joyful tune, Tristan rises to greet, and no longer to resent, the sun and the light of day. As if in reckless repudiation of any further concealment, he tears the bandages from his wound. Isolda runs in; Tristan sinks dying into her arms. Kurwenal desperately fights off the crew of a second ship, killing and being killed by Melot, and just finding the strength to drag himself to Tristan's side—as faithful in death as he had been in life. But Brangaena has told Mark about the love potion, and was bringing him not in enmity but in reconciliation. Mark's grief now is sadder then ever.

Then, like Brynhilda at the end of *Götterdämmerung*, Isolda takes over. We are brought back to the music of the glorious love scene of Act II, as the long arch of Isolda's "love-death" soars above the glowing orchestra, and she seems to see Tristan opening his smiling eyes to sink with her through waves of oblivion. Taken at face value, this is the somewhat pessimistic language of Nirvana, borrowed by Wagner through Schopenhauer. But Wagner himself was never really pessimistic, and he was temperamentally much more interested in transformation than in any literal oblivion. The image of the encompassing waves recalls the end of *The Flying Dutchman*, and both the beginning and the end of *The Ring;* it is traditionally a rebirth symbol. Wagner's interest in redemptions and renunciations and deaths as transfigurations makes good practical sense only in the context of his need to work out symbolically the problems of his own development. The idea of rebirth always carries some implication of a new start through growth of character. The symbolism in *Tristan* may be dark, but it is not gloomy; the music may be yearning, but it is not depressing. The astonishing score of *Tristan* marks the great divide of nineteenth-century romantic opera.

That Wagner worked something dark out of his system and made of it a splendid masterpiece in *Tristan* seems to be confirmed by the bright contrast next afforded by *Die Meistersinger von Nürnberg* ("The Mastersingers of Nuremberg"), performed in Munich in 1868. The poem as first sketched in 1845 was an amusing but relatively insignificant and unfeeling comedy. As reworked and finished by 1862, it is Wagner's mellowest libretto, in which Hans Sachs has become the real hero (as Wotan is in *The Ring*): a spokesman of ripe wisdom

EXAMPLE 20    Wagner, *Tristan und Isolde*, (a) the "love potion" motive which starts the overture; (b) the horns off stage in the first scene of Act II; (c) Kurwenal early in Act III tells Tristan how he brought him home; (d) the love motive from Act II in its recapitulation for Isolda's "love-death" (*Liebestod*) at the end of Act III.

and accepting philosophy in remarkable contrast to Wagner's own troubled fortunes and mental agitation at the time. The music was composed from 1862 to 1867, and is the warmest and serenest of all his scores. This is, in fact, a particularly interesting example of a great artist's power to compensate for instabilities in his ordinary living by sureness in his creative work, and fully confirms Wagner's own premonition, when he started composing *Rhinegold*, that life would essentially flow for him not through outward but through inward channels.

The overture, as often in Wagner, anticipates his drama in orchestral outline, while following the basic pattern of sonata form. A very grand motive of some length and substance suggests the guild of the Mastersingers themselves, and a very lyrical sequel, like a second subject, contrasts the human love story whose impact upon their worthy conventionality, as it begins to unfold in the first act, will prove in the end so valuable for either side. This more or less formal exposition leads to a development section in which a diminution of the Master-singers' motive indicates their sprightly apprentices; these are much to the forefront in the second act, which their turbulence climaxes. There follows an abbreviated and modified recapitulation, which foreshadows the eventual reso-lution of all the conflicts by combining three of the main themes in one of those relaxed but resourceful passages of simultaneous counterpoint which are so characteristic a feature of Wagner's mature technique.

The curtain goes up on a stroke of musical and theatrical inspiration. We are in a great church, and the congregation is singing a chorale, catching us up on the instant into the quiet faith which unites this small but prosperous German middle-class community of Nuremburg, and upholds its very real virtues. No doubt it is also a little pompous and self-satisfied, and indeed we have heard these bourgeois weaknesses in the overture, together with the solid honesty and practical good sense which go with them. But it is a community. The orchestra, however, intersperses the feelings of a very romantic individual, young Walther of Stolzing, a visiting knight, poet and singer. He keeps catching the responsive glances of Eva, daughter of a leading citizen, Pogner. Still younger as she is, she cleverly makes sure of a few private words with him. It soon reaches his ears and ours that her hand is to be the prize next day in a contest of song. And then and there, a preliminary trial is held in which he is courteously encouraged to enter. But the Marker, Beckmesser, who is the dry and no longer so young town clerk, fails Walther with a squeaky chalk mark on his slate for every breach of the appointed rules, until there is no more room on the slate for any further bad marks. Now this Beckmesser, unsuitable as it may appear, is himself a candidate for the radiant prize; and whatever else he may or may not know, he does know the rules. There is one master present, however, who hears the same crude faults, but also hears a certain fresh vitality which, if it could be tactfully assimilated and adjusted to the real (not pedantic) principles of form and order, would be exactly what the solid traditions of this admirable little community need to offset its undoubted tendency toward complacency—and we somehow know that he is not just thinking of their musical style, but also of their lifestyle.

This is Hans Sachs, the cobbler, a man in middle years, who would like to marry Eva himself (and he has certainly the skill and inspiration to excel in the contest) were it not that he knows at heart that she should have a younger husband—Walther, as he now begins to suspect, ruefully enough; but it is this situation which is going to be his own test of character.

In Act II, Walther and Eva, despairing of lawful success, are on the point of eloping, when Sachs stops them, for their own benefit, by letting the light fall on them from his window. Beckmesser also arrives to serenade Eva, at whose window he thinks he sees her; but it is actually her maid-servant Magdalena, who has changed clothes with Eva to deceive him and help the young couple to escape notice. As he tunes up with a perfectly correct yet somehow ridiculous prelude on his lute, and begins his poor little song, Sachs, now cobbling right at his doorway, strikes up with his hammer—for every mistake (and Beckmesser is getting nervous now) a stroke. Their increasingly crazy counterpoint (mingled with impetuous phrases from the concealed lovers) brings heads peering out of windows; Sachs' hasty young apprentice, David, seeing his beloved Magdalena being serenaded (though in error) by Beckmesser, rushes out to attack him, followed by other apprentices until a noisy and confused street battle results. Walther draws his sword to escape with Eva, but Sachs pulls him firmly into his own house, and she is quietly drawn indoors by her father. The street empties as quickly as it had filled; the old nightwatchman blows his ancient horn and sings his simple song in the sudden moonlit quiet—one of those inspired moments which only opera can achieve; and the curtain falls.

In Act III, Sachs reflects in his famous monologue (Ex. 21b) on that streak of madness, that fatal flaw of blind unconsciousness, which runs through human nature and sets men fighting without knowing the reason. He reflects, too, on his own lonely state, which Eva might have shared if Walther had not come along. But when Walther enters full of a dream he has just had, Sachs writes it down for him and helps him to shape it into a song fit to win him the contest, and Eva with it. The stage empties, and Beckmesser, much the worse for his beating, finds the song and pockets it with the ink still wet. Sachs catches him in the act—and gives him the song, knowing that he can only make a bungle of it. Eva consults Sachs ostensibly about her shoe, but really about her heart; for when Walther comes back, her feelings are plain to read on her face. He sings a further stanza of his dream song; she weeps, her head on Sachs's shoulder, but her eyes on Walther. She thanks Sachs for helping her to grow wise, and tells him that she would have married him if her heart left her any choice; he answers that he knows the tale of Tristan and Isolda, and does not want to end up like King Mark—while a fragment of *Tristan* in the music (compare Ex. 20a) shows up by a momentary darkness the immense distance which separates this complementary pair of operas. And here to balance the human picture come David and his Magdalena, the simple couple set as so often against the complex couple. Sachs makes David his journeyman with a cuff on the ear; and to bless Walther's new "morning dream's melody" a great quintet builds up, one of Wagner's rare ensembles and a very high point in the opera.

Outside the town, the guilds arrive with processions and ballet to build up a fine scene of grand opera, which the drama justifies; and last comes the master-singers' guild, whereupon the terms of the contest are announced. Beckmesser fails ludicrously to sing Walther's new song, and is laughed, not too unkindly, off the podium. Walther sings it joyously, with further elaborations on what we heard before (Ex. 21c). He sings first of the morning sunlight and the golden tree of life, with Eva radiant in his poet's dream of Paradise; next of the evening starlight and the fountain of inspiration, with Eva as the Muse in his dream of Parnassus; and then of waking to find woman and muse in one, and of winning both Paradise and Parnassus by his song. And win he does, by the joint acclaim of masters and populace. As his muse, Eva crowns him with the traditional laurel wreath once sanctified by Apollo's Dafne. As his bride, she leads him to her father Pogner, who gives the young couple his blessing—not unmixed with relief at the happy outcome of his somewhat rash promise to make her the prize. But Walther, still a little moody over his previous rejection, spurns the master's chain. It is the crucial conflict; and Sachs resolves it in a long arioso of extraordinary vocal and orchestral eloquence which sums up the purpose of the opera: to reconcile the heart's inspiration and the head's ordering. Sachs thereby speaks, and so yet more strongly have his actions spoken, for that mature acceptance of life which is itself a reconciliation. Eva confirms this sense of reconciliation by a gesture so unexpected, yet so right, that it brings to a sudden focus the great final scene, with its flood of warm sound, its contrapuntal virtuosity, and above all its abounding feeling. Taking the wreath from Walther's head, and coming up unseen from behind, she crowns Sachs as the master of them all, the spokesman for their vital principle. It is his moment of reward: he is deeply moved, and so are we. Walther accepts the chain from him with understanding now; and on a chorus of general rejoicing, the curtain falls.

EXAMPLE 21    Wagner, *Die Meistersinger von Nürnberg*, (a) the motive of the master-singers which opens the opera; (b) Sachs' sad monologue which opens Act III; (c) Walther's prize song in its final form for the contest in Act III.

(b) Sachs

Wahn! Wahn!  Ue - ber-all  Wahn!
*Mad! Mad!  Ev - ery-where mad!*

(c) Walther

Mor - gen - licht  leuch - tend__  in__  ro  -  si - gem  Schein
*Morn - ing - time  shin - ing__  with__  ros  -  y__  light*

At the end comes *Parsifal*, composed from 1877 to 1882, and performed at Bayreuth in 1882. The poetry is more relaxed than before, ranging all the way from easy narrative to intense emotion; it is partly in free verse and partly in regular meter, at times rhyming but most often not. The music follows this varied poetic line with an equal boldness and adaptability, ranging from quietly flowing arioso with almost the quality of accompanied recitative, on the one hand, to violently leaping melodies of powerful agitation, on the other hand. The harmony, too, is sometimes quiet and solemn, sometimes audaciously harsh and exacerbated. On the whole, the pulse of the music is slow, to correspond with the ritual broadness of the action; yet some of the harmonic progressions are so compressed that their tonality is only just to be followed by rapid adjustments of the mind. As music drama, *Parsifal* certainly goes the limit; but it can give an experience which justifies the severe demands it makes on everyone concerned—the audience included.

The prelude is built on a musical subject (Ex. 22) which throughout the opera is associated with the Holy Grail. This is the central symbol, as the ring is in *The Ring*; next to it in importance is a spear, which corresponds in importance to the sword in *The Ring*. The Grail is the cup from which Christ drank at the Last Supper, and which also caught the blood from his wound on the cross; and this Grail became one of medieval Christendom's great symbols for the feminine principle. The spear is that which wounded Christ, and (like the sword) has to do with the masculine principle. In the course of Act I, we learn from an old knight of the Grail, Gurnemanz, that the leader Amfortas was seduced by a certain archetypal enchantress, Kundry, who had brought on herself a doom somewhat like that of the Flying Dutchman; for she laughed at Christ on the cross, and has been around ever since, alternatively seeking redemption and functioning as a character-testing temptation to those who serve the Grail. The early-thirteenth-century *Parzival* of Wolfram von Eschenbach, Wagner's chief source for the legend, explains that "he who would to the Grail do service, he shall woman's love forswear."[9] But since the knights of the Grail do not have to be celibate (Parsifal himself became the father of Lohengrin, who became—on terms—the husband of Elsa), it seems once again not to be real love so much as love's compulsive counterfeit that needs to be forsworn.[10] It was that unmanning temptation which some time ago seduced Amfortas, with the result that he was robbed of the spear, and wounded with it, by the enchanter Klingsor, himself a fallen knight of the Grail who had been a previous victim to the same temptation. And this wound can only be healed by a touch from the spear which made it, and which in turn is only to be recovered by an innocent champion, a "pure fool," who is expected (too optimistically as it turns out) to understand what is required of him by simple unspoiled intuition.

Young Parsifal now wanders on, having just shot down one of the Grail castle's wild swans. Gurnemanz immediately forms the highest hopes of him, though he rebukes him for this seemingly thoughtless and destructive act. In fact, Kundry, who has second sight, announces that his mother at that very moment died of a broken heart; and since this mother had gone to great lengths to keep Parsifal from all contact with the world, that passing shot may have been symbolically the beginning of his growing up to be himself. His father had died in battle before he was born, which leaves him now doubly parentless, like Tristan and so many other legendary heroes deprived of an ordinary upbringing so as to stress their suitability for extraordinary deeds. But when Gurnemanz takes Parsifal to see Amfortas, in great pain, unveiling the Grail for the ritual of communion (Ex. 22), and when this musically and dramatically magnificent scene leaves Parsifal merely bewildered and unable either to answer the question "do you know that which you saw?" or to ask some saving question of his own, then Gurnemanz dismisses him in anger and disappointment. This pure fool has obviously still much to learn.

In Act II, we watch him learning it. Kundry, in her negative aspect, is commanded by Klingsor to seduce Parsifal in his magic garden. A rather conventional chorus and ballet of flower maidens leave Parsifal understandably indifferent. But Kundry, after singing to him most insidiously of his dead mother, kisses him on the mouth with almost irresistible sweetness. He starts away from her in terror, his expression showing some "fearful transformation" (*Veranderung*), which is certainly the right word for it. "Amfortas!" he cries out, "the wound!" By making this connection, Parsifal signifies his escape from the lethal fascination of the mother's image; and when Klingsor now hurls that double-edged spear at him, he catches it harmlessly in midair. This puts him in token possession of his own manhood; but to confirm it, he requires many years of adventurous wandering, under Kundry's equally double-edged curse, before in Act III he finds his way back to that castle of the Grail which betokens his own deeper self. Kundry is there already, but in her positive aspect as a penitent anxious to make reparation; and she washes his feet and anoints his head to make a redeemer of him in deliberate resemblance to Christ. He resolves her conflict and his own by baptizing her. In a yet more splendid recapitulation of the ritual and the music of Act I, Parsifal heals the wound of Amfortas by touching it with the very spear that once caused it, and himself unveils the Grail to yet serener music under the same flood of light; but now the white dove flies down in token of grace descending. Kundry sinks to the ground; but Parsifal, having done his own redeeming this time, rather than leaving it, like so many of Wagner's previous heroes, to the heroine to do for him, lives on to lead the renewed knighthood. We have the impression that Wagner himself had gained much in maturity of character, and that when he died in 1883 six months after the first performance of *Parsifal*, his work was finished and his story told.

EXAMPLE 22    Wagner, *Parsifal*, the motive of the Holy Grail.

## Notes

1. Arthur Schopenhauer, *Collected Works*, repr. Leipzig, n.d., esp. Vol. I, p. 345: quoted and well discussed by Jack Stein, *Richard Wagner and the Synthesis of the Arts*, Detroit, 1960, p. 150—a valuable and important book throughout.
2. While still in Dresden in 1848, Wagner completed the poem for a music drama on a subject drawn from Norse mythology, and called *Siegfried's Death*. But before he had attempted (apart from a few sketches) to compose the music, Wagner became dissatisfied with the text, which he decided relied too heavily on the narration of past events previous to the time depicted in the opera. He therefore wrote a text to precede it, under the title of *The Young Siegfried*, finished in 1851; but the same objection again arose in his mind; and he then planned a trilogy of three operas, with an introductory evening in front of these. In 1852 the texts of *Das Rheingold* ("Rhinegold") and of *Die Walküre* ("The Valkyries") were written, and later in the same year, *The Young Siegfried* was revised as *Siegfried*, and *Siegfried's Death* was substantially recast as *Die Götterdämmerung* ("The Twilight of the Gods"). The four poems as thus organized form the libretto of the entire cycle, known collectively as *Der Ring des Nibelungen* ("The Ring of the Nibelung"). *Rhinegold* was composed in 1853–1854, and first performed in Munich in 1869; *The Valkyries* was composed in 1854–1856, and first performed in Munich in 1870; *Siegfried* was begun in 1856, put aside in 1857 after the first two acts had been completed in an orchestral sketch, and (except for some full scoring in 1864) not resumed until 1869, after an interval of twelve years during which *Tristan* and *Die*

*Meistersinger* ("The Mastersingers") were composed. *Siegfried* was finished in 1871, but not then separately performed. *The Twilight of the Gods* was composed in 1869–1874, but not then separately performed. The entire *Ring* was first performed at Bayreuth on August 13, 14, 16, and 17, 1876, more than a quarter of a century after the great undertaking was first begun.

3. Reported by kind permission of Ursula Vaughan Williams: see her *R.V.W.: A Biography of Ralph Vaughan Williams*, London, 1964.
4. In *Beowulf*, the really dangerous monster is the mother of Grendel.
5. Robert Donington, *Wagner's Ring and Its Symbols*, rev. ed., New York, 1974.
6. See note 1 above.
7. See Ernst Kurth, *Romantische Harmonik und ihre Krise in Wagners Tristan*, Bern, 1920.
8. Joseph Kerman, *Opera as Drama*, New York, 1952, Ch. 7—another book of outstanding value and importance.
9. Wolfram von Eschenbach, *Parzival*, attr. to *c.* 1205, transl. Jessie L. Weston, London, 1894, I, p. 284.
10. In some sources, Titurel is father to Frimutel who is father to Amfortas; in others, as in Wagner, Titurel is father to Amfortas—at all events, neither a celibate nor a barren brotherhood.

# 11

# France, Russia, and Italy

Italian opera was dominated for much of the nineteenth century by Verdi, and German opera by Wagner. There were, however, composers of other nationalities who preserved a greater or lesser degree of independence, and who displayed national characteristics of their own. The chief of these were French and Russian: no English composer of the first rank was at work then in the field of opera, or in any field since Purcell and prior to Elgar at the end of the century.

## French Restraint

Though grand opera in Paris was more or less international, Hector Berlioz (1803–1869), a composer of striking but uneven genius, maintained at least some aspects of that classical restraint and lucidity which have always tended to characterize the French tradition. His *Benvenuto Cellini*, produced at the Paris *Opéra* in 1838, is an uneven work based on some remarkable incidents from Cellini's autobiography, the librettists being de Wailly and Barbier. *Les Troyens* ("The Trojans") has an undisciplined libretto drawn by Berlioz himself from Virgil's *Aeneid*, with additions under the influence of Shakespeare. The music was composed from 1856 to 1858. The second part only was performed in Paris in 1863; the first part not until 1890, at Karlsruhe in a German version; the whole not until the present century. We are taken almost without overture into a restless chorus of Trojans rejoicing gullibly over the feigned retreat of the Greek besiegers, and preparing to drag within their city walls the great wooden horse in which Greek soldiers are concealed. Cassandra prophesies disaster in a long scene, largely in arioso of the most remarkable vocal intensity above a sustained symphonic development in the orchestra: the same advanced technique which Verdi had been evolving. But other passages are old-fashioned number opera; and the crude conventions of Parisian grand opera are reflected in some irrelevant ballet and some lengthy choruses of which the excitement seems sometimes more artificially contrived than genuinely dramatic—for example in the second act when Troy has been sacked and the vestal virgins under Cassandra are choosing suicide rather than submit.

Cassandra was a true prophetess under the curse of never being believed, rather as we may not always believe our own saving intuitions or have them believed; and Berlioz may well have identified himself with this rejected visionary, and again with the abandoned Dido, Queen of Carthage, who is the heroine of his second part. She begins by offering trite congratulations to her people, who reply in choruses no more inspiring. Then in poignant arioso she reveals to her sister Anna's keen senses a greater discontent with her present widowed loneliness than she yet wants to admit. Aeneas and his escaping Trojans seek refuge from a fateful storm, and repay their welcome by helping to defeat an invading army. There follow (but in different order in different versions) some scenes of divertissement, among them a wonderful hunting scene in which water nymphs, wood nymphs, and satyrs seize the opportunity for some Parisian dance and spectacle, until another timely storm drives the hero and heroine into a cave—where they become lovers. At court, they are entertained with long and repetitive and in parts rather trivial dances, songs, and choruses. Then an extraordinarily intense and continuous closing scene develops, in which recitative and arioso, ensembles and choruses, arias and duets are fused with prolonged inspiration; and here the shapely melody and the melting harmony recall not the excesses of Meyerbeer but the sensibility of Bellini, while the scoring, and something in the broad sweep of the tonality, look forward not so much to Wagner as to Richard Strauss. Suddenly Mercury, the messenger-god, appears to remind Aeneas that his destiny is not to rule in Carthage but to found Rome in Italy. His departure in the last act leaves Dido an angry and embittered woman. She does not seem capable of that dignified acceptance and inward reconciliation which might make of her suicide a redeeming symbol of transformation, like Brynhilda's; the chorus of Carthaginians end this intermittently very great though sprawling opera in mere "hate eternal to the race of Aeneas." Yet we hear in the orchestra a theme (Ex. 23) which the chorus of Trojans have sung long before, at the end of Act I, and which has also been recalled in the love duet of Dido and Aeneas at the height of their ecstatic union. It is as if the music, although not the words, were able to drop us some small hint of potential resolution.

*Béatrice et Bénédict*, also with words (adapted from Shakespeare's *Much Ado about Nothing*), and music by Berlioz, and also rather uneven, was composed from 1860 to 1862, and first performed, in a German version, at Baden-Baden in 1862.

EXAMPLE 23   Berlioz, *Les Troyens*, recurring theme (a) as in the Trojan March of Act I, and again (this quotation) in the final chorus of the opera; (b) as recalled in the love duet of Dido and Aeneas; (c) reduced to its underlying progression.

French comic opera and operetta were cultivated by a number of gifted though hardly great composers. The line ran through François Boieldieu (1775–1834), with his extremely successful *La Dame Blanche* ("The White Lady") of 1825; Daniel François Esprit Auber (1782–1871), with his *Fra Diavolo* ("Brother Devil") of 1830; Louis Joseph Ferdinand Herold (1791–1833) with his *Zampa* of 1831; Adolphe Adam (1803–1856) with his *Postillon de Longjumeau* ("Postilion of Longjumeau") of 1836; and—best out of so many—Jacques Offenbach (1819–1880), whose enchanting operetta *La Belle Hélène* ("The Beautiful Helen") is a minor masterpiece in its own melodious kind, and whose brilliant *Les Contes d'Hoffmann* ("The Tales of Hoffmann") has the further recommendation of being sung throughout (it was performed posthumously in 1881). The influence of this French school of light opera was especially strong in Vienna, where Johann Strauss the Younger (1825–1899) produced one of the most exhilarating examples of the style in his operetta (based on Viennese waltzes) *Die Fledermaus* ("The Bat") of 1874. The same lively Parisian influence is evident in the splendid English partnership of W.S. Gilbert (the librettist) and Arthur Seymour Sullivan (1842–1900), whose sparkling "Savoy operas" still give the keenest pleasure to a vast public; perhaps the best of the long and excellent series is *The Mikado* of 1885. Other strong favorites are *H.M.S. Pinafore* (London, 1878); *The Pirates of Penzance* (Paignton, 1879); *Patience* (London, 1881) with its transparently amusing take-off of Oscar Wilde and his fellow aesthetes; *Iolanthe* (London, 1882); *Ruddigore* (London, 1887); and *The Yeomen of the Guard* (London, 1888). But Sullivan's serious *Ivanhoe* of 1891 failed from simple lack of genius and excess of solemnity.

Ambroise Thomas (1811–1896) based his graceful *Mignon* of 1866 on Goethe's *Wilhelm Meister*. Charles Gounod (1818–1893), a much finer composer, achieved a valid though somewhat sentimental masterpiece with his *Faust* of 1859, for which the libretto was drawn by Jules Barbier and Michel Carré from Part I of Goethe's *Faust*, dealing with Faust's seduction of Gretchen but not with his subsequent growth of character: the dialogue was spoken in the original version for performance at the *Théâtre-Lyrique*, but it was set as recitative, and a ballet was added, for production at the *Opéra* in 1869.

Georges Bizet (1838–1875) overshadows all his French contemporaries, not by his uneven earlier operas such as *Les Pêcheurs de Perles* ("The Pearl Fishers") of 1863 or *La Jolie Fille de Perth* ("The Pretty Girl of Perth") of 1866, but by his last—*Carmen*, performed in Paris in 1875, on an excellent libretto by Meilhac and Halévy after a powerful short novel by Mérimée. The form is technically *opéra comique*, with spoken dialogue (the recitatives added later should not be used); the music has a certain French clarity and directness to which the economical yet brilliantly colorful orchestration greatly contributes. The overture is short. There is first a catchy tune (Ex. 24a, p. 175) which suggests the Spanish pride of the townspeople of Seville, and which only becomes prominent subsequently in the last act of the opera. A second tune (Ex. 24b, p. 176), much in the same mood, and associated throughout the opera with the mettlesome bullfighting on which that pride centers, and with Escamillo, the brash toreador who embodies it; then the first catchy tune returns. There is a coda (Ex. 24c) of contrasting mood and chromatic insinuation, in which the tonally unstable interval of the augmented second not only makes for uneasy feeling but also recalls the idiom of the Spanish *flamenco;* this motive does not recur very often in the opera, but when it does, it evokes Carmen herself and her unsettling effect on men in general and José in particular. Other associations of musical material with specific characters and situations occur; but the overall unity comes chiefly from a sustained exotic atmosphere—Spanish in imagination rather than in actuality—to which the chromatic intervals and the piquant rhythms contribute. A further touch of glamor comes from having Carmen as a gypsy heroine.

To our left, a guard-house with soldiers passing in and out; Micaela, whose music suggests a simple but affectionate purity of character, inquires after her betrothed, José—but he is not yet on duty. To our right, a cigarette factory, from which the girls come out for their midday break and flirt with the soldiers as their habit is. The guard is changed, the children join in hilariously, José makes his entry modestly among the soldiers, and Carmen makes hers immodestly with her famous Habañera, a tune which Bizet borrowed—seemingly taking it for a folk tune, though actually it is by the Spanish-American composer Yradier. As

The Habañera, *Carmen,* Act I. The Metropolitan Opera Company.

improved by Bizet, the restless melody with its brazen words presents us immediately with the cruel and sensual aspect of Carmen's complex character. "If you do not love me," she boasts tauntingly, "I love you," and then "look out for yourself!" We know at once—in a way, she even knows herself—that she is one of those fortunately somewhat exceptional women who are so possessed by their own seductiveness that they use it to the destruction of any vulnerable man within reach of them. José is a vulnerable man, and Carmen sets about provoking him to such disquieting effect that he takes her for a witch. Micaela, once she is alone with José, gives him a fond message and a chaste kiss from his mother (who is an important background figure in Bizet's opera though not in Mérimée's novel). José feels like a man saved from great danger. But is he saved? Carmen next draws violent attention to herself by stabbing another factory girl; and when arrested and put in the charge of José, she dances so insinuating a Sequidilla for him (Bizet's own music but with *flamenco* rhythms and intervals) that he weakly lets her escape.

In a riotous second act, gypsy men and women are singing, dancing, and playing guitars in a low tavern when Escamillo enters boastfully; as the chorus greets him, his flaunting aria culminates in a refrain on the bullfighting motive (Ex. 24b), which the chorus picks up in raucous unison. Escamillo is drawn predictably to Carmen, gets a typically evasive answer, and departs to the same bold motive in the orchestra. José, just out of prison, where he was sent for letting Carmen escape, arrives to find her, and produces the now-withered flower which Carmen tossed to him contemptuously in Act I; but we hear in the orchestra her seductive theme with its sensuous augmented seconds (Ex. 24c), and we are left in no doubt of how deeply her taunting gesture cut into him. The bugles now recall him to the barracks, but she entices him into staying on; what is worse, when Lieutenant Zuniga comes to fetch him (and himself shows an interest in Carmen), José fights him, and has thus no alternative but to take refuge with the gypsies in their mountain fastness. There, in Act III, Carmen soon tires of José, leaving him to rue at leisure an intolerable situation from which he is still quite incapable of releasing himself. But the cards tell Carmen that she is soon to die, and José not long afterward. Escamillo risks and nearly loses his life by coming up after Carmen; he sings his habitual refrain (Ex. 24b) and departs after inviting all who love him (with a meaningful glance at Carmen) to his next bullfight. Micaela, too, bravely makes her way up to tell José that his mother is dying, which so affects him that he goes off to see her after warning Carmen to expect him back; the orchestra sounds Carmen's motive in confirmation; but Escamillo, off stage, has the last word with his toreador refrain.

The first tune of the overture (Ex. 24a) at last comes back in the excitement of Act IV, as the crowds pass into the arena for the bullfight; and Escamillo himself, the great man of the occasion, exchanges a brief but satisfactory declaration of love with Carmen on his way through. But we remain outside, where Carmen, after being warned that José is looking for her, not only lets him find her alone, but rejects his plea insultingly, almost goading him into attacking her. The tension of this charged and concentrated scene is heightened as we hear sounds of triumph from within the unseen arena. "Never will Carmen yield," she sings, talking of herself in the third person as if standing back indifferently from the fate she is now quite blatantly inviting. "Free she was born, and free she will die." This last word, *moura* ("die") actually overlaps the word *viva* (long "live" Escamillo) from the unseen chorus. Carmen throws José's ring at his feet; José stabs her; the crowd pours out to the motive (Ex. 24b) of Escamillo's triumph; José, to Carmen's own motive (Ex. 24c), gives himself up as Carmen's murderer.

There is intense dramatic irony in this pointed juxtaposition of death and life; and perhaps there is also some hidden but wishful reference to the basic theme of rebirth. For there was certainly something self-destructive in Bizet's own nature which corresponded to Carmen, and which for his very life's sake needed to be transformed. One of the clues to it is his liability to quite ungovernable rages, as though he were fighting off an inner enemy incomparably more formidable than the slight outer provocation might suggest. He once got a letter from his mother addressed from a hospital, and fell into such acute anxiety at the mere sight of it unopened that he picked a quarrel with a gondolier and attacked him as if he were about to strangle him. He wanted to live next door to his mother, yet have his mistresses come and go in despite of her—almost as it would seem by proxy for her. In his severe attacks of angina pectoris, he had visions of his mother laying her hand on his chest, when: "the agony would increase. I would suffocate, and it seemed to me that her hand, weighing on me so heavily, was the true cause of my suffering." In *Carmen*, it is as if Bizet were trying to objectify these conflicting but extremely dangerous fantasies by dividing them between the pure Micaela (with José's saintly mother behind her) and the seductive Carmen whom José has at least some real incentive to attack. As an intuitive bid for life, this did not succeed, though as a work of art it was a wonderful triumph of the creative spirit. Bizet became obsessed with fears of early death, yet took impulsive risks with his health. And in fact he did not long survive the production of *Carmen*. He fell into a psychosomatic crisis which his doctor stupidly thought so largely imaginary that he did not want to be recalled if it should recur. It did recur next evening; and by the time the doctor was recalled, Bizet was dead.[1] That same evening, Galli-Marié in the role of Carmen was singing of the deaths foretold by the cards when she was overwhelmed by terrifying foreboding, only just got through the scene, and fainted in the wings. Her terror, she insisted, was not for herself; but nobody paid much attention to it until the morning, when the first news of Bizet's death came through. Uncanny as it may seem, our fantasies in life and in art can come as close as that.

EXAMPLE 24   Bizet, *Carmen*, (a) opening tune; (b) Escamillo; (c) Carmen.

Among other very successful French operas, toward the end of the nineteenth century, of which the popularity has not endured, there are *Samson et Dalila* (1877) by Camille Saint-Saëns (1835–1921); *Manon* (1884) by Jules Massenet (1842–1912); and *Louise* (1900) by Gustave Charpentier (1860–1956). But *Pelléas et Mélisande*, the only opera by Claude Debussy (1862–1918), has the stuff of immortality. His genius, when compared with Berlioz or Bizet, was of a strangely withdrawn and inhibited quality; but it was just as French in its characteristic lucidity. His *Pelléas et Mélisande*, produced in Paris in 1902, is on a virtually unaltered prose play by Maeterlinck, the leading dramatist of the French "symbolists." It was Maeterlinck's intention to hint at deep mysteries by apparently simple images; and it was Debussy's intention to bring out further, as only music can, "the mysterious relationships between nature and the imagination," believing as he did that these "dream-like" words of Maeterlinck are in essence "more human" than any outwardly realistic action.[2] In harmony and in texture, Debussy's music was inevitably more under Wagner's influence than he wished it to be; and indeed there are Wagnerian leading motives in this opera. But they are so inconspicuous that they work subliminally and gain little from being analyzed. The mood is elusive and quite un-Wagnerian, following the shifting half-lights of the drama and hardly rising to a musical climax except, very moderately, in the orchestral interludes which link the scenes. It is a score as quiet as it is poetical, and in that quiet way one of the great masterpieces of opera.

The dark and rather sinister Prince Golaud is lost in a forest which envelops his gloomy castle sunlessly for many miles around, and which clearly stands like Dante's "dark wood" for that state of mind where "the direct way is lost," and can only be found again, if at all, by some hazardous encounter with the inner world.[3] Golaud encounters Mélisande, a princess of archetypal femininity, but so disoriented that she cannot even give him an account of her own identity or origins—except that she has just dropped her crown into a well from which she will not let him pick it out again. Golaud nevertheless induces her to come back to his home, where he marries her without finding out any more about her real nature. But Golaud's younger half-brother Pelléas, who is as lost to himself as Mélisande, feels an affinity with her which she shares. Playing by another symbolical well with him, she half-accidentally drops into it her wedding ring, as if in unavowed repudiation of her marriage; and at that moment, on the last stroke of midday, her husband Golaud is thrown dangerously from his horse in another part of the forest. He is more threatened than he yet knows; but on noticing with anger that she has lost his ring, he sends her out to look for it, at night, in the wrong place (for she has lied to him)—and with Pelléas to help her. They merely wander into a sea cave, and when the moon rises, they see three old beggars as pale and sinister as if the three fates themselves were sitting there. But when Mélisande lets her long golden hair fall from the window of her tower, and Pelléas outside fondles it and says "it loves me," Golaud overhears. All he says is "you are children"; but he later shows Pelléas the dangerously deep water in the castle vaults, his wish to murder him showing plainly to us though not yet to himself. In a scene longer and more developed musically than most, Golaud lifts up his little son Yniold to spy on Pelléas and Mélisande, but inconclusively. Golaud nevertheless suspects what is not yet a fact, and ill-treats Mélisande most brutally. And at last, in the castle grounds, the young pair recognize their love and avow it in most touching arioso (there is no concerted duet). Golaud surprises them, and kills Pelléas immediately—only to be overcome with remorse in Act V, as Mélisande too lies dying of a broken heart.

It is now Golaud's most bitter need to know what really happened. But press her as he may, he cannot learn from her what she does not know. None of them know: that is the meaning of the tragedy. Golaud, the villain, began well enough by asking questions of Mélisande, the heroine; but what answers could he gain from so pathetically repressed and disassociated a representative of the feminine principle? Nevertheless he brought her home, where Pélleas, the hero, instead of taking up the challenge to become a more conscious representative of the masculine principle, only found out within minutes of his death that he wanted anything particular at all. And this is indeed the tragedy of a personality so frightened that it dare not know itself, and so inhibited that very little real living is possible. To such a person, the world is like this gloomy castle, shut in by trees and mists which the light of the sun can hardly penetrate. But, of course, the world does not have to feel like that, and is not like that to more robust and fortunate personalities. Maeterlinck and Debussy were fortunate in being able to create out of their inhibitions and their genius combined such glowing art; but they were not robust personalities, and there lie the limits as well as the inspiration of this lovely opera. Only at the very end does King Arkel, that wise and compassionate old man who has been speaking for the authors more than once, sing "It is the turn of the poor little girl," Mélisande's newly born baby. He does not appear to be very hopeful about the baby's future, and indeed the children of neurotic parents have much to contend with in their own development. But there she is, the little mite, to show us that even in the grim chambers of Neurosis Castle, there can be a future.

# Russian Nationalism

Italian opera was long established in the Russian capitals, as it was in most of Europe other than France. Parisian grand opera was also familiar. A native idiom became noticeable when the lilt, the harmony, and the powerful coloring of Russian folk music entered, though not very strongly, into the operas of Mikhail Ivanovich Glinka (1804–1857), who as a child absorbed the soul-searching melancholy of his uncle's little orchestra of serfs, before acquiring a cosmopolitan acquaintanceship which included Bellini, Mendelssohn, and Berlioz. *A Life for the Tsar* was performed in 1836, and *Russlan and Ludmilla* in 1842, both at St. Petersburg. The native coloring became more distinctive with Glinka's younger friend Alexander Sergeyevich Dargomizhsky (1813–1869). His *Rusalka* of 1856 introduced an austere experiment in speech melody, halfway between recitative and arioso, which was still more rigorously maintained in *The Stone Guest*, on Pushkin's dramatization of the Don Juan legend; this was completed posthumously by Cui and Rimsky-Korsakov, and performed at St. Petersburg in 1872. Alexander Porfirievich Borodin (1833–1887) was more varied and more easygoing in his fitfully exhilarating *Prince Igor* (completed by Rimsky-Korsakov and Glazunov, and performed at St. Petersburg in 1890), on a legendary tale, and including some typically Russian humor in both the words and the music of two drunken musicians; it is now best known by the vigorous ballet sequence called the "Polovtsian Dances."

Modest Petrovich Mussorgsky (1839–1881) was an amateur, an unbalanced character who destroyed himself by drink, but was nevertheless possessed by a demonic if erratic genius. His *Boris Godunov*, on his own adaptation of a gloomy drama by Pushkin, survives in two versions of his own making, the second of which was performed at St. Petersburg in 1874; and in two revisions by Rimsky-Korsakov, which improved the lucidity of the progressions and the transparency of the orchestration at some cost to the crude but individual character of the original. There are many scenes of an extraordinarily somber power, such as the arioso of Boris' monologue and its continuation with the clock striking through the orchestra in Act II, and the grim scene in Act IV where Boris dies in an agony of tormented conscience, to which his broken speech melody perfectly corresponds. Debussy was to some extent influenced by Mussorgsky's poignant arioso, and by his succession of scenes not much connected in their dramatic or their musical material (but Debussy achieved in his *Pelléas et Mélisande* an overall unity of mood and texture which *Boris Godunov* does not). Mussorgsky's Russian coloring shows in the harmony and the rhythm, especially in some powerful choruses either using or resembling native folk tunes. We learn that Boris had gained his throne through the murder of the rightful heir, the boy Dimitri; his guilty remorse is the subject of the opera, into which Mussorgsky poured all the inspired intensity of his own deeply troubled state. But he had also the warmth to convey the love of Boris for his children, and especially for Feodor, his son and heir. The Polish scenes of Act III are an incongruously Italianate interlude only added to the second version, presumably for the sake of popular appeal; but greatness returns in Act IV where the chorus of Russian people break out in deep though misdirected resentment, leaving the Simpleton to sing (and maybe he sings it for Mussorgsky too) that "darkness will fall, night will take our sight away, there is no hope of dawn." In his second version, Mussorgsky made that the ending of his opera; but in his first version, he ended with the much stronger scene in which Boris dies. Rimsky-Korsakov restored this stronger ending, which focuses the drama more consistently on its central image.

Piotr Ilyich Tchaikovsky (1840–1893), though much less unstable than Mussorgsky, was subject to severe depressions, and may have fallen victim to some death wish of his own when, against the urgent protests of his friends, he drank unboiled water during an epidemic of cholera, and died of it. His *Eugene Onegin*, produced in Moscow in 1879, is on a disquieting libretto by his brother Modest, after yet another tale by Pushkin. With hardly any overture, there opens a provincial scene, in an elegantly Italian idiom of arioso, duets, ensembles, peasant dances, and choruses, as the young sisters Tatiana and Olga receive Olga's betrothed, Lensky, and his moody friend Onegin, by whom Tatiana is disturbingly attracted. During the night following, she writes an impetuous letter to him, of which she sings successive drafts in a wonderful alternation of arioso, recitative, and informal aria. But when at the end of the act Onegin calls upon her in response to it, he rejects her coldly as too unsophisticated for his serious attention. It becomes obvious that while he may be sophisticated, he has not much contact with his heart. He is so bored at Tatiana's birthday party in Act II that he makes cynical passes at Olga and gets involved in a duel with Lensky. This is no elegant divertissement. This is sudden tragedy, and the music responds to it with a rigid canon as Onegin and Lensky sing together of their brotherly friendship turned to murderous hatred. "Could we not throw away our pride, and let our quarrel end in laughter?" But no: the obsession which the canon signifies is too strong for them, and a moment later Onegin finds that he has killed his best friend, his other self, who had that warmth of feeling of which Onegin is now more than ever deprived. When in Act III he sees Tatiana, at a very sophisticated party indeed, as the wife of an elderly but distinguished and genuinely affectionate husband, he would like to have her, now that he cannot. She admits she loves him still; he insists he loves her to distraction, but Pushkin's poem made it somewhat plainer than the opera that the real calamity for Onegin is not so much losing Tatiana as being unable to recover from killing Lensky. No doubt he longs for her now in his own selfish fashion, and Tchaikovsky's rather too sentimentally Italian music leaves us to suppose that his heart is broken. It is not broken; it was dead already. That is the disquieting element in the libretto with which Tchaikovsky's own personality may have had more in common than superficially appears; for though he was in touch with grief, there is nothing in his life to suggest that he was in touch with love.

Something of this perhaps comes out in another fine but disquieting opera, *The Queen of Spades*, performed at St. Petersburg in 1890, on a prose story by Pushkin. The young but moody Hermann loves Lisa, the granddaughter of an old Countess who is known as the Queen of Spades owing to a strange tale of her youth. She once gave her favors to a sinister Count in return for the secret of three magically winning cards. Lisa has just become engaged to a reliable suitor, Yeletsky; but Hermann's not very reliable charm wins her away from him, and she gives Hermann a key together with instructions for making his way secretly through the old lady's room and into her own. But Hermann delays in order to press the old lady herself—at pistol point!—for her evidently diabolical secret. The shock kills her, but her ghost names three cards, of which the last betrays Hermann by showing up, not as the winning ace, but as the very Queen of Spades, so that he loses catastrophically to Yeletsky. Lisa has already committed suicide from romantic disillusionment; Hermann commits suicide from financial embarrassment—or do we sense something rather more lethal in the crucial scene between Hermann and the old lady, as if what really intercepted him and caused him to threaten her with that improbably phallic pistol might have been his immature fantasies of the mother who promises magic values but destroys real ones? Tchaikovsky corresponded intimately for thirteen years with an older woman who was his patroness but whom he never dared to meet; and when he tried to break out of this by getting married (quite against his own temperament) "to a woman with whom I am not in the least in love,"[4] it lasted nine weeks and sent him into a mental breakdown. Contemporary critics found *The Queen of Spades* unacceptably gruesome, and though its glorious vitality of melody and warmth of harmony soon gave it the popularity which it deservedly retains, there are still people who, for the same reason as with *Rigoletto*, experience something elusively distasteful about it. The tension between the confident surface and the veiled unease may well be part of what contributes to Tchaikovsky's greatness. His musical idiom is very personal, and he did not for long ally himself with the Russian national school.

Nikolai Andreyevich Rimsky-Korsakov (1844–1908), an altogether stabler character, was the one professional craftsman of the national school. For his subjects he had a preference for fairy tales, of which the implications may be deep but the treatment is light. His last and best opera is *Coq d'Or* ("The Golden Cockerel"), on an elusive libretto after Pushkin, and performed in Moscow in 1908. The theme of the Golden Cockerel (Ex. 25a) rings out unaccompanied on a muted trumpet—and a high one at that. The Astrologer's theme (Ex. 25b) is still higher, over a low bass with not much in between. Like Berlioz and Richard Strauss, Rimsky-Korsakov could spin an orchestral magic which is a musical dimension in itself (all three wrote famous treatises of orchestration). The Golden Cockerel gives warning of approaching danger, which takes the form of an exotic Queen; she seems like a wayward relative of the Queen of the Night. There is silly old King Dodon who goes out, after many evasions, to fight her army, and comes home thinking he has captured her; but it looks to us rather as if she has captured him. The Astrologer arrives to name his reward for services rendered: having been given the customary open option, he names the Queen. It is ridiculous—the King will have none of that, and knocks the Astrologer to the ground with his scepter. Clouds hide the sun, thunder peals, the Queen repudiates that foolish old monarch, and now the Golden Cockerel itself flies down and pecks him dead with one stroke of its beak. But the Astrologer tells us not to distress ourselves unduly; for of all these figures of imagination, "the Queen and I alone were human." He may mean, alone representative of more enduring human archetypes than the insubstantial fantasies we dream up merely to deceive ourselves. But it has been a dream of exquisite enchantment, for Rimsky-Korsakov's music, though not the greatest, is certainly the most felicitous of the Russian national school.

EXAMPLE 25    Rimsky-Korsakov, *Coq d'Or*, (a) the Golden Cockerel; (b) the Astrologer.

Near to the Russian school, though not of it, are the Bohemian and Moravian (now called Czech) composers. The pioneer was Bedřich Smetana (1824–1884) with his lively comic opera, *The Bartered Bride* of 1866, and others more serious of which the chief are the powerful *Dalibor* of 1868, and the patriotic *Libuša* of 1881; there is also a warm comedy with somber undertones, *The Kiss* of 1876. All these were produced in Prague—*Libuša* long delayed by powerful opposition. Antonín Dvořák (1841–1904) composed ten operas, but none have proved so significant as his famous symphonies. The most successful were the comic fantasy, *The Devil and Kate*, produced in Prague in 1899, and the enchanting folk tale *Rusalka*, in 1901. Their successor was the Moravian Leoš Janáček (1854–1928), with a long and interesting series of operas in which his experiments with speech-like arioso were cumulatively developed. *Jenufa*, produced at Brno in 1904, after a drama by Preissová, owes something both to Smetana and to Dvořák, and has an attractive peasant atmosphere (rather than actual peasant tunes); but it is already a very individual work. Here the line of the solo melodies ranges from drily conversational to passionately intense; and there is something about the texture and the harmony of the orchestral flow which brings to mind the tone poems of Richard Strauss. The idiom is warm and sympathetic. It has become a little more austere in *Káta Kabanová*, derived from Ostrovsky's play *The Storm*, and performed at Brno in 1921; but this is still a moving and human drama both verbally and musically. *The Cunning Little Vixen*, performed at Brno in 1924, withdraws a stage further by projecting most of what is sympathetically human onto animal figures, whose relationship to the ostensibly human characters is partly satirical and partly uneasy, as if the composer did not quite know how to take it himself. Much of his music here has the same effect of vicarious, not quite human experience, since it includes a stylization of natural sounds. Yet it is a touching fantasy. *The Makropoulos Affair*, performed at Brno in 1926, is on an adaptation by the composer of a very inhuman comedy by Karel Čapek, the music to which gets to be almost as dreary as its nearly immortal heroine has come to find life after some four centuries. Her one really lyrical passage comes when she is at last released and sings: "Marvellous, the gentle hand of death upon me." *The House of the Dead*, performed at Brno in 1930, was based by the composer on Dostoievsky's harrowing novel; it is a series of character studies in music of the wretched prisoners with whom the composer in his old age appears to have equated something in himself, and though it is musically quite uncompromising and for the most part bare, it carries a strange conviction by the splendid force of its integrity.

National folk material blended with Wagnerian influence to produce a German school of fairy-tale operas of which the first and best example is *Hänsel und Gretel* ("Hansel and Gretel") by Engelbert Humperdinck (1854–1921), on a libretto taken from the brothers Grimm by the composer's sister, and performed at Weimar in 1893. It is a work of very considerable musical charm and stature within its deliberate limitations of sentimentality.

## *Italian "Realism": Mascagni and Puccini*

Italian opera after Verdi exaggerated certain of his robuster qualities into a style commonly known as *verismo* ("realism"). This is not in fact any more realistic than other opera, but it was thought to be so because of a sort of inverted sentimentality which stresses the harsh side even more than the soft side of an essentially melodramatic idiom. Verdi, in *Rigoletto* or *Il Trovatore*, used extremely strong images without any deliberately symbolical intention, since the stories are meant to be taken literally while at the same time working rather disturbingly on our intuitions. The same naive use of strong but unassimilated images persists in *verismo* opera; but whereas Verdi kept his greatest intensity of melody, harmony, and scoring for his highest dramatic climaxes (such as Othello kissing Desdemona to the same music of Ex. 17 in three tragically different contexts), Verdi's successors were so anxious to go the limit that they tried for this intensity almost all the time. Such unremitting pressure defeats its own object, and in order to bring back enough contrast, somewhat artificial strokes of theater were contrived, which still further diminish the realistic effect intended. *Verismo* opera is not realistic; but it is often very good and heady theater, expressed in music which at its best is worth a very great deal for sheer melodic invention and vital energy.

Pietro Mascagni (1863–1945) was the composer of *Cavalleria Rusticana* ("Rustic Chivalry"), performed in Rome in 1890. Young Santuzza is jealous of Lola, a former (and, she suspects, revived) sweetheart of her lover Turiddu; she vindictively denounces him to Lola's husband Alfio, who kills him in an off-stage fight. The pace is unremitting except for two contrived contrasts: an Easter hymn sung devoutly by the villagers, and an orchestral interlude while they are in church. The tunes are bold; the harmony is obvious; the orchestration is blatant: but it all serves the raw and simple drama, and the little opera remains deservedly as popular as ever. It is generally billed with *I Pagliacci* ("The Clowns"), of which the librettist and composer was Ruggiero Leoncavallo (1858–1919), and which was performed in Milan in 1892. In a prelude, the clown Tonio sings that players, too, have hearts. His heart grieves for Nedda, the leading lady, who rejects him ignominiously. He contrives, in revenge, for her husband, Canio, to overhear her planning to go off with Silvio, who remains for the time unrecognized by Canio. Then we see a play within the play. Canio threatens Nedda, who tries to pass it all off as part of the play; but when she will not tell him her lover's name, he stabs her, and Silvio too as he rushes up to her. While the villagers voice their shock and horror, Canio rounds it off: "The play is ended."

Giacomo Puccini (1858–1924) had some success with *Manon Lescaut* at Turin in 1893, and very great success with *La Bohème* at Turin in 1896. This is his most gracious, pleasing, and melodious opera, and comes nearest to presenting a slice of real life, in the romantic poverty of a group of cheerful young Parisian artists and writers. The libretto, which was skillfully drawn by Giacosa and Illica from a popular novel by Mürger, is sentimental but not violent; and the music matches it with a directness of feeling which shows the *verismo* idiom at its warmest. A few relatively formal arias do little to interrupt the now customary flow of orchestrally supported recitative and arioso. Thus in the first act, when Rodolfo's hand meets Mimi's as they search for her lost key, the famous aria *Che gelida manina* ("Your tiny hand is frozen") emerges quite flexibly, and leads on into quite varied textures and actions, before the culminating love duet which closes the act. Almost all the melody of the opera, whatever the texture, is tense with emotion; and when at last Mimi dies of her consumption, the tension is merely a little heightened to enhance the pathos.

*Tosca*, performed in Rome in 1900, is a harsher and more characteristic example of *verismo* opera. The libretto was taken by Giacosa and Illica from a melodramatic play by Sardou. Three aggressively unrelated chords (Ex. 26) represent the villain, Scarpia, Chief of Police; whereupon the curtain goes up at once on the ironical peace and quiet of a great church. An escaped political prisoner, Angelotti, has just time to hide in a chapel before an old Sacristan comes in, followed by the hero, Cavaradossi, who gets to work on an almost finished painting of Mary Magdalen. His model is a beautiful unknown blonde he has seen worshipping there—actually Angelotti's sister, Attavanti. He compares her blue eyes and golden hair with the *black* eyes and brown hair of the singer Tosca, whom he loves. Angelotti, hearing the Sacristan leave, creeps out and is seen by Cavaradossi; but they are old friends. Tosca is heard outside; Angelotti hides again; Tosca asks suspiciously why the door was locked, but relents and invites Cavaradossi to an assignation for that evening. He seems preoccupied, having Angelotti on his mind; but Tosca, misinterpreting his mood, becomes jealous of the blonde in the portrait. He sings movingly of his art; and at an intuitive level we perhaps pick up a hint of that unformulated but often quite sharp jealousy a woman may feel when she senses rivalry in a man's creativity. Tosca takes her jealousy literally, and needs considerable persuasion before she will leave him to his painting, adding with some venom: "But let her eyes be black!" Cavaradossi sends Angelotti off to hide in his villa. The church fills with a congregation and some noisy choirboys, who are suddenly subdued as Scarpia enters. He finds a fan dropped by Attavanti; he pieces together the whole story of Angelotti's escape and Cavaradossi's involvement; and when Tosca returns, he uses the fan to play on her jealousy, since he desires her for himself. With a typical *verismo* touch, the church choir and organ now set up a sacred counterpoint to his lewd musings in the foreground. His own harsh chords (Ex. 26) bring down the curtain on this complicated, impetuous, and very skillfully constructed first act.

The second act shows Cavaradossi a prisoner under examination in Scarpia's apartments. Through an open window, a choral cantata with Tosca as soloist floats up. Now Tosca is sent for to witness Cavaradossi's ordeal; we and she hear from an inner chamber his involuntary cries and courageous denials under severe torture. To rescue him she reveals Angelotti's hiding place, and after singing her beautiful and plaintive aria *Vissi d'arte, vissi d'amore* ("I have lived for art, I have lived for love"), she promises her person to Scarpia as the price of Cavaradossi's freedom. Scarpia gives an order for a mock execution, in words which imply to his subordinates (though not to Tosca) an opposite intention. But she has found a sharp knife on the dinner table, and as he approaches her, she stabs him mortally, to an extraordinary outburst of fury in the orchestra. The third act opens quietly but not very convincingly with a shepherd boy's innocent singing, as Cavaradossi waits at dawn for his execution. Tosca comes to tell him that he has only to pretend to die, and explains the whole story in melting arioso. But when the bullets are fired, she finds him truly dead. As she is about to be seized for the murder of Scarpia, she leaps from the parapet to her own death on a magnificent top B flat. The music to this lurid libretto is not moving as Mozart or Bellini are moving; but it is almost consistently gripping. For beneath the surface, some very frightening fantasies are at work concerning the terrible father, the destructive woman, and the fatal deceptiveness of hope. They are not focused enough to redeem the gruesome improbability of the plot, but they strengthen its sinister undertones and come through powerfully in the dark energy of the music. It is altogether a shocking affair; but it captivates large audiences, as it always did, because its very crudeness imparts a primitive fascination.

*Madama Butterfly*, in which the same librettists drew upon a sad tale of Oriental innocence betrayed, was performed in Milan in 1904. For its American hero, his Oriental sweetheart might well have represented a fruitful contact with the unknown; but this potentiality was in no way developed, since the two sides never get into any real communication. In spite of much beautiful melody in

Puccini's most pathetic vein, the opera remains essentially heartless. *La Fanciulla del West* ("The Girl of the Golden West"), performed in New York in 1910, has not proved a popular success, and *La Rondine,* performed at Monte Carlo in 1917, is still less regarded. But the "triptych" (triple bill) of three one-act operas, performed in New York in 1918, shows an unexpected assimilation of contemporary idioms. *Il Tabarro* ("The Cloak") does not get much beyond bringing *verismo* melodrama rather impressively up to date. *Suor Angelica* ("Sister Angelica") verges on religiosity, and is musically a little trite. But *Gianni Schicchi* is an uncommonly elegant and vigorous comedy (Puccini composed no other comedies, though there is certainly humor in *La Bohème*), with a score of real sophistication and some very interesting resemblances to Richard Strauss. The unfinished *Turandot* (completed by Alfano and performed in Milan in 1926) is still more bold and experimental. But with that experiment, the long line of Italian opera based on vocal expressiveness came virtually to an end. It is ironical that Puccini, whose music depended supremely on the voice, made demands upon it which were more harmful to the art of singing than the great orchestra of Wagner, through which a properly trained technique of Italian voice production could always carry unimpaired. Caruso, above all, met Puccini's demands for extreme dramatization by departing over the years (as his phonograph recordings show) from pure *bel canto*—the traditional "fine singing" which had sustained Italian opera through three centuries of evolving idioms—toward a cumulative debasement both of vocal technique and of musical refinement, including a catch in the voice which was literally sob stuff. There lay one of the earliest causes of that decline in *bel canto* from which our present generation is doing its best to recover. In this and other ways, *verismo* opera contained the seeds of its own destruction.

EXAMPLE 26    Puccini, *Tosca,* Scarpia's harmonically disconnected chords.

## Notes

1.  For Bizet's life and music, Winton Dean, *Georges Bizet,* London, 1965, is the best discussion; for the peculiar circumstances of his death and their connection with his character, see Edmund Galabert, "La Maladie et la Mort de Bizet," *Le Passant,* February 1888; for Galli-Marié's premonitions, see Ernest Reyer, *Quarante Ans de Musique,* Paris, 1910, pp. 308–09.
2.  Letter to the Secretary-General of the *Opéra-Comique,* 1894. See Edward Lockspeiser, *Debussy: His Life and Mind,* London, Vol. I, 1962, Vol. II, 1965.
3.  *Inferno,* first stanza.
4.  Letter to Nadezda von Meck, July 15, 1897.

# 12

## The Romantic Strauss

Our times have greatly changed, and our music too, since the illusory certainties and the very real glories of the late nineteenth century. Mahler best expressed in music that more than personal nostalgia which may accompany the passing of an age; but he composed no operas. Nor did Elgar, nor Sibelius. But Richard Strauss (1864–1949), having anticipated in his symphonic tone poems, from *Tod und Verklärung* ("Death and Transfiguration") as early as 1889, some of the most radical developments of twentieth-century harmony, began a second career in opera with his unwieldy *Guntram* of 1894 and his moderately successful and amusing *Feuersnot* ("Fire Famine") of 1900. Strauss inherited from Wagner his seamless arioso, his rich orchestral commentary, and his unifying system of leading motives. But Strauss' arioso became more adaptable and less symmetrical than most of Wagner's (except perhaps in *Parsifal*). Strauss' orchestral commentary follows the smaller inflections of the drama more minutely, and has a sonorous translucency for which the nearest precedent was Berlioz. The leading motives in Strauss, however, are usually less compact and pregnant than in Wagner, and are more frequently expanded as melodies in their own right. In other respects, the musical events, and especially the modulations, are more closely packed: more happens in a shorter time, and more elliptically, so that this music used to seem harder to hear than Wagner's, until it grew in turn familiar. Strauss went even further than Wagner in the use of chromatically altered chords, and made cross-relationships a main ingredient of his harmonic progressions; but the direction of these progressions, though often very intricate, is never obscured, and the tonal pull is always clear and in general powerful. There is in Strauss a greater acceptance than in Mahler of the underlying opposites of our human existence. Strauss was more willing to take the rough with the smooth, and did not seem to feel Mahler's compulsion to give a wry twist in compensation for every warm or noble emotion. Strauss, more than any other composer of his time, was able to let the full tide of his emotions run on, without reacting with fear or guilt. This brought him increasingly out of touch with contemporary trends; but he is all the more valuable to us on that account, and his popularity is deservedly increasing.

## The Advanced Operas

In his first important operas, Strauss was far ahead of his time in his ruthless musical expression and virtuoso technique in the service of harsh dramatic situations. *Salome,* performed in Dresden in 1905, has a text derived from the play by Oscar Wilde, who made of this peculiar character from the Bible a pathological study. She is a destructive seductress, whose gruesome pleasure it is to kiss the severed head of John the Baptist, since in life he would not tolerate her compulsive advances. It is a distressing subject on any level, and captured with diabolical cleverness in a score which exceeded any precedent for exacerbated sonorities and strident harmonies. But there is also a colorful excitement and a rhythmic impetus about *Salome* which did not persist into *Elektra,* produced, also in Dresden, in 1909. This has the first libretto of Strauss' long and famous partnership with the Viennese symbolist poet, Hugo von Hofmannsthal. It is an adaptation of the classical Greek tragedy by Sophocles, with some touches from Euripides and a certain change of emphasis which brings out the obsessive hysteria of Elektra. Her obsession is that her brother Orestes, a fugitive since childhood, shall return to avenge on their mother, Clytemnestra, and the mother's lover, Aegisthus, the murder of their father, Agamemnon; their sister, Chrysothemis, only longs for a normal life and marriage, but she too is caught up in the family neurosis, and cannot seem to get away. The three women wrangle interminably, without the slightest prospect of real communication, and mostly in a high and agitated vocal register which grows to be unpleasantly monotonous. Orestes does return, and very sensibly in disguise. The scene in which he and Elektra recognize and greet each other brings a welcome change of vocal texture, and is the warmest scene of the opera. Orestes commits the mythologically necessary murders off stage, and when these are reported, Elektra dances to the point of collapse in a vindictive frenzy that does still less than her previous laments to engage our sympathies. In a later part of the myth, Orestes, after long and guilty self-torments personified as the Eumenides or Furies, at last resolved the family neurosis when bright Athene reconciled him with these dark and powerful figures of the underworld; but none of this comes into the present drama. The insights of Freud into Greek mythology were familiar to Hofmannsthal, who knew him in Vienna and read his writings; but in this opera there are no pointers toward reconciliation. It may be that Hofmannsthal, unlike Orestes, never did quite manage to forgive himself for having a dark underside. There is an element of self-torment in almost all his librettos which gave Strauss—so much the more open character—justifiable concern. On the other hand, the poetical imagination and felicity of language which Hofmannsthal contributed were advantages very rare in operatic poetry, and just as valuable as Strauss always gratefully acknowledged. The two men were by temperament complementary.

## The Romantic Operas

There was, moreover, another and entirely Viennese side to the genius of Hofmannsthal: his relish for social satire and refined comedy, tempered with genuine compassion. On this was built the one almost flawless masterpiece of the partnership: *Der Rosenkavalier* ("The Knight of the Rose"), performed in Dresden in 1911. The overture has a romantic ecstasy which at one point in the score is directed to be played as if parodied. The curtain rises on the great bedroom of the Princess (*Feldmarshalin* or *Marshalin*, Field-Marshall's wife), where it is plain that young Octavian (a "trousers role" sung by a mezzo-soprano) has spent the night with her, though they are both quite decently covered by now and there is nothing outwardly embarrassing except for his presence and the extreme sentimentality of his vocal endearments. Like a very youthful Tristan, he resents the coming of the day. He is forced to hide when noises without suggest that her husband has returned—but no, luckily it is only her country cousin Baron Ochs, a man positively boastful of his sensuality: by no means merely boorish; but certainly more than a little gross. When Octavian tries to slip out disguised as a servant-girl, the Baron takes an immediate interest in the pretty creature (a woman singing the part of a boy disguised as a girl—quite a baroque complication, but it all comes out perfectly clearly in the theater). And this notwithstanding that the very purpose of his visit is to tell the Princess that he is about to marry Sophie, the young and attractive daughter of the rich and newly ennobled Faninal. In the intervals of asking advice from the Princess about a suitable ambassador to carry to Sophie the traditional Silver Rose, the Baron tries to arrange an assignation with the disguised Octavian, greatly to the Princess' amusement and ours, especially when she shows the Baron a miniature of Octavian as a suitable ambassador—and he notices the likeness! The words are as witty as the situation, and the music is as delightful as the words, until suddenly the stage is flooded by petitioners and courtiers in a brilliant scene of artfully contrived agitation. But when they are all disposed of again, and the Princess is left alone, she recalls very pensively how once she was as young and unspoiled as this attractive Sophie—and now? How long will her Octavian love her? How soon must she accept that youth cannot last forever? He returns, and she cannot refrain from singing to him about her thoughts with wistfulness, to which he responds with passion and disbelief; but in her heart she knows that he will leave her for a younger woman, and that she must somehow take it lightly, lightly, to

Octavian arrives to present the Silver Rose, *Der Rosenkavalier*, Act II. New York City Opera Company.

save them both from intolerable pain. Abruptly she sends him off with the Silver Rose for Sophie, whom Baron Ochs expects to marry—but whom Octavian will marry. In Act II, to a long climax of Straussian excitement in the orchestra, Octavian arrives to give Sophie the Silver Rose; and now as they confront each other shyly but eagerly, the strangest of disconnected harmonies drop into the orchestra from high up on the shimmering celesta, with a touch of woodwind—and we hear in the music the fluttering of their youthful hearts (Ex. 27). "Where have I been before," she sings, "that I have been so happy?" He repeats the very words of her question, and they duet for a while about this present moment that seems for all eternity, both past and future. They have *not* been there before; but they do feel as if they have—and are simply recognizing what has always existed. This is because the situation into which they have fallen—love at first sight—is an archetypal situation which has always recurred down the generations of our human race. Nature herself has prepared them for it, so that they recognize, not literally each other, but certainly the intimations of the eternal masculine and feminine in each other. The strange harmonies in the orchestra appear to come from nowhere in the tonality, yet fit into it as if with foregone precision. It is beautiful music for a beautiful situation, and an excellent example of just what opera can do which other arts cannot.

For a while, the young couple are left to explore in rapt melody their new-old experience. Then that gross Baron arrives, and behaves, characteristically, with an insulting familiarity which enrages Octavian as much as it distresses Sophie. It all works up to a clash of weapons in which Baron Ochs gets a slight prick in the arm. He thinks he is mortally injured; but he cheers up quickly enough when a letter is brought to him (with an outpouring of that lovely waltz music which stands for his sentimental side and for the Viennese gaiety never far distant from this radiant score)—a letter of invitation from the supposed servant-girl. But it is actually, of course, a trap set by Octavian, into which Ochs falls in the third act, entertaining the pretty creature in a private room at a tavern so compromisingly, and surprised by so many hostile witnesses, that all prospects of his marrying Sophie are thrown to the winds. The Princess now takes entire command, dismissing the deflated Ochs, who is pursued off stage by the noisy crowd for payment of the large bills accrued; then with the stage left to Sophie, Octavian, and the Princess, there follows as touching a resolution as any opera has ever had. Octavian stands there filled with momentary shame and perplexity; but the Princess sends him over to Sophie, who can see how things have been with the Princess and Octavian, and feels that she is no more to him now than "empty air." The Princess knows better. She sings again, as she sang so sadly at the end of the first act, that she knew it had to come, only it is a little sooner than she might have hoped. She comforts Sophie, she encourages Octavian, she summons up the "whole and steadfast heart" to accept, like Sachs in *Die Meistersinger,* what is so obviously right for the young people. And because she accepts, it is also right for her: she has gained in stature by choosing freely what she could not in any case have prevented. The three of them then join in a trio as reconciling as the great quintet in *Die Meistersinger*. The Princess slips out; the young people pledge their union in a duet of which the music is appropriately simpler, but straight from the heart. They, too, leave the stage. But the Princess' little black boy runs on to retrieve Sophie's handkerchief, and to bring down the curtain lightly, lightly, just as the Princess herself has told us that she always intended.

EXAMPLE 27    Strauss, *Der Rosenkavalier,* the strange harmonies which express love at first sight in the scene of the Silver Rose.

Hofmannsthal's more tortured side played strange tricks again with *Ariadne auf Naxos* ("Ariadne on Naxos"), of which the third and final version was performed in Vienna in 1916. The opera was originally designed as a mere pendant to an adaptation (spoken) of Molière's *Bourgeois Gentilhomme;* that arrangement did not really work at all, and eventually a new first act (sung) was introduced instead. This develops dramatically and musically a theme originally worked into the spoken play, by which a serious opera company is confronted with a company of the traditionally improvising comedians of the *commedia dell'arte,* the comedy of arts. They have both been engaged, regardless of expense; now they are suddenly commanded to combine their entertainments, since there will not otherwise be sufficient time for the fireworks. This presents no particular problem to the comedians, who are nothing if not adaptable; but the serious musicians take considerable offense, until their young composer finds himself warmly attracted to the vivacious coloratura soprano, Zerbinetta, who is the chief attraction and virtuoso of the comic troupe. The second act, as in the original version, shows us the resulting entertainment, in which the serious drama has Ariadne abandoned by Theseus and desiring only the death which she seems to be expecting imminently; and the "improvising" comedians put on the most spontaneous and musically enchanting display to cheer the wretched woman up— only she will not be cheered up; and when in the end Bacchus himself discovers her with delight and longing, she takes him for Death in person until his persistence wins her into heavenly life. To this melancholy heroine and belated hero, Strauss gave some fine music, but he gave much finer music to the comedians (especially to Zerbinetta with her dazzling coloratura aria). Whenever for a moment he can bring the two worlds and the two idioms into a kind of contrapuntal communication, we hover on the verge of a very wonderful opera; but Hofmannsthal would not allow it to develop like that, and it is here that his own disposition to self-misgivings and self-tormentings became an obstacle. For Hofmannsthal, Ariadne and Bacchus represent a "world of the spirit" for which the "merely human" comedians can feel nothing but "incomprehension."[1] The real incomprehension, unfortunately, was Hofmannsthal's incomprehension of the earthy side.

In *Die Frau ohne Schatten* ("The Woman Without a Shadow"), which was performed in Vienna in 1919, the world of the spirit is represented by the mighty Keikobad, who is never seen but looms oppressively in the background from the first bars of the overture, where his leading motive sounds immediately with terrible menace (Ex. 28a). His daughter is a fairy-tale Empress whose mother was human, so that the Empress has the potential of either side; but so far she is all spirit and no solidity, in token of which she can bear no children and casts no shadow. She is warned by a stern messenger from Keikobad that if this is not remedied within the next three days, her husband the Emperor will be turned to stone (Ex. 28b). Keikobad here is being stern for their own good, like Sarastro in *The Magic Flute*, but much more frighteningly because he is neither visible nor approachable. There is also an old nurse who is almost as ambivalent as the Queen of the Night, and who certainly knows just how the transforming adventure has to be instigated. A shadow can be gained only by descending to the human level. This is represented by a very earthy couple: Barak, a simple dyer, of greater goodwill than diplomacy, and his nagging wife, who could give him children if she chose to do so—and has all too obviously an outsized shadow—but does not so choose. Strauss himself loved dearly his chronically nagging wife Pauline, with whom his relationship was of great solidity and value; and by far the best music in this opera is that which he composed most sympathetically for Barak as a bewildered but staunchly loving husband. The Empress, though warned by the nurse that she is not going to like it, opts firmly for going down; and the action begins.

There is not only nagging and quarreling in Barak's poor hut. There is a superabundance of symbols. The most self-conscious and inept of these are like more or less distorted recollections of the Arabian Nights, obviously much in Hofmannsthal's mind. Fishes are frying in the pan, and represent at the same time unborn children clamoring in chorus for attention: a symbol just about as cooked up as the fish are supposed to be. But the Nurse tempts Barak's wife with a most effective dream lover from the same Arabian tradition of fantasy, and gets her agreement to sell her own shadow to the Empress in return. The rest of the plot is a complicated demonstration that this plan will not succeed, since to trick Barak's wife by fantasy is itself a fantasy, and cruel and fraudulent in addition. The climax is reached when a fountain of water springs up, and a spirit-voice urges the Empress to drink from it. It seems that this is how she can get the shadow, but to the detriment of Barak's wife—and Barak and his wife have become as lost now, to themselves and each other, as the royal couple. So the Empress nobly refrains. The Emperor horrifyingly turns to stone; but still the Empress cannot bring herself to defraud Barak's wife, and this noble choice, we are given to understand, unlocks the obstacle, so that she gains on the instant a beautiful shadow. Like the rainbow in *Rhinegold*, her shadow forms a bridge, across which Barak and his wife find each other, while the Emperor returns to human form and rejoins the Empress; the characters break into very lengthy arioso and ensembles; the unborn children chorus hopefully rather than convincingly in the background—and the opera begins to seem as though neither the poet nor the composer knew quite how to finish it. Perhaps the symbolism took an artificial direction when Hofmannsthal turned his Empress away from what would traditionally represent the water of life, of which it is all too probable that he himself never really dared to drink very deeply. Wherever the text gets too contrived and tortuous, Strauss fills in with brilliant craftsmanship, but does not sound spontaneously inspired; and this is particularly noticeable in the concluding scene. Some of his finest music is to be heard in this opera, however, and as a flawed but splendid masterpiece it stands extremely high.

EXAMPLE 28    Strauss, *Die Frau ohne Schatten,* (a) Keikobad as the unseen menace; (b) the Emperor turned to stone.

As if to give himself a respite from so much earnest symbolism, Strauss next wrote his own libretto for an entertainment of great charm and vitality: *Intermezzo,* first performed in Dresden in 1924. This relates an episode from Strauss' own turbulent but rewarding marriage, and is, in fact, quite unconcealedly autobiographical. The text is in prose, and deliberately modeled on everyday language; the music is in a "conversational style" of which Strauss was very proud, and which he described in his preface as ranging in a "gradual transition from the spoken word to the sung and half-spoken word" all the way to "the so-called *bel canto*" where verbal distinctness may be a little "subordinated to beauty of melody." Most subsequent operas are to some extent indebted to Strauss' brilliant development of this varied conversational idiom; but he had a special way of using it to promote rather than to interrupt the musical and dramatic continuity of the whole, taking particular care to avoid obtrusive joins. He had always, as he reminds us, "paid the greatest possible attention to natural speech and to the timing of the dialogue." Between the scenes, the orchestra plays interludes which provide an emotional commentary of remarkable exactness and expressiveness.

*Die Ägyptische Helena* ("The Egyptian Helen"), performed in Dresden in 1928, has Hofmannsthal as librettist again, at his most subtle and least comprehensible, so that Strauss, who found it hard enough to understand the poetry, justifiably wondered whether the general public might not find it harder still. The main point made is the valid one that illusion is in vain, and that only the bitter truth holds a future if it can be courageously confronted; and this was a real enough issue to call from Strauss some admirable music, without quite carrying the opera through as a consistent drama, so episodical and improbable is its text. But *Arabella,* performed in Dresden in 1933, was intended to go beyond *Rosenkavalier* (in that same vein), and it does in fact come somewhere near to *Rosenkavalier* for verbal felicity and lyrical composing. It is neither dramatically nor musically so fine as *Rosenkavalier,* but it ends with a scene of Strauss' best vintage when the heroine brings to the hero a traditional glass of pure water (the water of life, and no mistake this time) in token of her commitment and her love after all misunderstandings have been cleared away.

Just before he was to finally revise the text of *Arabella,* Hofmannsthal died suddenly of a stroke—as he was about to set out for the funeral of his son, who had committed suicide. It was a tragic ending to Hoffmannsthal's own tormented but creative life story—and Strauss was thrown back on a series of alternative librettists. Stefan Zweig provided him with an excellent libretto, carrying warm undertones, for his one unqualified comedy, *Die Schweigsame Frau* ("The Silent Woman"), based on Ben Jonson's rather unfeeling play, and performed in Dresden in 1935. The score glows with some of Strauss' most relaxed "conversation-style" arioso, the orchestra in eloquent commentary throughout. The result is a beautifully composed comedy of types and situations rather than of subtle characters, and it certainly made a complete and timely change from Hofmannsthal's psychological preoccupations; but the Nazis broke up the partnership (Zweig was a Jew; Strauss' part in this affair was honorable toward Zweig and harmful to himself). All three of Strauss' following operas, to librettos by Josef Gregor, have points of some dramatic interest, and music of which the best is of memorable excellence, without quite fusing into masterpieces. *Friedenstag* ("Day of Peace"), performed in Munich in 1938, has reconciliation for its avowed theme in a historical setting from the Thirty Years' War; *Daphne*, performed in Dresden in 1938, and *Die Liebe der Danae* ("The Loves of Danae"), performed in Salzburg in 1952, have the advantage of traditionally mythological subjects; but the texts are not very satisfactory in construction and still less so in language. The last of these three is very much the best opera: "Something for a seventy-five-year-old man to be really proud of," Strauss said of the third act; and he certainly thought it was the end of him for opera. But this was yet to come—in *Capriccio*. When urged to write yet another opera, Strauss said of it: "One can only leave one testament."[2] The performance was in Munich in 1942; among others who had a hand in the libretto, Strauss himself took an influential and perhaps decisive share, though Clemens Krauss was given the official credit.

## The Last Testament

The prelude to *Capriccio* is a solo string sextet of quiet beauty, of which the theme (Ex. 29) recurs significantly throughout the opera. As the curtain rises, this sextet is being heard through open doors by three men: its composer, Flamand; Olivier, a poet and Flamand's rival for the love of a beautiful young Countess, in whose house they are; and a prominent theatrical producer, La Roche (who is at the moment comfortably asleep). "Enemies in love," sings Olivier; "Friendly foes," replies Flamand. "Words or music?" continues the poet; "She shall decide it," returns the composer. Their sentences drop at intervals of a few bars into the continuing sextet. Later, as the conversation grows brisker, the characters pick each other up more quickly, or break in on one another, or sing several at once in concerted ensembles, the orchestra maintaining its independent continuity meanwhile. There is room for all these gradations in Strauss' "conversational style"—mainly arioso, but sometimes virtually recitative, and sometimes more or less formal aria. And all these become topics of the conversation; for this is an opera about opera. It is no mere costume piece, but is set in a certain critical time of operatic history, about three-quarters through the eighteenth century, when the composer Gluck was a controversial reformer, and the poet Goldoni was another; and it must be staged in the decor of this time. But Strauss' own speculation shows through as well, from his equally historical position in the twentieth century. Strauss is actively exploring his own theory of opera. The beauty of it is that in this opera, the theory is the practice.

La Roche, when he wakes up, has his own contribution to make; for without the producer, opera could not appear, and even if he does his work, but does it incongruously, he can twist an opera out of its intended meaning. "Men of flesh and blood, and not phantoms," La Roche insists, as Strauss had so often asked of Hofmannsthal. And, La Roche protests with further irony, none of Gluck's "tumult in the orchestra"—a criticism Strauss had himself had to meet, though indeed his aim was to be as tuneful as Mozart, and as clear and natural in his setting of the words. The Countess has a brother, the Count, lightly in love with an actress, Clairon; the Countess on her part is drawn both to the poet and to the composer, and cannot lightly decide between them. The Count calls "beauty of living the truest reward"; the Countess calls "truth of living the most beautiful reward." As the characters unfold in all their separate distinctness, a sonnet (in fact translated from Ronsard) becomes the focal symbol for what is equally important, their mutual interdependence. The poet writes the sonnet for the Countess; the composer sets it to music for her. They can no longer say to which of them it belongs, but she replies: "To me!" The Count would like to know: "What's to come of this?" The Countess suggests: "Perhaps an opera!" And the Count brings the central issue into the open: "My sister as muse." The argument then grows long and heated, until she quiets them all by singing (to Olivier) "What the spirit of poetry has wonderfully begun" (to Flamand) "the power of music shall transform"; (and to La Roche) "On your stage it shall take place." And now it is the Count who proposes the subject: "The conflict as it moves ourselves," he sings, "the events of this day—what we have all lived through—write it and compose it—compose it as an opera!"

But the ending of the opera? That the Countess cannot decide, even at the end of the opera. As she sings her own sonnet, and as we hear matter from the opening sextet intertwining from the orchestra, she cannot choose between Flamand "the great soul" (*die grosse Seele*) and Olivier "the strong spirit" (*der starken Geist*). How should she choose? We do not have to choose between that feminine principle within us which can be called the soul and that masculine principle which can be called the spirit. Hopefully, we can reconcile them. As woman, the Countess cannot marry both the composer and the poet; as muse, she is undoubtedly for both of them. "The rivalry between words and music has been the problem of my life," wrote Strauss, "which *Capriccio* solves with a question-mark." To judge from the relaxed enchantment of the music as the curtain falls, he was well content to let it go at that.

EXAMPLE 29    Strauss, *Capriccio*, opening theme.

And so it is that Strauss, like some serene survivor from a securer age, brings us down to the middle years of our own restless century. The greatest by far of Wagner's direct heirs, Strauss began in his relatively early tone poems as the leader of late nineteenth-century advance, and continued in his first important operas to open one way forward into the twentieth century. But then he preferred (Hofmannsthal permitting) to let his heart take him into a belated romantic harvest no longer advanced or even contemporary, but nevertheless the pick of the crop so far in twentieth-century opera. It is as if Strauss, having confronted the harsher potentialities of our own century in *Salome* and *Elektra,* could turn somewhat away from them without in the least turning away from life itself. It is the buttoned-up composers who may be turning away from life; and for good and ill (but mostly for good), Strauss was preeminently not a buttoned-up composer. It is not that he was dodging the issue. There is darkness as well as radiance in Strauss' later operas, especially for that "woman without a shadow" who found that having one, or becoming aware of having one, is a necessary aspect of being human. But these polar opposites of light and dark are so deeply accepted and so wonderfully reconciled in the onward flow of Strauss' music that we experience the whole, rather than getting lost in too much sweetness on the one side or too much bitterness on the other. At the center of our being, pain and joy touch, because no life could be lived without some pain and some joy. However, we cannot live only at the center of our being. Not many of us can confront the violence of our age with the serene creativeness of Strauss' later years; and the diversity of the artistic idioms through which we have tried to come to terms with it is as exceptional as are the demands made upon us by a time of so much stress and insecurity. It is to the diversity of twentieth-century opera contemporary with Strauss that we have next to turn.

## Notes

1. Letter to Strauss, July 1911.
2. Quoted and discussed in William Mann, *Richard Strauss,* London, 1964, the most perceptive book on Strauss; see especially pp. 65 ff.

# 13

# Yesterday and Today

There seem to have been three possible ways of going forward musically into the twentieth century. One was to react either positively or negatively—or perhaps ambiguously—to Wagner, and in the end, there was not much future in that. The other two ways, as we shall see, had less to do with Wagner directly, but more to do with the future. We may first consider certain of the aftereffects of Wagner's influence. As we have already seen, Debussy reacted to Wagner with creative ambivalence, composing his own single masterpiece of opera, *Pelléas et Mélisande*, in a style of superb originality. It could not have been as it was without the harmony of *Tristan* or *Parsifal*, and yet it could not have been a more personal statement by Debussy himself. Indeed, Debussy's influence in its turn pervaded early twentieth-century music, but not as a directing force. It is not creative to imitate directly so individual yet so elusive a personality.

It is equally uncreative to fall too directly under the spell of so overwhelming a personality as Wagner. Strauss was strong enough to accept the romantic heritage of Wagner and develop it to his own fresh purposes. Not so a minor Wagnerian like Hans Pfitzner (1869–1949), whose reputation in Germany (it hardly spread elsewhere) climaxed with his *Palestrina*, on his own rather glamorized libretto. The opera, with music not quite inspired enough to match the obvious sincerity of his aspirations, was performed in Munich in 1917. Ethel Smyth (1858–1944) was an aggressively feminist rather than musically outstanding English Wagnerian. Her best opera, *The Wreckers*, was performed in German in Leipzig in 1906. The best opera of the English-born Frederick Delius (1862–1934) is *A Village Romeo and Juliet*, Wagnerian in its chromatic harmony but with a highly individual, dreamlike evasiveness and poignancy. It was first performed with its originally German libretto in Berlin in 1907. The English Rutland Boughton (1878–1960) achieved a partly Wagnerian but partly Celtic atmosphere, and a wistful but genuine charm of melody, in his once famous opera (on his own libretto) *The Immortal Hour*, performed in Glastonbury in 1914. The Hungarian Béla Bartók (1881–1945) was not yet the pioneer he later became when in 1911 he composed his beautiful *Duke Bluebeard's Castle* (on his own libretto after Maeterlinck). Performed in Budapest in 1918, it is a little reminiscent of Debussy, with perhaps a harsher touch from *Salome,* and we cannot help regretting that Bartók did not return to opera. The English Gustav Holst (1874–1934) composed in 1908 a very austere but individual chamber-music opera under a far-from-Wagnerian Hindu influence in his *Savitri,* performed in London in 1916; and an equally un-Wagnerian one-act comedy of strongly personal inspiration, *The Perfect Fool,* performed in London in 1923.

The Englishman Ralph Vaughan Williams (1872–1958) poured so much of himself into his short pastoral drama drawn from Bunyan, *The Shepherds of the Delectable Mountains* (performed in London in 1922) that he gave it a lovingly revised and expanded reincarnation in the somewhat too static, but intensely moving opera of his late maturity, *The Pilgrim's Progress,* performed in London in 1951. Of his middle years, *Hugh the Drover* (1924) is a ballad opera and *Sir John in Love* (1929) is a more formal opera. Both works are strongly under that influence of English folk tunes which (with Tudor polyphony) he eventually assimilated so that their effects became an integral part of him rather than a borrowed element. This style certainly helped his own growth into the most individual and valuable of English composers since Elgar, as well as one of the least Wagnerian. His *Riders to the Sea* (1937) is a highly personal and intimate one-act setting of Synge's intentionally symbolic play: here the vocal lines are remarkably free and declamatory, above an orchestral texture of great concentration and suggestiveness. Both in its poetic symbolism and in its musical evocativeness, it is an uncommonly heartfelt little drama in music, and real opera in spite of its brevity. But the main importance of Vaughan Williams is as a symphonist.

## The Primary Divergence

The two composers who led most significantly onward into twentieth-century music, on parallel but contrasted paths, were the Viennese Arnold Schoenberg and the Russian-born Igor Stravinsky. The earliest compositions of Schoenberg (1874-1951) were in direct line from Wagner. They show a talent of abounding fertility and imagination, but without Wagner's sure instinct for where to stop. They are full of splendid passages, with a romantic beauty of detail that could hardly be more felicitous. So heavily worked up are the climaxes, however, and so complex and prolonged are the forms, that they tend to defeat themselves. There was nothing more to be achieved in Wagnerian romanticism thus merely enlarged and intensified, and the influential works of Schoenberg's maturity resulted from his early and very radical appreciation of this fact. His first approach to an operatic idiom was *Erwartung* ("Expectation"), a monodrama of one character, with a libretto written by Marie Pappenheim at Schoenberg's own suggestion. It was composed in 1909, though not performed until 1924, in Prague. The character is a woman wandering through a dark wood—symbolic, as usual, of the dark misery and confusion of a lost and searching soul. She seeks her lover, and finds only his murdered corpse near the house of another woman who has enticed him away. Schoenberg wanted the wood to be visibly staged, but it is deliberately left undefined how much if any of the woman's impassioned declamation relates to anything outside of her own troubled mind. The music was composed in one impulsive gesture lasting only sixteen days, and is thus of necessity an almost entirely unmodified upsurge from the unconscious. It lacks not only a consciously ordered form but identifiable themes which could give it a form. The idiom itself derives largely from the great monologues in Strauss' *Salome,* and it may therefore be seen as the next stage along that road which *Salome* opened up. The style corresponds to that which in painting is called "expressionism." Just as *verismo* ("realism") implied a violent juxtaposition of outer occurrences, supposed to be realistic, so expressionism implied a violent juxtaposition of mental experiences, presented as psychological. In both cases the intention is to make the strongest emotional impact, and although the techniques employed by expressionism may be more sophisticated, the two movements had something in common. On different planes, they were both designed to shock. Neither style persisted for very long unchanged, and both passed on some significant ingredients to later styles. But the importance of expressionism was artistically the greater.

In so far as expressionism includes a desire to shock, *Salome* was a pioneering masterpiece of expressionistic opera. There is another element in *Erwartung*, however, which was not present in *Salome*. This is the deliberately open invitation to the unconscious. Vienna at this time was humming with the new discoveries and ideas of Freud, which found a ready although superficial acceptance among those artists (especially the subsequent surrealists) who welcomed the encouragement to avoid too conscious a responsibility for their own creativeness. The unconscious is indeed always the ultimate source, but what wells up from the unconscious is not yet a work of art. What wells up is images for a work of art, together with innumerable subtle hints for exploring and connecting them. In *Erwartung,* Schoenberg gave himself scant opportunity for working over his material; and although his superb craftsmanship and technical experience saw to it that he turned out a serviceable article, it is not an article with much benefit of reason.

Schoenberg's next approach to an operatic idiom (again, not quite an opera) was *Die Glückliche Hand* ("The Fortunate Hand"), completed in 1913 though not performed until 1924, in Vienna. It resembles *Erwartung* in idiom, but Schoenberg was even more committed by this time to a new view of tonality first unmistakably established in his famous piano pieces, Op. 11, of 1908. Those well-defined centers of tonal force which we call keys, and which provided the dynamism for musical construction during the three previous centuries, had been shaken by *Tristan*, because of the extent to which diatonic notes proper to the key are replaced by chromatic alteration. Tonality itself is derived from the physical properties of the natural harmonic series, and cannot be avoided except by avoiding any consecutive sequence of tones definite in pitch.[1] But key tonality can be suspended by avoiding chords with a strong tonal direction, and by not allowing the music to settle to any one center of tonality such as might function in the traditional relationships of the tonic, the dominant, the subdominant, and the various mediants. The tonal pull is there so long as there are tones to pull, and Schoenberg himself would not call his music "atonal" (nontonal), preferring more accurately to regard it as "pantonal" (all-tonal). If not merely some but all chromatic notes are admitted as though they were diatonic, key may still linger (as major and minor lingered from modal tonality into key tonality, and other modal variants returned in Debussy or Vaughan Williams); but it does not remain as a structural dynamic. To replace it, Schoenberg evolved his famous method of "composition with twelve notes related only to one another," and not to any predetermined tonic. In "twelve-tone" music, what is predetermined is a "series" (or "set" or "tone row") of all the twelve notes of the complete chromatic scale, none of which is (basically) to be repeated until each has been sounded in the same order. Series of less than twelve notes are also used. In serial composition, there can be almost unlimited modifications, refinements, and extensions of the basic principle, but all have it more or less in common that, like fugal counterpoint, they are self-imposed limitations in which success depends upon the artist's capacity for turning a voluntary restriction into a creative opportunity. The element of imagination is just as necessary in serial composition as in any other; yet it is obvious that the intellectual element involved in organizing such formidable requirements must be exceptionally great. Here was Schoenberg's other side: the rigid control which he seemed to need to set up over against his impulsive energy. It is a polarity which has had much to do with twentieth-century music.

The first serial composition for the theater was Schoenberg's one-act comic opera, *Von Heute auf Morgen* ("From Today till Tomorrow"), performed at Frankfurt in 1930. From 1930 to 1932 Schoenberg composed the first two acts of *Moses und Aron* ("Moses and Aaron"), a tightly serial composition, to which he returned without being able to finish it in 1951. The completed acts were broadcast from Hamburg in 1954, and staged performances have been effectively given. The difficulty was probably inherent in the libretto Schoenberg prepared for himself: a dramatization of that very polarity of the head and heart which he spent his life in trying to reconcile. Aaron is an extrovert, a man of action and impulse, who expresses himself in sensuous melody; Moses is an introvert, a man of thought and reservation, who expresses himself in more or less inflected speech. There is no mediating woman, as there is so wonderfully in *Capriccio*, and unlike Strauss, Schoenberg seems not to have been content to end gracefully with an open question.[2] For all his genius, Schoenberg was a less integrated personality, and less able to bring his life's development to a quiet fulfillment. Yet *Moses and Aaron* remains a torso worth more than many completed statues.

Among Schoenberg's many devoted pupils, the Viennese Anton Webern (1883–1945) was a miniaturist so constricted that Schoenberg himself did not think he could ever contribute to the main stream of music. Some ten years after his death, however, Webern achieved an immense reputation and influence with more than one school of advanced twentieth-century music. This influence has been at the same time very intense and very narrowing, and has had an indirect effect on opera although Webern himself composed no operas—or any other music approaching an operatic scale. The reputation of the Viennese Alban Berg (1885–1935) has recently begun to overtake that of Webern. Berg has the further distinction of having completed the only advanced opera of our century to have found general acceptance in the international repertory: *Wozzeck*. The idea for this opera first occurred to Berg through a performance, in the spring of 1914, of some dramatic fragments by an oddly prophetic writer of almost a century before, Georg Büchner (1813–1837). From a selection of these fragments, Berg organized a connected drama in three acts of five scenes each. The music was not finished until 1921, and the first performance of the opera was in Berlin in 1925. Its reception was hotly divided, but evoked such keen interest that many further performances were given. It seemed to be recognized from the start that, like it or not, here was a remarkable expression, in opera, of the contemporary mood. Strauss, by then, was no longer attempting to be contemporary, concerned as he was with aspects of human experience not much subject to time or change. The mood of *Wozzeck* is also a part of our common humanity, but one which surfaces more urgently in the twentieth century than it did in the eighteenth, when opera had heroes of dauntless nobility and villains of Satanic grandeur. One could find no farther extreme from eighteenth-century serious opera than this unheroic tragedy, which has not only a non-hero for its leading character, but a non-heroine and several non-villains in its supporting roles.

With no more than a bar or two in place of overture, the curtain flies up on a petty tyrant of a military Captain, characterized by a jerky but strangely haunting motive (Ex. 30a) which follows him through the opera. Berg uses Wagner's technique of leading motives to excellent although quite un-Wagnerian effect. In the course of being shaved by Wozzeck, his orderly, the Captain needles him and humiliates him as no human spirit ought to be humiliated. And Wozzeck replies with an uncritical submissiveness that shows what a doormat of a man he has somehow become. It is the element of masochism in Wozzeck which both invites the Captain's sadism and meshes in with it. For the characters in this opera are acutely pathological specimens, standing for characteristics which are indeed latent in everyone, but which in most of us are active only from time to time and to a modified degree. The musical miracle is that Berg conveys these characters with a compassion which leaves us purged by the pity and the terror of his sordid story, just as Aristotle required in his celebrated definition of tragedy. Compassion is what makes a true tragedy of *Wozzeck*.

The second scene shows Wozzeck out in the fields with a friend and fellow

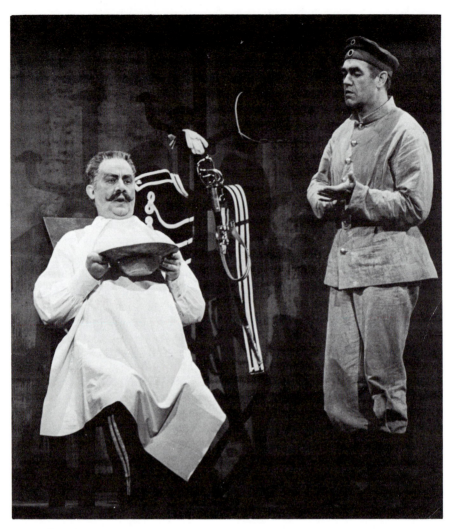

*Wozzeck,* Scene 1.

soldier who does not understand him any better, but at least does not try to bully him, so that we see Wozzeck's feelings of persecution haunting him just as much when he is not being bullied as when he is. The horror with which he reacts to a crop of real or imaginary toadstools, and to a fire in the sky which is in reality only a fiery sunset, reveals how near to hallucinatory paranoia he already stands. He is presently baited again by another sick character, the Doctor, who with cruel delusions of grandeur is using him as experimental material for some crackpot research; and meanwhile we have been introduced to Wozzeck's sluttish mistress, Marie, who thinks she sees a real hero in the resplendent Drum-Major, but is obviously mistaking the mere swagger of him for more than it is truly worth. She yields to him, and there follows in course of Act II an extraordinary scene of emotional as well as musical counterpoint, in a low tavern, where the stage orchestra blends its blatant "wrong-note" waltz tunes into the wry sophistication of the main orchestra, with the most oddly moving effect. Marie and the Drum-Major dance themselves into an erotic frenzy before the miserable Wozzeck's eyes. Back at the barracks he is taunted drunkenly by the returning Drum-Major, but can do no better in the way of protest than get himself knocked down.

Act III opens with a particularly touching scene as Marie, alone with her child, sits reading passages from the Bible, almost in speech, interspersed with outbursts of poignant melody as she decries herself with exaggerated guilt. Next she is alone with him, in very distraught condition, by the forest pool. They are quite incapable of talking over their problem constructively, and we hear the tortured obsession in Wozzeck's mind through an extraordinarily persistent pedal B ranging both high and low against the rest of the complicated orchestral texture. As his obsession works up, the moon rises—blood-red, it seems to them; and at the orchestral climax, he stabs his own mistress and only real companion, and is himself thereby a man destroyed. He is seen back in the tavern with blood on his hands, as an out-of-tune piano again counterpoints earthy music ironically yet movingly against the orchestra's compassionate commentary; he flies, returns to the pool, and in searching for the incriminating knife lets himself slip into the water and drown while the Captain and the Doctor walk indifferently by. A relatively long and very expressive orchestral interlude in deliberate D minor brings together the whole emotional complexity of the opera; this Berg told us that he was addressing directly to the audience, in token of all humanity. For it was more than Wozzeck's individual fate that Berg wanted to convey; and evidently he experienced his own plight, and that of humanity, as in some manner corresponding to the plight of his distressed and ill-fated antihero. The opera concludes with Marie's orphaned child playing in pathetic ignorance of his mother's death, yet to music so open-ended, and so like a ray of light glancing through the closing bars of this dark opera, that as with Mélisande's child at the sad ending of *Pelléas et Mélisande,* he seems to be holding out to us at least the hope that there will be a future.

EXAMPLE 30    Berg, *Wozzeck*, (a) the Captain's motive; (b) 12-tone series of passacaglia in I, 4.

The music of *Wozzeck* is not yet twelve-tone, except for an anticipation in the Passacaglia of Act I, Scene iv (Ex. 30b). Key-tonality, however, is not used structurally except in the D minor interlude. Berg gave himself confidence, if not much else, by using in rather odd ways such traditional forms as suite, rhapsody, military march, passacaglia, and rondo (Act I); sonata-form, fantasia and fugue, largo, scherzo, and rondo (Act II); and five "inventions" (Act III). But Berg insisted that we should not try to notice them in course of the performance.

There is also the formal symmetry of a long middle act flanked by two shorter acts. We certainly notice the extraordinary preciseness with which the characters are drawn in the music, and the wonderful flood of tonality which carries them along. For it is the tonal impetus, and not the relative obscurity of key, which now that we know it well comes uppermost in *Wozzeck;* and indeed as Erwin Stein (a fellow-pupil of Berg's under Schoenberg) explained: "It has been described as atonal, but there is no such thing as atonality. Tones are the very substance of music."[3] We have here the working principle of the Schoenberg school. For purely lyrical invention and quintessential joy of music, Berg perhaps surpassed Schoenberg, and certainly surpassed Webern. It is the warmth of musicianly feeling glowing through the array of ostensibly academic forms which makes *Wozzeck,* even in its rebellion against nineteenth-century romanticism, a romantic masterpiece of the twentieth century.

Berg's second opera, *Lulu,* was virtually finished when he died, though the last act was not scored and was withheld until the death of his widow; only incomplete performances have yet been given (first in Zurich in 1937). The libretto was adapted by the composer from Wedekind's *Erdgeist* ("Earth-Spirit") and *Die Büchse der Pandora* ("Pandora's Box"). Lulu is an archetypally sensual and disturbing representative of the eternal feminine, who like Marie ends her adventures by being squalidly stabbed to death. There seems to have been an obsession in Berg's unconscious with this symbolically destructive image, which like Bizet in *Carmen* he confronted courageously, but literally could not survive. The music of *Lulu* makes an intensive although very individual use of serial technique, and is far harsher than *Wozzeck,* perhaps because Berg was most unhappy in his marriage then, and at the end a dying man.

The line through Schoenberg into the twentieth century may in some aspects be regarded as neoromantic. The line through the Russian-born Igor Stravinsky (1882–1971) may in some aspects be regarded as neoclassical. Of his early ballets, *The Firebird* (1910), is as colorful as works of his great teacher Rimsky-Korsakov, and considerably more impetuous and inspired. *Petrushka* (1911) includes chains of unresolved discords used for atmosphere rather than for harmonic function, as Debussy had already used them; but there is an assertive piquancy of scoring and of rhythm in this riotous score which are unmistakable Stravinsky. By *The Rite of Spring* (1913) the riot had become a volcano, uncannily prophetic of the war about to explode in 1914, and of the disruption which it brought into the open within our much-shaken civilization. And it soon became evident that Stravinsky had frightened himself by his own success. In later years, he could give no account of this early achievement, nor recall anything of the uninhibited emotion which he certainly put into it at the time. It was after this that he turned to the safer regions of his neoclassical styles, for example in the austerely beautiful ballet *Apollo Musagetes* ("Apollo the Leader of the Muses") of 1928. Nature meant Stravinsky for a passionate composer; Stravinsky took precautions to keep these passions from getting the upper hand. So great was his musical genius that he still surpassed all others of our time: and on occasion, as with the radiant *Symphony of Psalms* in 1930, he held nothing back in a quietly glowing idiom (the text, however, is to be sung dispassionately in Latin). In opera, he composed an early work, *Le Rossignol* ("The Nightingale") performed in Paris in 1914, and a one-act comedy, *Mavra*, performed in Paris in 1922; this has arias and other set numbers in half-serious imitation of Italian opera. *The Soldier's Tale*, performed in Lausanne in 1919, has dance and mime, a narrator, and a little on-stage orchestra, including a violin to represent the soldier's soul—not an opera, but music-theater of a particularly novel, piquant, and successful kind; the libretto by C.F. Ramuz is of considerable psychological acumen; the music is at the same time incisive and compassionate. This is a small masterpiece. *Oedipus Rex*, which has an originally French text by Cocteau translated into Latin with the deliberate intention of keeping personal involvement at a distance, was performed in Paris in 1927: it is nearer to oratorio than to opera, having a narrator in modern dress (he greatly misinterprets the myth) and static actors and chorus in costume; but the controlled intensity of its music is magnificent.

The much later full-length opera, *The Rake's Progress*, on a libretto by W.H. Auden and Chester Kallman, was performed in Venice in 1951. On one level, it is a witty stylization of Hogarth's famous set of social caricatures; on another level it is a somewhat surrealist fantasy into which echoes of classical and medieval mythology enter confusedly. As usual with Auden, the poetical imagination is fresh and elegant, the feeling is lyrical, the mythology is somewhat misread, and the emotional commitment ultimately a little restricted. For every warm feeling there is a cynical sequel or a comic reservation, as if the authors dare not risk too much real passion without hedging their bets. It is the same with Stravinsky's remarkable score. The form is neoclassical: a number opera with recitative, arioso, and aria quite in the old-fashioned pattern, though not in an old-fashioned idiom. The music glitters and sparkles with inventive touches, and in its wry manner often glows with warmth and imagination. But it is not allowed to become genuinely moving for very long without being recalled by Stravinsky's involuntary determination to reinsure his emotional commitment. This he did for much of his career by hiding his own glorious imagination behind the most clever pastiche of other composers. At one time, it was supposed Pergolesi;[4] at another, it was actual Tchaikovsky;[5] here it was mainly Mozart, cunningly twisted around into astonishing Stravinsky, but nevertheless twisted. It does not really quite do. With all its intermittent beauty and its unfailing exhilaration, it escapes us in the end, leaving us more stimulated than satisfied.

We begin a little too idyllically to be true. The two young lovers, Tom and Anne, pledge their troth and win her father's qualified approval—qualified because Tom will not work to earn a living; but Nick Shadow conveniently relieves him of that necessity by informing him of a mysterious legacy and carrying him off to London to look into it. And this Nick Shadow is not only "shadow" to young Tom, but to the rest of us as well; for he is no other than that archetypal Prince of Darkness, the Devil, in disguise. He is Old Nick in very person. He soon has Tom ensnared by another archetypal personage, Baba the Turk, who follows his visit to a brothel (rather as Wagner's Kundry follows the faceless flower maidens), but who possesses the oddity of "a full and flowing black beard"—in short, she represents that mythologically familiar but ambivalent image, the man-woman who displays openly the dual sexuality concealed in all of us. Having got Tom to marry her unresistingly, she discards him graciously for Anne to recover if she can. Unfortunately, Tom is not only ruined by now, but in debt to the Devil, who demands not his money but his soul, to be staked upon three cards which must be truly named. The scene is a graveyard, and the grave is already open. Twice the promptings of apparent chance give Tom true answers; the third answer comes to him from seeing Anne enter, and naming rightly (for the second time) the Queen of Hearts. Nick is conquered, but "your sins, my foe, before I go, give me some power to pain: to reason blind shall be your mind; henceforth be you insane!" So poor Tom ends in Bedlam under the outward delusion that he is Adonis and his Anne is Venus. When she compassionately visits him, "the wild boar is vanquished," and very movingly they duet together; but then she leaves him in despair, and what might have been a positive and healing inner symbol gets turned the negative way around. Yet assuredly this is, with its amazing brilliance in both text and in music, another of those flawed achievements which are worth more than so many smoother and less disturbingly ambiguous accomplishments. Both Auden and Stravinsky were artists of genius, and even in their imperfections they were admirably suited to one another.

## *Secondary Directions*

The German Carl Orff (1895–   ) took over from Stravinsky some of his surface simplifications with little of his essential sophistication. There are pounding rhythms, there are unrelated dissonances, there are sometimes ornate flights of melody, all applied with a certain brusque unconcern for the grace and logic of organic development in music. *Carmina Burana* (1937) is a blend of staged dance and oratorio, musically impoverished but theatrically impactful; *Antigonae* (1949) and *Oedipus der Tyrann* (1959) are fringe opera designed to be of primitive force but perhaps deprived too far of the living stuff of music. The German Paul Hindemith (1895–1963) achieved great integrity and a massive output in negative reaction both to Schoenberg and to Stravinsky. His analysis of his own neoclassical system of harmony grew increasingly elaborate and infertile; he spent much energy in later life revising earlier works to the detriment of their original vitality and freshness. *Cardillac* (1926, revised 1952) is a number opera of a somewhat austerely classical construction, contrapuntal in the orchestra and basically instrumental even in the vocal melody, though some expressive recitative and aria occurs, and some energetic choruses. *Mathis der Maler* ("Matthias the Painter," 1938) and *Die Harmonie der Welt* ("The Harmony of the World," 1957) are large-scale blends of opera and oratorio, somewhat too dramatically immobile and (in the second case) too heavily allegorical to succeed altogether on the stage, though the orchestral suite from *Mathis* is deservedly familiar.

The Swiss Arthur Honegger (1892–1955) also inclined to mingled opera and oratorio, as in *King David* (1921) and the very successful *Jeanne d'Arc* ("Joan of

Arc," 1938); but *Judith* (1926) and *Antigone* (1927) are operas, of which *Antigone* is especially interesting for its almost continuous expressive recitative over a symphonic development of very individual character in the orchestra. The work of the French Darius Milhaud (1892–    ) is again mainly directed to marginal forms, including *trois opéra-minutes* (1927–1928), three miniature operas each complete within ten to fifteen minutes' duration, and of a half-mocking, twisted melodiousness which is still more evident in his three-act tragi-comic opera *Le Pauvre Matelot* ("The Poor Sailor," 1927). Of his larger stage works, *Médée* ("Medea") first performed in Antwerp in 1939, on a libretto by his wife Madeleine Milhaud after Euripides, comes nearest to genuine opera, from which his restlessly experimental combinations of sight and sound effects in the main took him some way distant. A quieter and perhaps sincerer composer was Francis Poulenc (1899–1963), whose slow and increasingly traditional development came to late fruition in his reticent but heartfelt tragic opera, *Les Dialogues des Carmélites* ("The Dialogues of the Carmelites"), on a libretto by Georges Bernanos after a short story by Getrude von Le Fort; it was performed in Milan in 1957. Key-tonality flows uneventfully but expressively through passages of melodious vocal recitative which look back to Debussy, and even in a manner to Lully, while orchestral interludes connect the individual scenes; at the end, the chorus enters appropriately and movingly into the drama, of which the theme is the persecution of the nuns and the strengthening of the heroine's personal courage through religious faith in the face of death. Poulenc is described by his friends as a man of much irrational anxiety and deep-seated fear throughout his life; and the emotion with which he evidently worked out his inner problem in this moving opera does more to make it convincing than any novelty.

The Russian Sergei Prokofiev (1891–1953) had all the qualities of a great composer except, perhaps, the quiet inwardness to be himself without self-mockery, of which the other side of the coin is mockery of us and ultimately of human values. The signs of irony are uncomfortable just because they do not usually come quite into the open, as they do, for example, with Stravinsky whenever he happens to be in an ironic mood. It is almost as if Prokofiev were defending himself against imaginary critics by hinting in his music that it is all very clever, but of course we must not really take him seriously. He found a good outlet for his irony in *The Love for Three Oranges*, on a zany story by Gozzi which the score matches agreeably and in certain scenes lyrically; it was deliberately made a little mellower than Prokofiev's previous style in the hope of pleasing American audiences, and was performed in Chicago in 1921, but only the orchestral suite derived from it achieved popularity. *The Flaming Angel*, with a libretto by Prokofiev after Brjussow, takes its story from sixteenth-century Germany, and is equally fantastic, but in a vein of macabre hallucination and superstitious cruelty to which the score fits well but painfully; it was composed from 1919 to 1927, but not staged until 1955, in Venice. Having moved from America, and worked for some time in Paris with frequent visits to Soviet Russia, Prokofiev decided from about 1935 to make Russia his permanent home, thus submitting himself to actual critics who perhaps seemed less alarming to him than those of his own self-punishing imagination. Here he was under the external necessity of simplifying his style to meet the political demands of the Union of Soviet Composers for plain tunes and easy harmonies. *The Duenna* is a social comedy based on Sheridan, performed in Leningrad in 1946, and giving official satisfaction with many formal arias and ensembles supported by relatively sustained orchestration of little harmonic severity and much rhythmic energy; the style is neoclassical, rather similar to Prokofiev's early Classical Symphony but with a better justification for its elements of irony. *War and Peace* is a long and rambling epic on a libretto derived by Prokofiev and Mira Mendelssohn from Tolstoy's great novel; the first complete staged performance was in Leningrad in 1955. It is an opera of loosely connected scenes, arranged in two parts—the first in time of peace, with a great deal of social divertissement and a prominent love interest; the second in time of war, with the emphasis on patriotic sentiment. The simplification of style is extraordinary, and not altogether convincing. Much of the first part somewhat recalls Tchaikovsky, and much of the second part somewhat recalls Borodin; but there are also many passages of finely drawn arioso, quite without disconcerting irony, which suggest that Prokofiev preserved and developed something of his own individuality under these very conditions of outside pressure as he seldom did during his years of free choice elsewhere. His overall contribution to opera is confusingly diverse, and less valuable both in itself and as an influence than his talent promised. No useful way into the future led on from Prokofiev.

Dmitri Shostakovich (1906–1975) was an undoubtedly great Russian composer whose sincerity survived the severe pressure of Soviet official policy, though his development was assuredly hampered. His vigorous opera on a libretto by Leskov, *Lady Macbeth of Mtsensk*, was performed in Leningrad in 1934 and was very favorably received until an official criticism in *Pravda* viciously condemned it as "a mess-up instead of music" (a revised version appeared in 1962). His symphonies show many fluctuations under the same official pressure, but they represent an impressive achievement provided we do not look to them for advances of style which the circumstances of his work precluded. He was, perhaps, a worthy heir to Mahler; but he was indebted neither to Schoenberg, nor to Stravinsky in any important degree; nor did he (any more than Prokofiev) open any viable road toward the future. The Italian Luigi Dallapiccola (1904–1953), on the other hand, became indirectly indebted, by way of Webern, to Schoenberg's serial technique, which he adapted to his own typically Italian and lyrical gift for melody, in an idiom which influenced such younger Italian composers as Luigi Nono. Dallapiccola's short opera *Il Prigioniero* ("The Prisoner"), first staged in Florence in 1950, concerns the alternating hopes and despairs of a "prisoner" doomed never to escape, and serving like Wozzeck as a symbol for a certain dark aspect of our human condition; and like *Wozzeck* itself, this is one of the rare modern operas (it is in twelve-tone technique) which reach the heart both as music and as theater. The Viennese Ernst Křenek (1900–   ) had his one great popular success, the lively jazz opera *Jonny spielt auf* ("Johnny Strikes Up," Leipzig, 1927) before taking up serial techniques increasingly, as in his ambitious *Karl V* (Prague, 1938). The German and American Kurt Weill (1900–1950) had an equally popular and more enduring success with his brilliant and piquant ballad opera, containing elements of jazz, *Die Dreigroschenoper* ("The Three-Penny Opera," Berlin, 1928), on a free adaptation by Bertolt Brecht of *The Beggar's Opera.* The orchestra, on stage (as in *The Soldier's Tale*), is very small; the melody is impertinent and catchy; the harmony is sharp but poignant; and the whole effect has a wry pathos which is oddly moving. Weill's more serious collaboration with Brecht, *Mahagonny,* called a *Singspiel* (a "singing-play") is a harsh and unfair satire of current life in America; it was produced in Baden-Baden in 1927, and in a revised version in Leipzig in 1930. After settling in America himself in 1935, however, Weill turned his keen talents mainly toward a series of admirable musicals.

In this direction, American composers were in the lead, and remain so, but not many musicals unfold a drama as much in the music as in the words, and for this reason, they do not for the most part fall quite into the category of opera. There is one important and valuable American work which is on the margins between an opera and a musical, but should certainly be accepted as an opera because of the continuity and dramatic characterization which the music throughout displays. This is *Porgy and Bess,* an opera of folk-like character for Negro singers, based on a book by DuBose Heyward, and composed by George Gershwin (1898–1937); it was performed in Boston in 1935. A combination of witty jazz and haunting Negro melodies is absorbed into a symphonic flow, not with complete technical success, but sufficiently for drama to unfold in the music as in the words. There is no other opera quite resembling *Porgy and Bess,* and it could hardly be repeated; but it is a moving achievement of complete sincerity and very real stature. Of other important American composers of opera, Douglas Moore (1893–1969) remained traditional through his long though comparatively uneventful development, in which his response to indigenous American folk music has been the formative element. *The Devil and Daniel Webster* was performed in New York in 1939; *The Giants in the Earth* in 1951; and (perhaps the most characteristic of his direct appeal) *The Ballad of Baby Doe,* in Central City, Colorado, in 1956. Here the libretto by John Latouche narrates in a relaxed and colloquial but not unpoetical idiom one of those legends of Colorado's mining days which in its main outlines actually happened: a myth seen in the making. Horace Tabor, the mayor and very nearly the owner of Leadville, appears impressively enough with his wife at the height of his hard-won prosperity— outside the little opera house he has had built to give tone to the place. The attractive adventuress and supposed widow known as Baby Doe arrives, causing considerable stir by her evident accessibility; he overhears her singing a soft aria of her lost love, showing that the adventuress is not the only side of her; and he confesses to her the impression she makes on his own half-recognized unhappiness. By contrast, his wife Augusta is seen to be a nagging woman, though her feelings for him are more genuine than her manner yet shows. They quarrel about his seeing Baby Doe, and part in anger. He sets up confidently with Baby Doe; but not long afterward, Augusta would like to warn the two of them, if only he would listen, that silver will fall and gold will rise—the moon and the sun become symbolically equated with these contending metals, and as silver sinks, so do Horace Tabor's fortunes, until he is a ruined and broken man. The opera ends with a visionary recall of past happiness and present failure; but Baby Doe comes to bring him home, though it is death that is intended by this sad homecoming. It is a sentimental story, and the music expressing it is sentimental also; but it flows warmly enough in arioso and aria and ensemble above an effective orchestral texture; and like *Porgy and Bess*, it gains from its folklore roots an integrity which carries its simple message to the heart. We are once again in the mood rather of the American musical than of American opera; but the drama does genuinely and continuously unfold in the music. It is naive, but deliberately so, in the wish to be primitively American as the next generation of American opera was not.

For the next generation of contemporary composers became deeply involved in a situation quite different again. In the first half of the twentieth century, the two main streams of advance flowed through Schoenberg on the one hand and Stravinsky on the other hand, and can be very approximately called neoromantic and neoclassical. No other channels, not even from Strauss with his sunset radiance, nor from Hindemith with his once-promising but ultimately false dawn, actually led into the future. But that future, now that it has become present, proves to be a matter not just of two main streams, but of a more complex divergence. We have finally, therefore, to consider the recent achievements and future prospects of opera during the second half of the twentieth century, under conditions in which music itself has a very complicated present, and a future as yet quite unpredictable.

*Notes*

1. For the acoustic aspects, and their connection with the artistic aspects, see Robert Donington, *The Instruments of Music*, London, 1949, but see greatly revised ed. of 1974.
2. Eric Salzman, *Twentieth-Century Music: An Introduction*, Englewood Cliffs, New Jersey, 1967, p. 120.
3. Erwin Stein, *Orpheus in New Guises*, London, 1953. See also Berg's own essay of 1929 on *Wozzeck*, given in Hans Redlich, *Alban Berg*, London, 1957.
4. In the ballet *Pulcinella*, Paris, 1920.
5. In the ballet *Le Baiser de la Fée* ("The Fairy's Kiss"), Paris, 1928.

# 14

# Today and Tomorrow

During the middle years of the twentieth century, the broad distinction between neoromantic composers related to Schoenberg and neoclassical composers related to Stravinsky gave place to a more complex situation, in which some composers retain elements variously drawn from the past, while others depart from the past not only more radically than usual, but also more diversely. No doubt this novelty and this diversity will both appear much diminished when seen from the perspective of some future time; yet it is already clear that our age, when compared with earlier ages, is short on tradition and still shorter on agreement about the shape of things to come.

The most obvious novelty of our times in music concerns the difference between tones definite in pitch (notes) and sounds indefinite in pitch (noises). The use of untuned drums (i.e., other than kettle-drums) in the traditional orchestra is an example of sounds indefinite in pitch but assimilated into a flow of tones definite in pitch, so that tonality still prevailed. This is a method which has been greatly extended in the modern orchestra by a splendid growth in the percussion department, both pitched and unpitched; but unless the flow of tones is actually suspended or overwhelmed, tonality still prevails. However, it is also possible to dispense with tones or reduce them to insignificance in a flow of sounds wholly or mainly indefinite in pitch, or alternatively to keep tones so shifting in perpetual glissandos that they settle to no one stable pitch. In these cases, tonality does not prevail. When tones are replaced or diluted in effect by unpitched sounds, it does make sense to talk of atonality. The difference between tonal and atonal music has become a reality today for the first time in known Western music.

These extremes of contrast between notes and noise are farther both from tradition and from one another than any of the divergencies we have so far had to consider. In addition, there are many intermediate degrees in which some balance is struck. Moreover there are other elements of music in which departures almost as extreme are cultivated by various schools and individuals composing at the present time. In some schools, early represented by the American composer Milton Babbitt (1916–    ), all parameters, including rhythm, tempo, dynamics, and texture, may be wholly or partly controlled by mathematical calculations artificially derived from a tone row, under rules of serial composition originally intended to apply only to controlling pitch. In other schools, largely deriving from John Cage (1912–    ), various attempts are made to reduce as far as possible the composer's control, and to increase the performer's—or, still more radically, to minimize all control other than that exercised by chance, in what are therefore called *aleatory* (random) passages or pieces. Olivier Messiaen (1908–    ), a French composer of much poetic talent, ranges (especially for rhythm) from mystical or mathematical controls of the utmost subtlety to the impersonal imitation of such external and nonhuman sounds as bird calls. Some of these methods go farther than others beyond the intrinsic function of music as a communication between human beings, but beneath their evident diversity they show at least one factor in common. They all carry a considerable insurance against the alarming responsibility of just being one's own fallible human self, and showing it. None of the advanced composers just named has composed operas. But other advanced composers have done so, besides the more traditional composers whose contact with the operatic past is often close and meaningful. It is under these unusual circumstances of novelty and diversity that we have now to consider the present state and future prospects of opera.

## Traditional Opera Today

The oldest of the living composers whose work in opera has been both rooted in the past and significant for our present generation is the Englishman Michael Tippett (1905–    ). His early music showed the temporary influence of Hindemith and Stravinsky, and also, more enduringly, of the Elizabethans and of Vaughan Williams. His real breakthrough came with his first opera, *The Midsummer Marriage,* on his own libretto, performed at London in 1955. It is an extraordinary lyrical outpouring of impassioned modern music, indebted to no current fashion, and altogether without cautionary insurance against the hazards of letting personal feeling and individuality take over. Not since Strauss has there been so fine and memorable an opera. The brief overture sets up a breathless momentum continued in the orchestra while the chorus find their way to a meeting place, close to a strange building (which is not always there) on the open hillside. It looks so uncanny in the morning mist that they hide again in the woods nearby. We shall find that it stands for that other side of our human personalities, not often seen so tangibly, but sensed elusively as the underlying dynamism within us which does most to shape our conscious ends. A troupe of dream-like dancers comes out (Ex. 31a, p. 214), followed by two ancients— certainly parental images, and very positive ones. Still more are they images of that archetypal masculinity and femininity within us, as old as our human species, but as often renewed as any pair of lovers take up the perennial story in youthful freshness. Two such pairs come into this opera: Mark and Jenifer, who will need to work their story through in relative awareness, like Tamino and Pamina in *The Magic Flute;* and Jack and Bella, who will go as far as their simpler natures need by good intuition, and considerably further than Papageno and Papagena went.'This resemblance to the initiation depicted in *The Magic Flute* was intentional. There is also the chorus here, who sing at the end of Act I: "Let Mark and Jenifer endure for us the perils of the royal way. We are the laughing children. . . ." The villain is Jenifer's father, King Fisher, who precipitates the crisis in the usual manner of fairy tales: he recalls (and is meant to recall) the desolated Fisher King of the Grail legends as reflected by T.S. Eliot's *The Waste Land;* and so does a still more timeless clairvoyant, called Sosostris. The dance which now begins is no other than the dance of life. Mark wants it changed in honor of his wedding day this midsummer morning, but the change will prove more painful than he as yet anticipates.

Mark sings of his love in a long arioso of the most ecstatic freedom. When Jenifer arrives, however, she brusquely puts off the wedding because, for the time at least, "It isn't love I want, but truth." She means truth about herself, and in search of it she climbs a topless stair into that traditional realm of spirit and consciousness, the sky. He counters this by going down through the gates of a cave into the traditional underworld of instinct and unconsciousness—in search of his own dark shadow. They return in still stranger state, and no better reconciled than before, but now it is Mark who mounts the stairs and Jennifer who plunges into the infernal cave.

The second act shows us the turn of Jack and Bella. She brings their courtship to a head with naive and touching art, and in lyrical arioso and enchanting dialogue (at times passing into aria) they agree to marry at once. Their initiation begins through seeing in all innocence three ritual dances, representing Earth, Water, and Air. The dances instruct them, without their knowing it, in the same ambivalent archetypal forces that meanwhile have Mark and Jenifer more consciously in their grip. The prolonged orchestral interludes accompanying these ballets have an imaginative freedom that is conspicuous even in this uncommonly free-moving score. Act III completes the initiation as King Fisher, in his villain's role as initiator in disguise, strips the veils from the mysterious Sosostris, only to reveal Mark and Jenifer in ritual union as if they were Shiva and Parvati from Hindu mythology. It is a weakness of this scene that Hindu mythology does not immediately relate either to the Druidic imagery of the opera so far or to anything native to our Western heritage. But if we in the audience are willing to accept the change of image, it symbolizes exactly what is necessary, namely the reconciliation of our inner components of masculinity and femininity in preparation for a genuine outer mating—which at the same time benefits from it and expresses it. The fourth ritual dance follows as Fire is made by a revolving stick in a hollow block—primitive symbolism not only for physical mating but for seasonal renewal and psychological rebirth. The flames spread to the couple and seem to consume them, but the fire dies down. We are left in darkness until the quiet light of an ordinary dawn returns and Mark and Jenifer appear in their everyday clothes and their everyday persons. "After the visionary night," sings Mark, "the senses purified, my heart's at rest"; and Jenifer confirms that "truth is assumed in love." They have absorbed enough deep archetypal awareness for the moment, it seems, to go forward to the next stage of their development together.[1]

EXAMPLE 31    Tippett, *The Midsummer Marriage*, (a) The temple doors open for the dance of life; (b), (c), (d) the elusive presence within us of the archetypal world in different aspects.

Tippett's next opera was *King Priam*, on his own libretto after Homer's *Iliad*, performed in Coventry in 1962. In form, it is a return to "scene" opera somewhat in Berg's manner. In content, it is extremely lucid and often of the most haunting beauty; but it has not the glorious freedom of *The Midsummer Marriage.* At some deep level, Tippett must have been too overwhelmed by his own courageous experience to go on in quite such romantic abandon; and somehow he seems to have felt that he had to submit his genius all too often to a classical austerity for which nature never really meant him. *The Knot Garden,* produced at London in 1970, has rather a tortured libretto by the composer, and a score which is no more than fitfully inspired. *The Icebreak,* performed at London in 1977, has a simpler libretto, as usual by the composer, and a score of which the best passages are strong and warm enough to stand out above the younger generation, but not to compare with his own prime in *The Midsummer Marriage.* The overall effect is probably too terse to add up successfully.

Benjamin Britten (1913–1976), Tippett's English near-contemporary, developed a style earlier and died sooner. His music rapidly caught attention by its lyrical innocence at a time when current trends of music, particularly in England, seemed all too earnest and complicated, not to say a little dreary. His first opera, *Paul Bunyan,* on a fine libretto by W.H. Auden, was performed in New York in 1941. It is halfway to a musical, but shows already some of Britten's most characteristic freshness and enchantment. *Peter Grimes,* whose libretto was drawn by Montague Slater from Crabbe's poem *The Borough,* was performed in London in 1945, and has since become almost as well established internationally as *Wozzeck.* The curtain goes up without overture on a dramatic scene in court. The fisherman Peter Grimes is under investigation for the death of his boy apprentice, from thirst, when the boat was blown off course at sea. The orchestral theme (Ex. 32a) against which the coroner intones has a strong resemblance to the Captain's theme (Ex. 30a) at the start of *Wozzeck.* To some degree this resemblance extends to the general mood and idiom of the opera, although it is profoundly modified by Britten's English traditions and gentler temperament. Peter Grimes is not an antihero like Wozzeck, but a hero tormented by unresolved ambivalence so that in another aspect he is also the villain of the piece. The heroine, Ellen Orford, is frustrated by circumstances, not by any special insufficiency of her own. There is, moreover, a chorus that is deeply involved in the action—the members of a tight small-town community, the Borough. Peter is at odds with the Borough, there being a certain amount of fault on both sides. Peter has, it comes out, acted like a man in saving his boy from drowning in a recent storm; a verdict of "accidental death" is given, but with a warning that Peter take no further apprentice unless he gets some woman to help look after him. Ellen, a widow of about forty, would like to be the woman, and Peter would like her to be—but not until he has proved himself to the Borough, for the sake of his pride, by making enough money to be sure she will not be marrying him out of pity alone. This pride is his flaw and his undoing, but the music expresses Britten's compassion for his hero's feelings and his heroine's as well.

The first of six substantial and very beautiful orchestral interludes now develops, rather like a delayed overture. It depicts the sound of the sea quietly beating on the shore at dawn. But the sea is the perpetual background of the Borough's life, and it is not always quiet. There is a warm undertow of brass in the major, entering against keen, high strings and swirling woodwinds in the minor. The same music continues in the orchestra while the chorus and some of the soloists take up their normal daytime actions by the shore. It is the choral writing—very typical of Britten's inwardness and intensity—which really confirms the mood. Another apprentice is now to be fetched for Peter, and Ellen will help bring him by the carrier, but a storm blows up, in a second interlude (for which Britten, sure of his own innate individuality, was not ashamed to owe a little to Richard Strauss). The next scene, in the Boar Inn, has grown lively by the time that Ellen, the carrier, and the new apprentice come in drenched and exhausted from struggling through the river, after finding the bridge down. Both the storm and the broken bridge seem to relate to Peter's state as he takes the boy off in angry hostility and willful isolation. The third interlude restores the quiet of a sunlit Sunday morning, but against the bells and the church service in the background, there is a bitter scene. Ellen has seen a fresh bruise on the boy's neck, and Peter wants to force the boy to sea although it is the Sabbath, for he is obsessive in his eagerness for the money "to buy us a home, respect, freedom." He actually strikes her, and she goes off full of foreboding. A long passacaglia on the theme shown in Ex. 32b, impresses Peter's obsessiveness relentlessly on our attention, and here he is in his poor hut, again forcing the boy to sea, where the water is boiling with a fine shoal of fish. Having reduced the boy to tears, Peter comforts him with clumsy kindness, and falls to gentle thoughts of marrying Ellen. At that moment, a thumping drum leads up a whole procession of suspicious neighbors. Peter's persecuted fears rise intolerably—has the boy been talking against him? He urges the boy down the cliff path by the back door, bidding him go carefully, but the boy slips and falls with a scream, and Peter goes after him, so that the neighbors find only the empty hut. The fifth interlude is warm and tranquil for the moonlit night, but pierced by sharp reminders, on flute and harp, of Peter's tortured state of mind. A dance is in progress off stage, a little like the tavern scenes in *Wozzeck*. Ellen and the old sea captain Bulstrode agree to give Peter what help they can, but the neighbors begin their cruel hunt again. The sixth interlude is thick with a mist as dense as Peter's confusion, and he is soon seen down on the shore, singing distractedly, while the recurrent moaning of the distant foghorn deepens our sense of relentless destiny. Bulstrode tells him: "Sail out till you lose sight of land. Then sink the boat." And so Peter returns himself to the embrace of the sea, with some hint, at least, of the traditional image of transformation. Very healingly, the music brings back the shimmering mystery and the slow warm surge of the first interlude and chorus, in Britten's own special blend of intensity and innocence. It is the new day beginning, the tides of the sea and of life itself ebbing and flowing in constant renewal. And so the opera ends not in tragedy but in gentle reminder of our common lot.

EXAMPLE 32    Britten, *Peter Grimes*, (a) opening orchestral theme; (b) basic theme of passacaglia.

*Peter Grimes.* Royal Opera House, Covent Garden.

None of Britten's later operas has music quite so rich as this early maturing, but it is remarkable how each of them revolves around much the same preoccupation with isolation, deprivation, and innocence betrayed. With all of his repeated triumphs and honors, Britten could never quite believe that the Borough did not despise and reject him, or that it was permissible to be happy and successful. The least criticism distressed him disproportionately. He felt compassion for Peter Grimes and his other hero-victims because on one level he could so readily identify himself with them. Peter being harsh to his boy apprentice was like Britten being harsh to Britten, in some part of his own repressed potential. It is as if the child in him were caught up for life in some unrecorded damage from infancy, made evident by his choice of subjects and his manner of handling them. In *The Rape of Lucretia,* the heroine is not only raped but feels so excluded by the experience from her own or society's tolerance that she kills herself. (The libretto was drawn by Ronald Duncan, mainly from Livy, and the opera was performed at Glyndebourne in 1946.) *Albert Herring* (on a libretto drawn by Eric Crozier from a story by de Maupassant, and performed at Glyndebourne in 1947) would be bitterly cynical if it were not so brilliant a comedy. *Billy Budd* (on a libretto by E.M. Forster and Eric Crozier, and performed in London in 1951) has no feminine character at all, and achieves a measure of belated reconciliation only after one ambivalent hero (Vere) has hanged the other, simple-minded Billy, from the ship's yardarm. *Gloriana* (on a libretto by William Plomer, produced for the coronation celebrations in London in 1953) does more for the self-destroying Essex than for Elizabeth, who was the reluctant instrument of his destruction. *The Turn of the Screw* (on a skillful libretto by Myfanwy Piper after the tormented ghost story by Henry James, performed in Venice in 1954) is another study in unlived potential returning to haunt its true victim—the person who has not lived it. Indeed, there was much the same unlived potential in the life (though not in the art) of Britten as in that of Henry James.[2] *A Midsummer Night's Dream* (performed at Aldeburgh in 1960) follows Shakespeare in treating the fairies and the artisans more imaginatively than the ordinary mortals, in a score which even for Britten is uncommonly colorful and evocative. *Owen Wingrave* (on another libretto by Myfanwy Piper after Henry James, televised in 1971) has a hero victimized for being, like Britten, a pacifist; it makes an undramatic opera, of no great musical inspiration. But the last opera, *Death in Venice* (libretto by Myfanwy Piper after the famous short novel by Thomas Mann, performed at Aldeburgh in 1973), brought Britten's life and work around full circle from his early promise in *Paul Bunyan* and his first masterpiece in *Peter Grimes.*

The curtain goes straight up on a famous but elderly writer, Aschenbach. He is brooding because the flow of ordered inspiration on which he has built his books and his life is failing him. A spectral Traveler voices Aschenbach's own unrecognized longing to break away from order and seek who knows what fresh experience in the sensual South. At once we see him on the boat for Venice, among a crowd of flirtatious young men. An elderly fop joins them. Aschenbach is disgusted, knowing at heart as he does that it is not the young men but the elderly fop who holds up the mirror to himself. The fop is the same bass-baritone who was the Traveler, and who is next the Gondolier rowing him (in excess of his instructions) to the Lido—with a glance at Charon, ferryman of the dead, who indeed cannot be instructed. A flowing orchestral interlude brings us to the hotel, whose manager is again no other than this same disguised messenger of the fates. Against every fear and every scruple, Aschenbach falls most desperately in love with an adolescent guest, the boy Tadzio, who dances without singing or speaking, and on whom he projects in mythological imagery not only the ideal beauty of Apollo but the dangerous allurement of Dionysus. This second level is depicted in ballet, and in avant-garde orchestration with vibraphone predominating. Aschenbach never quite dares to speak to Tadzio, and indeed it is to his own fantasies that he must really speak. For Tadzio stands for the same unlived potential which in *The Turn of the Screw* drew the children to their ghostly seducers. Thomas Mann knew, like his hero, that his life had been spent in the austere service of his art, cut off from the common passions he so regretted by that ineradicable compulsion which is at once the artist's inhibiting prison and his creative drive. Britten identified with Thomas Mann and with Aschenbach—

sung by his friend and interpreter of so many years, Peter Pears. Can we wonder that his finest powers were so beautifully renewed, in this last and most revealing masterpiece of his well-fulfilled story?

A near-contemporary of Britten is the Italian-born but American resident Gian-Carlo Menotti (1911–   ), who comes as close to being an heir of Puccini and of *verismo* opera as would be possible in this day and age. His style is aimed, as that was, at popular effect. It is melodious in aria and arioso, flexible in recitative, and broad in ensemble (there is hardly ever any chorus). The scoring is for small and practical orchestras, admirably handled. Menotti has always been his own librettist, and both in text and in music he is served by a sure sense of theater. His popular success began with *The Medium*, performed in New York in 1946. It has a nice irony: a fraudulent spiritualist who takes the spirit voices for more real than ever she herself supposed them to be, leaving us in splendid suspense. This short opera fully deserved the very long run which it achieved together with its frequent companion piece, an amusing comedy of misunderstandings called *The Telephone*, first performed in New York in 1947. *The Consul*, performed in New York in 1950, on the other hand, is a strongly felt tragedy on the uncaring persecution of a group of political refugees. It is ingenious in its dramatization and compassionate in its sympathy, though lacking the musical intensity quite to transform this all too topical theme into the universality of a modern myth. *Amahl and the Night Visitors* (1951) is a deliberately simple and sincere little Christmas piece composed for television. *The Saint of Bleecker Street* is an urban tale set in New York itself, where it was performed to warm critical acclaim in 1954. *Maria Golovin* was composed for the International Exposition at Brussels, and performed there in 1958. Later operas include *Le Dernier Sauvage* ("The Last Savage," Paris, 1963; in English, New York, 1964); *Martin's Lie* (a chamber opera, Bath, England, 1964); *Help, Help, the Globolinks!* (a one-act opera "for children and those who like children," including electronic sounds, Hamburg, 1968); and *The Most Important Man*, commissioned and performed by the New York City Opera, New York, 1971). Menotti also wrote the libretto for an attractively traditional opera by the American Samuel Barber, *Vanessa*, performed in New York in 1958.

A composer in whom a variety of advanced effects rather obscure than illumi-nate a fundamentally conventional idiom is the Austrian Gottfried von Einem (1918–   ). Two of his most ambitious operas are *Dantons Tod* ("Danton's Death") on a libretto drawn from a drama by Georg Büchner and performed in Salzburg in 1947, and *Der Prozess* ("The Trial") on a libretto drawn from Franz Kafka's surrealist novel, and performed in Salzburg in 1953. His more recent opera, *Der Besuch der Alten Dame* ("The Visit of the Old Lady"), from a text by Freidrich Dürrenmatt and performed in Vienna in 1971, is so weighty in the orchestra that the very rapid words are unduly covered. The effect in the theater is therefore less than the musical and verbal intensity the drama promises.

Another very substantial composer of our own day who draws upon a variety of traditions both conventional and novel is the German Hans Werner Henze (1926–   ). His commitment to opera is serious, but his musical idiom is not an entirely settled one; even within the confines of a single work it is apt to change from scene to scene. Of his long list of operas, a characteristically startling and satirical comedy is *Der Junge Lord* ("The Young Lord"), on a libretto by I. Bachmann after W. Hauff, performed in Berlin in 1965. The satire is against the conventional hypocrisy and social snobbery of a small town visited by a caricature of an English milord and his companion. This companion gains a reputation for charming eccentricity until he (or it) turns out to represent all too literally the ape in us. This is a bitter work in both words and music, but it moves with admirable energy and invention, and is extremely good theater. *The Bassarids* is a mythological drama on a modernized adaptation by W.H. Auden and Chester Kallman of Euripides' classical tragedy, *The Bacchae;* it was first performed in Salzburg in 1966, under the German title *Die Bassariden.* The adaptation is in part reasonably faithful to the spirit and the manner of its great original, in part distorted and expanded in a misguided attempt to give the myth a new and contemporary interpretation. The reasonably faithful parts make excellent opera; the distorted and interpolated parts do not. The score is similarly inconsistent and uneven. If it were all as inventive as its finer passages it would indeed be memorable, but too much of it is clever pastiche and too little of it shows a distinctive individuality. Nevertheless, its theatrical effectiveness is altogether very considerable. Dionysus, the god of wine and of manic inspiration, has entered Thebes in disguise, and King Pentheus attempts to suppress his worship as a fraudulent blasphemy. In fact, Dionysus stands for something dark but creative within us which cannot be suppressed (though the authors of the libretto mistake it for unmotivated cruelty). The real power and fascination of the god is shown when he causes Pentheus himself to long to witness his orgiastic celebrations. In his mother's hand mirror, Pentheus is then shown his own sexual fantasies in a farcical interlude which misuses the tragic prophet Teiresias as a lewdly undignified figure of comedy, having no connection either with Euripides or with genuine mythology. This is supposed to be Oedipal psychology, but it is in fact quite artificial, and in addition it is a dramatic miscalculation. Later Pentheus, caught spying on the Dionysiac orgy, is torn to pieces by the frenzied women, led by his own mother Agave. The most moving scene in the opera, both dramatically and musically, unfolds in very expressive arioso the grief of Agave when she comes out of her trance and realizes what she has done to her dreadfully dismembered son. A more recent work by Henze, *We Come to the River* (1976), is not called an opera, but "actions for music," and these actions are simultaneously presented on three parts of the stage to the accompaniment of three separate orchestras, which makes a consecutive drama in words and music deliberately impossible. As music theater this may be an interesting experiment, but it is edging away well outside the boundaries of opera. The plot is naively Marxist, and the music is of only intermittent interest.

A less ambitious but more rewarding recent composer of opera is the Scottish Thea Musgrave (1928–    ). Her chamber opera *The Abbott of Drimock* appeared in 1955 and her three-act opera *The Decision* in 1964, but her best so far is *The Voice of Ariadne* (libretto by Amalia Elguera after "The Last of the Valerii" by Henry James, performed at Aldeburgh in 1974). The score is in a most sensitive musical style which, while retaining some traditional elements, is nevertheless sufficiently advanced. The action, according to the current fashion, mainly unfolds in flexible arioso, with the orchestra in support as an expressive commentary (not, as in Wagner or Strauss, as an independent rhetoric). We learn of an old family legend (one which fascinated Henry James, who got the essence of it in part from *La Vénus D'Ille*, Mérimée's haunting story, and in part from "The Marble Faun" by Nathaniel Hawthorne). The legend tells of the buried statue of a goddess which will bring happiness to its finder, and it seems that Count Valerio, in whose estate it lies, has found it and is preparing to unveil it ceremonially. The Countess, who is one of Henry James' expatriate Americans, merely expects to have her own perfect married happiness confirmed, but from some of the comments of the guests, we begin to wonder whether that marriage is quite as perfect as she is making out. One of these guests is in love with the Count, another with the Countess—there is at least the possibility of the threads getting crossed. How much more so when the "goddess" proves to be no deity but a woman, long dead indeed and certainly mythological (since she is that same Ariadne so sadly left on Naxos by her lover Theseus), yet capable of singing alluringly off stage and disturbing the impressionable Count with the most unsettling fantasies. To show her archetypal remoteness, her part is on pre-recorded tape (an interesting and meaningful use of electronics in live opera). But once unearthed, she is a living force, standing as she so plainly does—yet again—for some unfulfilled potential, presumably in Mérimée, undoubtedly in Henry James, and now operatically in Count Valerio, on whom she takes it for granted that she has some prior claim. Unearthing her was the best thing to do about her, provided that what she stands for can be assimilated into the present situation. Henry James could at least work her out of his system in his story, as he did with so many of his inner problems. The Count and his Countess work out her implications in their actual relationship, which poor Henry James never managed to do with any woman. The rest of the opera depicts this working out, and a very satisfying drama in words and music the librettist and the composer together have made of it.

Krysztof Penderecki (1933–   ) of Poland is a composer who tempers very actively advanced sonorities with other, more accessible elements skillfully concealed, and has consequently a wider appeal than usual to middle-of-the-road listeners. He is a distinguished leader of a group of Polish composers whose courage in pursuing avant-garde objectives has changed their national climate of musical theory and practice to valuable effect. His opera *The Devils of Loudun* (first performed in Hamburg in 1969) is on his own libretto, drawn from Erich Fried's German translation of Aldous Huxley's novel and from Desmond Clayton's adaptation of John Whiting's play. The orchestra employed is very large, and includes much powerful percussion. The chorus shrieks, roars, laughs and prays; there is solo monologue of rhythmic force or declamatory freedom; there are ensembles including a quartet of nuns and a male quintet. The music is more explosive than flowing, and incorporates many tone-clusters to blanket out the tonality. From one angle, perhaps too much happens in the music to make an entirely satisfactory opera. From another angle, too little.

## *Advanced Opera Tomorrow?*

How do the prospects for opera look, now that we have brought our story to the threshold of the future? If opera is drama unfolding as much in the music as in the words, and as much in the words as in the music, then the influence of the avant-garde is not favorable to opera, although it may be favorable to other forms of musical theater. For with regard to the words, it is argued that their freshness for poetic meaning is so worn out that they are best confined simply to evocative sonority, by fragmenting or prolonging or distorting or overlapping them rather than letting them take their natural shapes as verbal units and grammatical sentences—as if some new fear of meaning were infiltrating into our previous fear of feeling. And with regard to the music, it is argued that all manner of sounds, not only notes of definite pitch, are found in the world, and may as well be included in the composer's resources—as if selection and judgment and the self-imposed limitations of the creative artist were responsibilities too alarming to face, and were best left either to impersonal mathematics or to open-ended permissiveness. There are gains and losses, of course, but some of these extremes look more like abdications of human choice than liberations. The voice heard so seductively in some of the primeval and fragmented sounds of the avant-garde today is the voice not of our bright reason but of our dark shadow. It was no doubt a necessary reaction against too much vain confidence; for we get broadly the art that we need, and reject it only when it does not meet our need. What art brings to us is in itself only one half of the experience; the other half is what we bring to it, which is why good judges may differ. The unconscious is very often our strongest part, but the conscious is our most distinctive part as human beings. The artist who can function as a mediator serves us best. The extent of our differences in the arts today can only suggest that our needs are not being altogether satisfied.

But tomorrow? The very young composers, who will be the established composers of tomorrow, concern themselves very little either with serial composition or with random composition. They take tonality as a natural field of force, like magnetism, which is always available and open to further uses. Key tonality is another matter. Yet key is certainly latent in tonality, and for so large a structure as opera, there are advantages in the subtle deployment of tonal areas as well as in the sophisticated exploitation of the tonal pull. We have seen this in Britten's last opera, *Death in Venice*, where the melody is a free and eloquent vehicle for the words, the orchestral sonority is advanced and original, but the tonal areas and the tonal pull are clear and dynamic beneath the considerable surface ambiguity and dissonance. By comparison, a moderately avant-garde opera such as *The Royal Hunt of the Sun* by the Scottish Iain Hamilton (1922–   ) is static. This is not in fact Hamilton's latest opera, but it was given its belated but excellent London performance in 1977. The libretto is by the composer, who kept close to an interesting play by Peter Shaffer on the Spanish conquest of Peru, seen as an inner clash of characters. The declamation is in a speech-like arioso whose melodic felicity and verbal naturalness are quite close to Britten. The orchestra has a preponderance of percussion, both pitched and unpitched, and used with great sensitiveness and sonorous beauty. As the harmonies pile up, they generate implications of tonality, but these are not gathered together into any sort of tonal momentum. There are neither keys nor modulations, nor are any of the other resources used—whether of rhythm, volume, texture, or timbre—adequate to get the music moving. In the text, the characters are obviously aspects of one another, but they do contrast and interrelate and, in a manner, grow. In the music they almost stand still. Lacking modulation, the score lacks that forward dynamism which should be the driving power behind the opera.

Historically and artistically, modulation and opera arose together. No alternative resource previously or subsequently available is nearly so powerful a force as modulation for on-going development in music. Perhaps it will even turn out that opera has been a period piece, the period coinciding with the period of modulation. More probably, both opera and modulation are merely going through an unusually acute but passing transition. Words as irrational but meaningful as Beckett's or Pinter's wonderful extensions of our verbal drama are certainly acceptable in opera; for music is particularly successful at bringing out the deeper layers. Gesture is expressive; dance is expressive; music is expressive. But words are what articulate a drama, and while a drama without verbal articulation may also be valuable, it is not opera.

On the whole, the more typical an avant-garde opera is of the avant-garde, the less typical it is of opera. When Henze, in *We Come to the River,* wanted his drama not so much to unfold as to overlap, he rejected "opera" as "too archaic and inflexible," and called his piece "actions in music" (although his is not a very deeply avant-garde idiom in other respects).[3] The Italian Luigi Nono (1924–    ), who is truly of the avant-garde, stands in line from Webern by way of Dallapiccola; his *Intoleranza* (1960), performed in Venice in 1961, is called a "scenic action," and combines, in his own libretto, quotations from Marxist writings with compassionate protests against all authoritarian persecution. The music is serial with some original sound effects. The Italian Luciano Berio (1925–    ), also influenced by Dallapiccola, had a "spectacle for mixed media" performed in Santa Fe in 1971, which is called *Opera* and is indeed a sort of opera-like exploration of space and time, related to his celebrated *Circles* of 1960. This is a path, however, which in practice leads away from opera. Similarly, Bruno Maderna (1920–1973), another of this distinguished school of Italian pioneers, opened his non-opera *Hyperion* of 1964 with a flutist unpacking his flutes of different sizes as a prolonged theatrical gesture before arriving at any direct act of performance; and when he does, it proves to be the unleashing of a powerful onslaught of highly amplified electronic tape. Also on tape, the chorus is heard ejaculating deliberately jumbled words in different languages; yet the piece ends with a strangely lyrical melody, almost an aria, for soprano solo.

In these areas of advanced music theater, action and gesture are more important objectives than drama, and quite as important as music. There are gestures by actors, performers, dancers, even the audience if it can be induced to interact; verbal gestures without grammatical sense; gestures of decor; and gestures by stage lighting, sometimes spreading to the auditorium. There are gestures directed toward stage properties like the hanging bird-man in *Musik im Bau*, a recent work by the German Karlheinz Stockhausen (1928–   ) which hovers between the conditions of a concert hall and a theater stage, and produces a powerful response by methods not in the least traditional for either. In the background of this work there is again the strong influence of Webern, and in the foreground there is the more recent influence of Messiaen—whose promised opera is certain to raise and may well answer some further questions in the matter. Stockhausen, who was one of Messiaen's pupils, shares with him an extraordinary predilection for the *ostinato* principle: the obsessive persistence, often under very rigorous precompositional control, of the same small piece of musical material. The French Pierre Boulez (1925–   ), who was also a pupil of Messiaen, shows on the contrary a temperamental inclination to flexibility and waywardness—and responsiveness, true performer that he is, to the presence of an audience. These twin leaders of our current generation are variously involved in musical theater, but their idioms do not blaze any very obvious path forward into the opera of the future.

An extreme but logical consequence of the current situation is described by the noncommittal but appropriate term, "happening." Works of art, of course, do not really "happen," even at their most seemingly casual; for what the conscious does not choose to decide, the unconscious all the more autonomously imposes. But the artist may well feel that he is merely allowing something to happen of its own accord. Surrealism remains the most interesting and accomplished of these "let it happen" schools of art. Their only serious deficiency is that they are out of balance between two poles of our human experience which were called by Nietzsche the Dionysiac and the Apollonian. A very good example of the Dionysiac is *Einstein on the Beach*, which after extensive European trial runs was mounted at great expense in the Metropolitan Opera House in New York in 1976. The stage was filled with engineering structures, electronic equipment, and movable properties with aerial orbits and special lighting effects, including a simulated spaceship. Singers and dancers and even instrumentalists climb and are hoisted around; there is a chorus in the pit; there are multiple microphones and speakers everywhere for the powerful amplification of live and electronic sounds. The scenes and images connect by free association rather than by logic, so that the main thrust of the piece comes from the unconscious, and though some of the words are intelligible, they are not intended to unfold a drama. There are fragments of familiar archetypal imagery, but this is not in itself sufficient for a public work of art, since there is neither the reliance on tradition nor the personal genius which might fuse them into some sort of common relevance (as Blake was able to fuse mythological images of his own invention into a sufficiently though not a very accessibly public communication). The deviser of this and several similar stage events is Robert Wilson, and the composer is Philip Glass. There is no librettist, because there is no libretto, which caused the critic David Sargent to comment with some understatement that "it is hardly an opera." It is not an opera at all, but then, "opera as a living, on-going art is dead," he firmly added; "new operas that are both intellectually respectable and decently popular simply are not forthcoming."[4]

This might largely be true, if only because so many of the most interesting new stage works, even when they are called operas, are not operas, but something else again. The most interesting new composers are so suspicious of the operatic form that they go to great lengths to keep away from it, in fact if not in name. The English Opera Group, where old and new are well balanced in the repertoire, did find it more honest and more politic to change its name to the English Music Theatre. But the end of the story is not yet. Already the next chapters are being written, by Jack Beeson, Harrison Birtwistle, Gordon Crosse, Peter Maxwell Davies, Alan Hoddinott, John Tavener, and many others. Above all, in the great civic centers and universities of the United States, it is not so much the standard opera companies as the inspired opera groups and the experimental opera workshops which are so active and so creative at the grassroots level. All of this skilled direction and talented response is going somewhere; if we do not yet know quite where, we may be the better off for it in the long run. For at the moment, we do not have *music* so much as *musics*. The next very great composer to come along may well find the answer we cannot yet predict, not only about the future of opera, but about the future of music.

## Notes

1. A fuller account is in Robert Donington, "Words and Music," in *Michael Tippett: A Symposium*, ed. Ian Kemp, London, 1965, pp. 94–108.

2. A classic study of the relationship between the work of Henry James and the strange course of his life story will be found in Leon Edel, *Henry James*, 5 vols., London, 1953–1972.

3. Quoted in the interesting article by Peter Heyworth, "Activating Opera," *The Observer Review*, London, July 18, 1976.

4. *The Village Voice*, New York, November 22, 1976.

# Additional Reading

A very full bibliography of opera may be found in Grout's *Short History of Opera* (see below), including both special studies and biographical "life and works" of individual composers. The suggestions below are merely hints for quite general reading, either to fill in further details, or to open up new ideas.

Donington, Robert. *Wagner's "Ring" and its Symbols: The Music and the Myth*, London, 1963, 3rd ed. 1974. [A "words and music" discussion.]

Grout, Donald. *A Short History of Opera*, New York, 1947, 2nd ed. 1965. [A magnificent compendium.]

Hamm, Charles. *Opera*, Boston, 1966. [A composer's-eye view of the nature and history of opera.]

Harewood, the Earl of, ed. *Kobbé's Complete Opera Book*, London, revised ed. 1977. [Still a very popular introduction, but more reliable under its new editorship.]

Jacobs, Arthur, and Stanley Sadie. *The Pan Book of Opera*, London, 1964, now as *Opera: A Modern Guide*, Newton Abbot, 1971, and New York, 1972. [Admirable for a quick spot-check.]

Kerman, Joseph. *Opera as Drama*, New York, 1956. [Still one of the most thought-provoking and valuable books ever written on opera.]

Loewenberg, Alfred. *Annals of Opera, 1597–1940*, 2 vols., Geneva, 1943, 2nd ed. revised, 1955. [The most solid and reliable general work for quick reference on the basic facts.]

Orrey, Leslie. *A Concise History of Opera*, London, 1972. [Possibly the best of the short introductions, and tells a very good story.]

Rosenthal, Harold, and John Warrack. *Concise Oxford Dictionary of Opera*, London, 1964; with corrections, 1966. [A remarkable alphabetical condensation.]

Smith, Patrick J. *The Tenth Muse: A Historical Study of the Opera Libretto*, New York, 1970. [Valuable for "words" as opposed to "music."]

Stein, Jack M. *Richard Wagner and the Synthesis of the Arts*, Detroit, 1960. ["Words" *and* "music" in their Wagnerian interrelationships.]

Strunk, Oliver, ed. and transl. *Source Readings in Music History*, New York, 1950. [An invaluable introduction to the sources *contemporary* with the operas, well selected and reliably translated.]

Weisstein, Ulrich, ed. and transl. *The Essence of Opera*, London, 1964. [Quotations resembling Strunk, but restricted to opera, and not quite so dependably translated—nevertheless a valuable doorway.]

# Index

E
F
G
H  3
I   4
J   5